COMMANDANT
OF AUSCHWITZ
The Autobiography of Rudolf Hoess

Translated by
Constantine FitzGibbon

Introduced by
Primo Levi
Translated by Joachim Neugroschel

PHOENIX

A PHOENIX PRESS PAPERBACK

First published in Great Britain
by Weidenfeld & Nicolson in 1959
This paperback edition published in 2000
by Phoenix Press,
a division of The Orion Publishing Group Ltd,
Orion House, 5 Upper St Martin's Lane,
London WC2H 9EA

10 9 8 7 6 5 4

A CIP catalogue record for this book
is available from the British Library.
Printed and bound in Great Britain by
Clays Ltd, St Ives plc

ISBN 1 84212 024 7

www.orionbooks.co.uk

Contents

TRANSLATOR'S NOTE

This autobiography was written in a Polish prison, and for the following facts concerning Hoess and the writing of it I am principally indebted to Dr Martin Broszat, who wrote the introduction to the German edition.[1]

Hoess was arrested by the British Military Police near Flensburg, in Schleswig-Holstein, on 11 March, 1946. He was interrogated by Field Security on 13 and 14 March. Later that month he was handed over to the Americans and taken to Nuremberg, where he was again interrogated, in April, in connection with the trial of Kaltenbrunner, the so-called 'Pohl Trial' and the 'IG Farben Trial'.[2] During the period 9–16 April he had several conversations with the American prison psychiatrist, Dr Gilbert.[3] On 25 May, 1946, he was handed over to the Polish authorities and removed to Cracow and later to Warsaw to await trial. The trial did not take place until the following March. He was condemned to death, and executed in April 1947.

What Hoess wrote in prison, the greater part of which is translated and reproduced here, falls into two parts. There is his autobiography, which constitutes pages 29 to 181 and which is given in its entirety so far as it is legible. This was written in January and February of 1947, that is to say after the preliminary enquiries had been completed, but before he faced trial. The remainder of this book, here given in the form of appendices, was written in connection with that preliminary enquiry or with other enquiries being simultaneously carried out by Dr Jan Sehn, the examining judge. These documents are of varying interest, and are not all reproduced in full here.[4] The diary is handwritten and a careful comparison of the handwriting with other documents known to have been written by Hoess, both before and after his arrest, proves its authenticity

---

[1] *Kommandant in Auschwitz*, Deutsche Verlags-Anstalt, 1958.

[2] The relevant documents are IMG XXXIII, Doct. PS–3868: IMG XI, S.438 et seqq: Nuremberg Doct. NI–035/037: and Nuremberg Doct. NI–039/041.

[3] G. M. Gilbert, *Nuremberg Diary*, New York, 1947.

[4] Omissions are explained in footnotes.

beyond a shadow of doubt. The other documents are in most cases type-written, some being stenograms, but internal evidence proves them to be certainly genuine as well. The original documents are the property of the *High Commission for the Examination of Hitlerite Crimes in Poland (Gltowne Komisja Badania Zbrodni Hitlerowskick w Polsce)*, but the Auschwitz Museum made a photostat available to Dr Broszat, who has fully tested its authenticity.

These documents were first published, in part, in 1951, in a Polish translation edited and introduced by the well-known Polish criminologist, Dr Stanislaw Batawie, who had had some thirteen conversations with Hoess in Cracow prison, and who had then suggested to him that he write his autobiography. This edition contained all the autobiography and a selection of the other documents. The first complete edition, containing all the documents as well as Hoess's last letters to his wife and children,[1] was also a Polish translation, appearing in 1956 and with an introduction and various explanatory notes by Dr Jan Sehn.[2]

The autobiography and the other documents have, as a result of these Polish editions, been known to scholars for many years, and are quoted in most of the books dealing with Nazi atrocities or allied subjects.[3] But this English edition, and the edition being simultaneously printed in Germany, are the first to appear in any language other than Polish. In the German edition the autobiography has been broken up and given chapter headings; but in this English edition it has been considered better to print the text exactly as Hoess wrote it. Furthermore, the German edition is not unabridged. For example, the incident of the Rumanian prince has been omitted, presumably for reasons of squeamishness. Here the autobiography is given in its entirety: where there are gaps, indicated by . . . . . , this is in all cases save one because such brief gaps, all of only a few words, exist in the transcribed typescript and are due to the illegibility of the original manuscript.

The translator would like to express his personal gratitude to Mr Andrew Foster-Melliar for his help both in preparing the first draft of this translation and in correcting the proofs.

---

[1] Here omitted.

[2] See also *Auschwitz-Birkenau*, by Dr Jan Sehn, Wydawnictwo Prawnicze, Warsaw, 1957. This is published in English, as well as in Polish and German, and is the best short description of Auschwitz known to me.

[3] For example: *The Scourge of the Swastika*, by Lord Russell of Liverpool, Cassell, 1954.

Illustrations

Introduction by Primo Levi

Introduction

Usually when you agree to write the introduction to a book, you do so because you truly care about the book: it's readable, it's got a high literary quality, so that you like or at least admire the author. This book, however, is the extreme opposite. It's filled with evil, and this evil is narrated with a disturbing bureaucratic obtuseness; it has no literary quality, and reading it is agony. Furthermore, despite his efforts at defending himself, the author comes across as what he is: a coarse, stupid, arrogant, long-winded scoundrel, who sometimes blatantly lies. Yet this autobiography of the Commandant of Auschwitz is one of the most instructive books ever published because it very accurately describes the course of a human life that was exemplary in its way. In a climate different from the one he happened to grow up in, Rudolph Hoess would quite likely have wound up as some sort of drab functionary, committed to discipline and dedicated to order—at most a careerist with modest ambitions. Instead, he evolved, step by step, into one of the greatest criminals in history.

We survivors of the Nazi concentration camps are often asked a symptomatic question, especially by young people: Who were the people 'on the other side' and what were they like? Is it possible that all of them were wicked, that no glint of humanity ever shone in their eyes? This question is thoroughly answered by Hoess's book, which shows how readily evil can replace good, besieging it and finally submerging it—yet allowing it to persist in tiny, grotesque islets: an orderly family life, love of nature, Victorian morality.

Precisely because the author is uneducated, he cannot be suspected of deliberately perpetrating a colossal falsification of history: he would have been incapable of that. His pages teem with mechanical rehashes of Nazi rhetoric, white lies and black lies, attempts at self-justification, at embellishment. Yet these are all so ingenuous and transparent that the most unprepared reader will have no trouble seeing through all these things—they stick out from the texture of the narrative like flies in milk.

On the whole, this book is substantially truthful: it is the autobiography of a man who was not a monster and who never became one even at the height of his career in Auschwitz, when at his orders thousands of innocent people were murdered daily. What I mean is that we can believe him when he claims that he never enjoyed inflicting pain or killing: he was no sadist, he had nothing of the satanist. By contrast, satanic features can be found in Hoess's portrait of his peer and friend, Adolf Eichmann; however, Eichmann was far more intelligent than Hoess, and we are left with the impression that Hoess took some of Eichmann's bragging at face value, even though it doesn't hold up to a serious analysis.

Rudolph Hoess may have been one of the worst criminals of all time, but his makeup was not dissimilar from that of any citizen of any country. His guilt, which was not inscribed in his genes or in his German birth, lay entirely in the fact that he was unable to resist the pressure exerted on him by a violent environment even before Hitler's takeover.

To be fair, we have to admit that the young boy got off to a bad start. His father, a businessman, was a "fanatical Catholic" (but be careful: for Hoess, as in the overall Nazi vocabulary, the adjective 'fanatical' always has a positive ring). The father wanted his son to be a priest, yet he simultaneously subjected him to a rigid, military-like upbringing, while totally ignoring the boy's inclinations and aptitudes. Understandably the son felt no affection for his parents and became taciturn and introverted. Soon orphaned, he suffered a religious crisis, and when the Great War broke out he did not hesitate. His moral universe was now reduced to a single constellation: Duty, Fatherland, Comradeship, Courage. After enlisting in the army, the seventeen-year-old was shipped to the savage Iraqi front. He killed, was wounded, and felt he had become a man—that is, a soldier: for him the two words were synonymous.

War was the worst school—anywhere, but especially in a defeated and humiliated Germany. Yet Rudolph Hoess did not try to reintegrate himself in normal life. Amid the terrible conditions of post-war Germany, he joined one of the Freikorps, the volunteer corps, with their basically repressive aims. After participating in a political assassination, he was sentenced to ten years in prison. Life behind bars was hard, but it suited him. He was no rebel, he liked discipline and order, he even liked expiating: he was a model prisoner. His heart was in the right place: he had accepted the violence of war because it was ordered by Authority, but he was disgusted at the violence committed by his fellow inmates because their acts were spontaneous. That was to become one of his leitmotifs: order is necessary in everything;

directives have to come from higher up, they are good by definition, and they are carried out conscientiously and without discussion; personal initiative is permissible only if it fosters a more efficient execution of orders. Hoess was suspicious of friendship, love, and sex; he was a loner.

After six years he was amnestied and he then found work in a farming community. He got married, but he admits that he never succeeded in communicating intimately with his wife—either then or later on, when he needed even more to do so. It was at this point that the pitfall opened before him: he was invited to join the SS and he accepted, drawn as he was by the "prospect of a rapid career" and "the concomitant financial advantages." And it is also at this point that he lies to the reader for the first time: "Reading [Heinrich] Himmler's invitation to join the SS service in the concentration camps. I did not think even minimally about the actual reality of those camps. . . . They were an absolutely unknown concept, and I failed to have any idea of them." Come now, Commandant Hoess. Lying requires a lot more mental agility. That was the year 1934. Hitler was already in power and had never pulled any punches. The term 'concentration camp' was already well-known in its new meaning: few people knew what went on in the camps, but everyone knew that these were places of terror and horror —and enough was known about them in the world of the SS. The "concept" was anything but "unknown," it was already being cynically utilised in the regime's propaganda: 'If you don't behave, you'll end up in a concentration camp' had become an almost proverbial turn of phrase.

Rudolph Hoess's career was indeed rapid. His prison experience was not useless: his superiors, who rightfully viewed him as a specialist, turned down his feeble requests to go back to the troops. Both forms of service were equally valid: after all, the enemy was ubiquitous—at the borders and on the inside. Hoess had no reason to feel slighted. He accepted. If it was his duty to be a jailer, then a jailer he would be with all possible diligence. "I must confess that I did my job conscientiously and attentively, I had no regard for the prisoners, I was severe and often harsh." No one doubts that he was harsh, but the statement that his "stone mask" concealed an aching heart is not only an indecent but also a childish lie.

Still, he is not lying when he repeatedly maintains that once he entered the Nazi machine it was difficult to get out. He would certainly not have been risking death, or even a severe punishment, but leaving would indeed have been difficult. Life in the SS involved a skilful and intense 're-education' that fed the ambitions of the recruits, who, mostly uneducated and frustrated outcasts, felt their self-esteem thus boosted and exalted. The uniform was elegant, the pay was good, the power was virtually unlimited, and impunity was guaranteed. Today they were the masters of Germany and tomorrow—according to one of their anthems—the entire world.

At the outbreak of World War II, Rudolph Hoess was already the *Schutzhaftlagerführer* (leader of the protective-custody camp—at Sachsenhausen, which was no small position. But he deserved a promotion. And when, to his surprise and delight, he was named Commandant of a new camp, he accepted. The camp, which was still under construction, was located far from Germany near a small Polish town named Oswiecim or, in German, Auschwitz.

He was truly—as he puts it without irony—an expert. At this juncture, his text becomes agitated: the Hoess who is writing this has already been condemned to death by a Polish tribunal, and since this sentence has been handed down by an authority, he fully accepts it. But this is no reason for him not to describe his finest hour. He pontificates, supplying us with a veritable treatise on city planning, his knowledge must not be lost, nor his patrimony scattered. He teaches us how to plan, build, and run a concentration camp so it will function smoothly, *reibungslos* (without friction), despite the ineptness of subordinates and the blindness and internal conflicts of superiors, who sent him more trainloads than the camp could handle. And what about him, the Commandant? Well, he makes do as best he can. Here, Hoess becomes downright heroic: he asks for the reader's praise, admiration, even commiseration. He was a highly competent and zealous functionary, sacrificing everything to *his* camp: his days, his nights of rest, his feelings for his family. But the Inspectorate had no understanding for him, they sent him no provisions—so that he, the model bureaucrat, squeezed between the upper and lower jaws of authority, had to "literally go and steal the most urgent minimum of barbed wire. . . . I had to attend to my own concerns!"

He's less convincing when setting himself up as a pundit for the sociology of the *Lager*. With righteous disgust he bemoans the infighting among the prisoners. What riffraff! They know neither honour nor solidarity, the great virtues of the German people. But then several lines later he nevertheless admits that 'those struggles were stirred up and cultivated by the head of the camp"—that is, Rudolph Hoess. With professional hauteur he describes the various categories of inmates,

mingling his old-fashioned scorn with jarring cries of post-facto hypo-
critical piety. The political prisoners were better than the common
criminals, the Gypsies ("the inmates I cherished most") were better
than the homosexuals, the Russian POWs were animals, and he never
liked the Jews.

In regard to the Jews his false notes become more strident. He feels
no conflict, his Nazi indoctrination never collides with a new and more
humane vision of the world. Quite simply, Hoess has understood nothing, he has not transcended his past, he is not cured. When he says (and
quite frequently at that), "Now I realize . . . Now I understand. . . .", he
is brazenly lying—as do today's political 'penitents' and all those who
express their remorse in words rather than deeds. Why does he lie?
Perhaps in order to leave us with a better image of himself, or perhaps
only because his judges, who are his new superiors, have told him that
the correct opinions are no longer the earlier ones but are now entirely
different ones.

The theme of Jews shows us how heavily Goebbels's propaganda
weighed on Germany and how hard it is to wipe out the effects it had—
even on a pliant individual like Rudolph Hoess. He admits that the Jews
were "quite persecuted" in Germany, but then he quickly points out
that their mass presence had a pernicious impact on the moral level of
the camps: the Jews, as is well-known, are rich, and money can corrupt
anybody, even the highly ethical officials of the SS. But the puritan
Hoess (who had an affair with an Auschwitz prisoner and extricated
himself by sending her to her death) does not agree with the pornographic anti-Semitism of Streicher's *Der Stürmer*: his newspaper "caused
a lot of harm; it was totally useless for serious anti-Semitism." But this
is not surprising since, as Hoess ad-libs, "the editor was a Jew." It was
the Jews who spread (Hoess doesn't dare say, 'invented') the atrocity
stories about Germany, and for that reason the Jews deserve to be punished. However, Hoess the Righteous disagrees with his superior Eicke,
who wanted to stop the leaking of information by applying the intelligent system of collective punishment. The campaign about atrocities
"would have continued *even* if hundreds or thousands of people had
been shot to death" (the stress on *even*, a gem of Nazi logic, is mine).

In the summer of 1941, Himmler "personally" notified Rudolph
Hoess that Auschwitz would be something different from a place of
affliction; it had to be "the largest extermination centre of all time," and
Hoess and his colleagues would have to come up with the best tech-
nology. Hoess didn't bat an eye, it was an order like any other, and

orders are not to be questioned. Experiments had been conducted in other camps, but mass machine-gunnings and toxic injections were inconvenient; they needed something faster and more reliable. Above all, the Germans had to avoid "bloodbaths," because they had a demoralising effect on the executioners. After the bloodiest actions, several SS-men killed themselves, others got methodically drunk. What they needed was something aseptic, something impersonal, to safeguard the mental health of the soldiers. Collective gassing set off by motors was a step in the right direction, but it had to be perfected. Hoess and his assistant got the brilliant idea of resorting to Cyclon B, a poison used on rats and cockroaches, and it was all for the best. After testing it on nine hundred Russian prisoners, Hoess felt "greatly at ease": the mass killing had gone well both quantitatively and qualitatively – no blood, and no trauma. It's one thing machine-gunning a bunch of naked people on the edge of a pit that they themselves have dug; but inserting a container of poison through an air conduit is fundamentally different. Rudolph Hoess's highest aspiration was reached, his professionalism had been demonstrated and he was the finest technician of mass slaughter. His envious colleagues were clobbered.

The most repugnant pages of this autobiography are those on which Hoess is quick to describe the brutality and indifference of those Jews who were assigned to get rid of the corpses. These passages contain a loathsome charge, an accusation of complicity, as if these unfortunates (weren't they too 'carrying out orders'?) could assume the guilt of the people who had created and delegated them. The crux of the book, and its least credible lie, then appears on page 154: in regard to killing children, Hoess says, "I felt such immense pity that I wanted to vanish from the face of the earth, but I wasn't allowed to show the slightest emotion." Who would have prevented him from "vanishing"? Not Himmler, his supreme superior, who, despite Hoess's great esteem, comes across as both a demi-urge and a pedantic, incoherent, and intractable idiot.

In the final section, which takes on the tone of a spiritual testament, Hoess again fails to gauge the horror of what he has done or to find a touch of sincerity. "Today I understand that the extermination of the Jews was a mistake, a colossal mistake" (not a 'crime'). "Anti-Semitism was absolutely useless [for us]; quite the contrary, Judaism took advantage of it in order to get closer to its ultimate objective." A short time later, Hoess says he felt "faint" upon "learning of the horrible tortures applied in Auschwitz and also in other camps." If we recall that the man writing those words is about to be hanged, we are stunned by his obstinacy in lying until his very last breath. There is only one possible explanation: Hoess, like all of his ilk (not only Germans; I'm thinking of the confessions of terrorists who have repented or dissociated themselves), spent all his life assimilating lies from the very air he breathed and therefore lying to himself.

We can wonder—and someone will certainly ask himself or others —if it makes any sense putting this book out again today, forty years after the end of the war and thirty-eight years after the execution of its author. To my mind there are at least two good reasons for doing so. The first reason is a contingent one. Several years ago, an insidious trend was launched when people began affirming that the number of victims of the Nazi era was far less than stated by 'official history,' and that no poison gas was used to kill human beings in the camps. In regard to both these points, Rudolph Hoess's testimony is complete and explicit, nor would he have formulated it in such a precise and articulate manner, and with so many details confirmed by survivors and by material evidence, if he had been acting under coercion, as the 'revisionists' allege. Hoess often lies to justify himself but never about facts; indeed, he seems proud of his organisational work. He and his supposed instigators would have had to be very shrewd to concoct such a coherent and plausible story out of thin air. The confessions extorted by the Inquisition, or by the Moscow Trials of the nineteen-thirties, or by the witch-hunts had an entirely different tone.

The second reason for republishing Hoess's book is an essential one with a permanent validity. At present, when many tears are being shed over the end of the ideologies, it strikes me that this text reveals in an exemplary fashion how far an ideology can go when it is accepted as radically as by Hitler's Germans, indeed by extremists in general. Ideologies can be good or bad, and it is good to know them, confront them, and attempt to evaluate them. But it is always bad to espouse an ideology even if it is cloaked with respectable words such as 'Country' and 'Duty.' The ultimate consequences of blindly accepted Duty—that is, Nazi Germany's *Führerprinzip*, the principle of unquestioning devotion to a Great Leader—are demonstrated by the story of Rudolph Hoess.

Primo Levi
March 1985
Translated from Italian by Joachim Neugroschel

Commandant of Auschwitz

Autobiography

In the following pages I want to try and tell the story of my inner-most being. I shall attempt to reconstruct from memory a true account of all the important events and occurrences in my life and of the psychological heights and depths through which I have passed.

In order to give as complete a picture as possible, it is essential that I first return to the earliest experiences of my childhood.

Until I was six years old, we lived in the remoter outskirts of Baden-Baden, in a neighbourhood consisting of scattered and isolated farmhouses. The children in the neighbourhood were all much older than I and consequently I had no playmates, and was dependent for companionship on grown-up people. I derived little pleasure from this, and tried, whenever possible, to escape their supervision and go off on voyages of solitary exploration. I was fascinated by the immense woods with their tall, Black Forest pines, that began near our house. I never ventured to go far into them, however, never beyond a point where I was able, from the mountain slopes, to keep our own valley in sight. Indeed, I was actually forbidden to go into the forest alone, since when I was younger some travelling gypsies had found me playing by myself and had taken me away with them. I was rescued by a neighbouring peasant who happened by chance to meet us on the road and who brought me back home.

A spot that I found particularly attractive was the large reservoir that supplied the town. For hours on end I would listen to the mysterious whisper of the water behind its thick walls, and could never, despite the explanations of my elders, understand what this was. But most of my time I spent in the farmers' byres and stables, and when people wished to find me it was always there that they looked for me first. The horses particularly delighted me, and I never tired of stroking them and talking to them and giving them tit-bits. If I could lay my hands on a brush or a curry-comb, I would at once begin grooming them. In spite of the farmers' anxiety, I would creep between the horses' legs while I brushed them, and never to this day has an animal kicked or bitten me. Even a bad-tempered bull that belonged to one of the farmers was always most friendly towards me. Nor was I ever afraid of dogs and none has ever attacked me. I would immediately forsake even my favourite toy, if I saw a chance to steal away to the stables. My mother did everything possible to wean me of this love of animals, which seemed to her so dangerous, but in vain. I developed into a solitary child, and was never happier than when playing or working alone and unobserved. I could not bear being watched by anybody.

Water, too, had an irrestible attraction for me, and I was perpetually washing and bathing. I used to wash all manner of things in the bath or in the stream that flowed through our garden, and many were the toys or clothes that I ruined in this way. This passion for water remains with me to this day.

When I was six years old we settled in the neighbourhood of Mannheim. As before, we lived on the outskirts of the town. But to my great disappointment there were no stables and no cattle. My mother often told me how, for weeks on end, I was almost ill with homesickness for my animals and my hills and forest. My parents did everything in their power at that time to distract me from my exaggerated love of animals. They did not succeed: I found books containing pictures of animals and would hide myself away, and dream of my cows and horses. On my seventh birthday I was given Hans, a coal-black pony with sparkling eyes and a long mane. I was almost beside myself with joy. I had a comrade at last. For Hans was the most confiding of creatures, and followed me wherever I went, like a dog. When my parents were away, I would even take him up to my bedroom. Since I was always on good terms with our servants, they accepted this weakness of mine and never gave me away. I had plenty of playmates of my own age where we now lived. We played the games that children play all over the world, and I took part in many a youthful prank. But my greatest joy was to take my Hans into the great Haardt Forest, where we could be entirely alone together, riding for hour after hour without meeting a soul.

School, and the more serious business of life, had now begun. Nothing happened during these first school years that is of importance to my story. I was a keen student, and used to finish my homework as quickly as possible, so that I might have plenty of free time to wander about with Hans.

My parents let me do more or less as I wished.

My father had taken a vow that I should be a priest, and my future profession was therefore already firmly laid down. I was educated entirely with this end in view. My father brought me up on strict military principles. I was also influenced by the deeply religious atmosphere that pervaded our family life, for my father was a devout Catholic. While we lived at Baden-Baden I saw little of my father, since he spent much of his time travelling, and his business sometimes kept him away from home for months at a time.[1] All this changed when we moved to Mannheim. My father now found time almost every day to take an interest in me, either checking my school-work or discussing my future profession with me. My greatest joy was to hear him talk of his experiences on active service in East Africa, and to listen to his descriptions of battles against rebellious natives, and his accounts of their lives and customs and sinister idolatories. I listened with passionate enthusiasm when he spoke of the blessed and civilising activities of the missionaries, and I was determined that I myself should one day be a missionary in the gloomy jungles of darkest Africa. They were red-letter days indeed when we were visited by one of the elderly, bearded African Fathers whom my father had known in East Africa. I did not let one word of the conversation escape me, becoming so absorbed that I even forgot my Hans.

My family entertained a great deal, although they rarely visited other people's houses. Our guests were mostly priests of every sort.

As the years passed, my father's religious fervour increased. Whenever time permitted, he would take me on pilgrimages to all the holy places in our own country, as well as to Einsiedeln in Switzerland and to Lourdes in France. He prayed passionately that the grace of God might be bestowed on me, so that I might one day become a priest blessed by God. I, too, was as deeply religious as was possible for a boy of my age, and I took my religious duties very seriously. I prayed with true, child-like gravity and performed my duties as acolyte with great earnestness. I had been brought up by my parents to be respectful and obedient towards all grown-up people, and especially the elderly, regardless of their social status.

[1] Rudolf Hoess's father, Franz Xavier Hoess, was a salesman.

I was taught that my highest duty was to help those in need. It was constantly impressed upon me in forceful terms that I must obey promptly the wishes and commands of my parents, teachers and priests, and indeed of all grown-up people, including servants, and that nothing must distract me from this duty. Whatever they said was always right.

These basic principles on which I was brought up became part of my flesh and blood. I can still clearly remember how my father, who on account of his fervent Catholicism was a determined opponent of the Reich government and its policy, never ceased to remind his friends that, however strong one's opposition might be, the laws and decrees of the State had to be obeyed unconditionally.

From my earliest youth I was brought up with a strong awareness of duty. In my parents' house it was insisted that every task be exactly and conscientiously carried out. Each member of the family had his own special duties to perform. My father took particular care to see that I obeyed all his instructions and wishes with the greatest meticulousness. I remember to this day how he hauled me out of bed one night, because I had left the saddle-cloth lying in the garden instead of hanging it up in the barn to dry, as he had told me to do. I had simply forgotten all about it. Again and again he impressed on me how great evils almost always spring from small, apparently insignificant misdeeds. At that time I did not fully understand the meaning of this dictum, but in later years I was to learn, through bitter experience, the truth of his words.

The relationship between my parents was one of loving respect and mutual understanding. Yet I never remember any display of tenderness; but at the same time I never heard them exchange an angry word. While my two sisters, who were four and six years younger than I, were very affectionate and were always hanging about their mother. I had always, from my earliest years, fought shy of any sign of tenderness, much to the regret of my mother, and of all my aunts and other relatives. A handshake and a few brief words of thanks were the most that could be expected of me.

Although both my parents were devoted to me, I was never able to confide in them the many big and little worries that from time to time beset a child's heart. I had to work all my problems out, as best I could, for myself. My sole confidant was my pony, and I was certain that he understood me. My two sisters were very attached to me, and were perpetually trying to establish a loving and sisterly relationship. But I never wished to have much to do with them. I shared in their games only when I had to, and then I would nag at them until they ran crying to my mother. Many were the practical jokes that I played on them. But despite all this, their devotion to me remained unchanged and they always regretted, and still do to this day, that I was never able to have any warmer feelings for them. They have always been strangers to me.

I had the greatest respect, however, for both my parents, and looked up to them with veneration. But love, the kind of love that other children have for their parents, which I myself later learnt to know, I was never able to give them. Why this should have been I have never understood. Even today I can find no explanation.

I was not particularly well-behaved, and certainly not a model child. I was up to all the tricks normal to a boy of my age. I ragged with the others and took part in the wildest games and brawls, whenever the opportunity came my way. Although there were always times when I had to be on my own, I had enough friends to play with when I wanted to. I stood no nonsense, and always held my own. If I were the victim of an injustice, I would not rest until I considered it avenged. In such matters I was implacable, and was held in terror by my class-mates. Incidentally, during the whole of my time at the grammar school I shared a bench with a Swedish girl who wanted to be a doctor. We always remained good friends and never quarrelled. It was the custom at our school for the same pupils to share a bench during the whole time they were at school together.

When I was thirteen years old, an incident occurred which I must regard as marking the first shattering of the religious beliefs to which I adhered so firmly.

During one of the usual scuffles that took place at the entrance to the gymnasium, I unintentionally threw one of my class-mates downstairs. He broke an ankle as a result. During the years, hundreds of school-boys must have tumbled down those stairs, I amongst them, and none had ever been seriously hurt. This particular boy was simply unlucky. I was given three days' confinement. It was a Saturday morning. That afternoon I went to confession as I did every week, and I made a clean breast of this accident. I said nothing about it at home, however, as I did not wish to spoil my parents' Sunday. They would learn about it soon enough next week. My confessor, who was a good friend of my father's had been invited to our house that same evening. Next morning I was taxed by my father concerning the accident, and duly punished because I had not told him about it straight away. I was completely overwhelmed, not on account of the punishment, but because of this undreamed-of betrayal on the part of the confessor. I had always been taught that the secrets of the sacred confessional were so inviolable that even the most serious offences there confided to the priest would never be revealed by him. And now this priest, in whom I had placed such implicit trust, to whom I regularly went for confession, and who knew by heart all the ins and outs of my petty sins, had broken the seal of the confessional over a matter as trifling as this! It could only have been he who had told my father of the accident, for neither my father nor my mother nor anyone at home had been into town that day. Our telephone was out of order. None of my class-mates lived in the neighbourhood. No one, other than this priest, had visited us. For a very long time I brooded over all the details of this incident, so monstrous did it appear to me. I was then, and still remain, completely convinced that the priest had broken the seal of confessional secrecy. My faith in the sacred priesthood had been destroyed and doubts began to arise in my mind for the first time. I no longer went to this priest for confession. When he and my father took me to task on that account, I was able to make the excuse that I went to confession in our school church, to the priest who gave us religious instruction. This seemed plausible enough to my father, but I am convinced that my former confessor knew my real reason. He did everything to win me back, but I could no longer bring myself to confess to him. In fact I went further, and gave up going to confession altogether, since I no longer regarded the priesthood as worthy of my trust.

I had been taught at school that God meted out severe punishment to those who went to Holy Communion without first making their confession. It might even happen that such sinners would be struck dead at the communion rail.

In my childish ignorance I earnestly beseeched our Heavenly Father to make allowances for the fact that I was no longer able to go to confession, and to forgive my sins which I then proceeded to enumerate. Thus did I believe that my sins had been forgiven me, and I went with trembling heart, uncertain as to the rightness of my actions, to communion in a church where I was unknown. Nothing happened! And I, poor, miserable worm, believed that God had heard my prayer, and had approved of what I had done.

My spirit, which in matters of belief had up to then been so peacefully and surely shepherded, had been severely shaken and the deep, genuine faith of a child had been shattered.

The next year my father died suddenly. I cannot remember that I was much affected by this. I was perhaps too young to appreciate my loss fully. And as a result of his death my life took a very different turn from that which he had wished.

The war broke out. The Mannheim garrison set off for the front. Reserve formations were created. The first trainloads of wounded arrived from the front. I was hardly ever at home. There was so much to see, and I did not want to miss anything. I pestered my mother until she gave me permission to enrol as an auxiliary with the Red Cross.

Amongst all the crowded impressions of that time it is now impossible to recall exactly how I was affected by my first contact with wounded soldiers. I can still remember the gory bandages around heads and arms, and our own field-grey uniforms and the pre-war blue tunics and red trousers of the French, all stained with blood and mud. I still hear their stifled groans as they were loaded into hastily-prepared tramcars. I ran hither and thither, handing out refreshments and tobacco. When not at school, I spent my whole time in the hospitals, or the barracks, or at the railway station meeting the troop transports and hospital trains and helping with the distribution of food and comforts. In the hospitals I used to tiptoe past the beds on which the seriously wounded lay moaning, and I saw many who were dying, or even dead. All this made a strange impression upon me, although I cannot now describe my sensations in any greater detail.

The memory of these sad scenes, however, was quickly dispelled by the unconquerable barrack-room humour of the soldiers who had only been slightly wounded or who were not in pain. I never tired of listening to their tales of the front and of their first-hand experiences. The soldier's blood that ran in my veins responded. For many generations all my forebears on my father's side had been officers; in 1870 my grandfather had fallen in battle, as a colonel at the head of his regiment. My father too had been a soldier through and through, even though once he had retired from the army his military enthusiasm had been quenched by his religious ardour. I wanted to be a soldier. I was determined at all costs not to miss this war. My mother and my guardian, in fact all my relations, did their best to dissuade me. I must first pass my matriculation, they said, and then we would talk it over. It had been decided in any case that I was to be a priest. I did not argue, but went on trying by every means to get to the front. I often hid in troop trains, but I was always discovered, and in spite of my earnest entreaties was taken back home by the military police on account of my age.

All my thoughts and hopes were directed at that time towards becoming a soldier. My school, my future profession and my home faded into the background. With quite extraordinary and touching patience and goodness, my mother did her best to make me change my mind. Yet I stubbornly went on seeking every opportunity of achieving my ambition. My mother was powerless in the face of such obstinacy. My relations wanted to send me to a training college for missionaries, although my mother was against this. I was half-hearted in matters of religion, even though I conscientiously followed the regulations of the Church. I lacked my father's strong, guiding hand.

In 1916 with the help of a cavalry captain whom I had got to know in hospital, I finally succeeded in joining the regiment in which my father and grandfather had served.[1] After a short period of training I was sent to the front, without my mother's knowledge.

I was to see her no more, for she died in 1917.

I was sent to Turkey and then to the Iraqi front.

The fact that I had enlisted secretly, combined with the ever-present fear that I be discovered and sent back home, made the long and varied journey that took me through many lands on my way to Turkey a deeply impressive event in the life of a boy not yet sixteen years old. The stay in Constantinople, which at that time was still a richly oriental city, and the journey by train and horse to the far-distant Iraqi front were likewise packed with fresh experiences. Nevertheless these were not of fundamental importance to me and do not remain clearly imprinted on my mind.

I remember, however, every detail of my first encounter with the enemy.

Soon after our arrival at the front we were attached to a Turkish division and our cavalry unit was broken up to act as a stiffening force with the three Turkish regiments. We were still being trained

[1] The 21st (Baden) Regiment of Dragoons.

in our duties when the British—New Zealanders and Indians—launched an attack. When the fighting became intense, the Turks ran away. Our little troop of Germans lay isolated in the vast expanse of desert, amongst the stones and the ruins of once flourishing civilisations, and we had to defend ourselves as best we could. We were short of ammunition, and the dressing-station had been left far behind with our horses. The enemy's fire became even more intense and accurate, and I soon realised how serious our situation was. One after another my comrades fell wounded and then suddenly the man next to me gave no answer when I called to him. I turned and saw that blood was pouring from a severe head-wound, and that he was already dead. I was seized with a terror, which I was never again to experience to the same extent, lest I too should suffer the same fate. Had I been alone I would certainly have run away, as the Turks had done. I kept glancing round at my dead comrade. Then suddenly, in my desperation, I noticed our captain, who was lying behind a rock with icy calm, as though on the practice range, and returning the enemy's fire with the rifle that had fallen from the hands of my dead neighbour. At that, a strange calm descended on me too, such as I had never before known. It dawned on me that I too must start shooting. Up to then I had not fired a single round and had only watched, with mounting terror, as the Indians slowly came nearer and nearer. One of them had just jumped out from a pile of stones. I can see him now, a tall, broad man with a bristling, black beard. For an instant I hesitated, the image of my dead comrade was before my eyes, then I let fly and, trembling, I saw how the Indian plunged forward, fell, and moved no more. I cannot honestly say whether I had even aimed my rifle properly. My first dead man! The spell was broken. I now fired, shot after shot, as I had been trained to do, and had no further thought of danger. Moreover, my captain was not far away and from time to time he would shout words of encouragement to me. The attack was halted as soon as the Indians realised that they were faced with serious resistance. Meanwhile the Turks had been driven forward once more, and a counter-attack was launched. On that same day a great deal of lost ground was recaptured. During the advance I glanced with some trepidation and nervousness at *my dead man*, and I did not feel very happy about it all. I cannot say whether I killed or wounded any more Indians during this battle, although I had aimed and fired at any enemy who emerged from behind cover. I was too excited about the whole thing.

My captain expressed his amazement at my coolness during this, my first battle, my *baptism of fire*. If he had only known how I actually felt deep down! Later I described to him my real state of mind. He laughed, and told me that all soldiers experience much the same sort of feelings.

I had an implicit and unusual confidence in my captain. He became, so to speak, my soldier-father and I held him in great respect. It was a far more profound relationship than that which had existed between myself and my real father. He kept me always under his eye. Although he never showed any favouritism towards me, he treated me with great affection, and looked after me as though I were his son. He was loth to let me go on long-distance reconnaissance patrols, although he always gave way in the end to my repeated requests that I be sent. He was especially proud when I was decorated or promoted.[1] He himself, however, never recommended me for any distinction. I mourned his loss deeply when he fell in the second Battle of the Jordan, in the spring of 1918. His death affected me very profoundly indeed.

At the beginning of 1917 our formation was transferred to the Palestine front. We were in the Holy Land. The old, familiar names from religious history and the stories of the saints were all about us. And how utterly different it all was from the pictures and stories that had filled my youthful dreams!

At first we took up positions on the Hejaz road, but later we moved to the Jerusalem front.

Thus one morning, as we were returning from a lengthy patrol on the far side of the Jordan, we met a column of farm-carts in the valley, filled with moss. As the British were using every imaginable means of supplying arms to the Arabs and the mixed races of Palestine, all only too anxious to shake off the Turkish yoke, we had orders to search all farm-carts and beasts of burden. We therefore told these peasants to unload their carts, and interrogated them with the help of our interpreter, a young Indian.

When we asked them where they were taking their moss, they explained that it was destined for the monasteries of Jerusalem, where it would be sold to the pilgrims. We were somewhat mystified by this explanation. A little later I was wounded, and sent to a

---

[1] Hoess was twice wounded, in Mesopotamia and Palestine. In 1917 and 1918 he received the Iron Cross, 1st and 2nd class, the Iron Crescent and the Baden Service Medal.

hospital in Wilhelma, a German settlement between Jerusalem and Jaffa. The colonists in this place had emigrated from Wurtemberg for religious reasons some generations before. While I was in hospital, they told me that a very profitable trade was carried out in the moss that the peasants brought to Jerusalem in their carts. It was a kind of Icelandic moss with greyish-white streaks and red spots. It was described to the pilgrims as having come from Golgotha, the red spots being the blood of Jesus, and it was sold to them at a high price. The colonists explained quite frankly that in peacetime, when thousands visited the holy places, the sale of this moss was an extremely lucrative business. The pilgrims would buy anything that was in any way connected with the saints or the shrines. The large pilgrim monasteries were the greatest offenders. There every effort was made to extract the maximum amount of money from the pilgrims. After my discharge from hospital, I had a chance of seeing with my own eyes some of these activities in Jerusalem. Owing to the war, there were only a few pilgrims, but this shortage was made good by the presence of German and Austrian soldiers. Later on I came across the same business in Nazareth. I discussed this matter with many of my comrades, because I was disgusted by the cynical manner in which this trade in allegedly holy relics was carried on by the representatives of the many churches established there.

Most of my friends were indifferent, and said that if people were so silly as to be taken in by these swindlers they must expect to pay for their stupidity. Others looked on the whole thing as a kind of tourist trade, such as always flourishes in places that have a special interest. But a few of them who, like me, were devout Catholics, condemned this traffic carried on by the churches, and were sickened by the way they cashed in on the deep, religious feelings of the pilgrims, many of whom had sold all they possessed in order to visit the holy places just once in their lives.

For a long time I failed to sort out my feelings in this matter, but nevertheless they probably played a decisive part in my subsequent renunciation of my faith. I should, however, mention in this connection that my comrades were all convinced Catholics, from the strongly Catholic Black Forest district. Never during this period did I hear a word spoken against the Church.

At this time I also experienced my first love affair. When in the hospital at Wilhelma, I was looked after by a young German nurse. I had been shot through the knee, and at the same time I went down with a severe and protracted bout of malaria. I therefore had to be given particular care and attention lest I harm myself during a feverish delirium. Not even my mother could have looked after me better than did this nurse. Gradually I became aware that it was not mother-love alone that made her bestow such loving attention on me. Until then I had never known love for a member of the opposite sex. I had of course heard a great deal of talk about sexual matters amongst my comrades, and soldiers do not mince their words on this subject. But, perhaps through lack of opportunity, I had had no personal experiences. In addition the hardships of that particular theatre of war were not exactly conducive to love-making.

At first I was distressed by her tender caresses and by the way in which she would hold me up and support me longer than was strictly necessary. For, ever since my earliest childhood, I had shunned all demonstration of affection. But at last I too fell under the magic spell of love, and began to regard the woman with new eyes. This love affair, which developed under her guidance stage by stage until its final consummation, was for me a wonderful and undreamed-of experience. I would never have been able on my own to summon enough courage to bring it about. In all its tenderness and charm, it was to affect me throughout all the rest of my life. I could never again speak flippantly of such matters; sexual intercourse without real affection became unthinkable for me. Thus I was saved from casual flirtations and brothels.

The war came to an end. The upshot of my army service was that I had reached manhood, both physically and mentally, long before my years. My wartime experiences had left their mark on me, a mark that would never be erased. I had broken away from the narrow safety of my parents' home. My attitude to life was wider. I had seen and experienced a great deal during the two and a half years that I had spent in foreign lands. I had got to know all sorts and conditions of men, and had observed their needs and weaknesses.

The frightened schoolboy who had escaped from his mother's care and fought his first action against the enemy had become a tough and hardened soldier. I became a non-commissioned officer at the age of seventeen, the youngest in the army, and was decorated with the Iron Cross, First Class. After my promotion I was engaged almost entirely on long-range reconnaissance and sabotage behind the enemy lines. Meanwhile I had learnt that the ability to lead men depends not on rank, but on skill, and that in difficult situations it is icy calm and unshakeable imperturbability that are decisive in a commanding officer. But I had also learnt how hard it is always to be an example to others and to keep up an appearance that does not betray one's real feelings.

The armistice found us in Damascus. I was determined at all costs not to be interned, and decided on my own initiative to fight my way home. The Corps had warned us against this. After a discussion, all the men of my troop volunteered to come with me. Since the spring of 1918 I had commanded an independent cavalry troop of which all the men were in their thirties, while I was just eighteen.

We had an adventurous journey through Anatolia, sailed across the Black Sea to Varna in a miserable coaster, travelled on through Bulgaria and Rumania and made our way, in deep snow, through the Transylvanian Alps to Hungary and Austria. We eventually reached home after almost three months of travelling. We had no maps to help us and had to rely on a school atlas. We were always short of food both for ourselves and our horses and we had to force our way through a Rumania which had now become hostile again. Our arrival at the regimental depot was completely unexpected. So far as I know no other complete unit from our theatre of war succeeded in reaching home.

During the war I had repeated doubts concerning my suitability for the priesthood. The affair of my confession, and the trade in sacred relics that I had seen in the Holy Land, had destroyed my faith in priests. I also had doubts concerning various established customs of the Church. Gradually I became of the opinion that I must refuse to follow the profession that my father had vowed should be mine. I discussed this with no one. In the last letter that she wrote before her death, my mother had told me never to forget the future that my father had foreseen for me! The respect that I had for my parents' wishes, and my rejection of the profession they had chosen for me, threw my mind into a turmoil, and I was still unable to see matters clearly when at last I arrived home.

My guardian, and indeed all my relations, badgered me to go at once to a training college for priests, so that I might find the right surroundings and prepare for my predestined profession. Our household had been completely broken up, and my sisters had been sent to a convent school. I realised for the first time the full signifi-cance of my mother's death. I no longer had a home. My ' dear relations ' had shared out amongst themselves all those cherished possessions which had formed part of the home we had loved; they were certain that I would become a missionary and my sisters remain in the convent, and that therefore we would have no further use for such worldly things. Sufficient money had been left to buy our entry into the mission-house and the convent.

Filled with indignation at my relations' high-handed action, and, with distress at the loss of my home, I went that very day to my uncle, who was also my guardian, and told him curtly that I had decided not to become a priest. He tried to compel me to change my mind, by telling me that he was not prepared to find the money to set me up in any other profession, since my parents had decided upon the priesthood for me. I speedily resolved to renounce my share of the inheritance in favour of my sisters, and on the following day I got my lawyer to draw up the necessary documents. From then on I refused to accept any further help from my relations. I would battle my way through the world alone. Full of rage and without saying goodbye, I left this ' relation-ridden ' house, and travelled to East Prussia, in order to enlist in a Freikorps[1] destined for the Baltic States.

In this way, the problem of my profession was suddenly solved and I became a soldier once more. I found a home again, and a sense of security in the comradeship of my fellows. Oddly enough it was I, the lone wolf, always keeping my thoughts and my feelings to myself, who felt continually drawn towards that comradeship which enables a man to rely on others in time of need and of danger.

The fighting in the Baltic States was more savage and more bitter than any I had experienced either in the World War or later with the Freikorps. There was no real front, for the enemy was everywhere. When it came to a clash, it was a fight to the death, and no quarter was given or expected. The Letts excelled in this kind of fighting. It was there that I saw for the first time the horrors endured by a civilian population. The Letts exacted a terrible revenge on those of their own people who sheltered or cared for the German or Russian soldiers of the White Army. They set their houses on fire and burned the occupants to death. On innumerable occasions I came across this terrible spectacle of burned-out cottages containing the charred corpses of women and children.

[1] Volunteer units of former soldiers which sprang up in Germany at this time, and which were originally formed to safeguard the frontiers and prevent internal disturbance. The one he belonged to was the Freikorps Rossbach, with which he fought in the Baltic States, Mecklenburg, the Ruhr and Upper Silesia.

When I saw it the first time, I was dumbfounded. I believed then that I was witnessing the height of man's destructive madness.

Although later on I had to be the continual witness of far more terrible scenes, yet the picture of those half-burned-out huts at the edge of the forest beside the Dvina, with whole families dead within them, remains indelibly engraved on my mind. At that time I was still able to pray, and I did.

The Freikorps of the years 1918 to 1921 were peculiar phenomena of the times. The government of the day needed them whenever trouble started either on the frontiers or within the country, and when the police force, or later the army, was too weak to deal with the situation or for political reasons dared not put in an appearance. Once the danger had passed, or when France made pointed enquiries, the government promptly disowned them. They were then dissolved and the new organisations which succeeded them, and were awaiting employment, were prosecuted.

The members of this particular Freikorps consisted of officers and men who had returned from the war and who found themselves misfits in civilian life, of adventurers who wanted to try their hand at this game, of unemployed men anxious to escape from idleness and public charity, and of young enthusiastic volunteers who hastened to take up arms for love of their country. All of them, without exception, were bound by a personal oath of loyalty to their Corps leader. The Corps stood or fell with him. As a result there developed a feeling of solidarity and an *esprit de corps* which nothing could destroy. In fact the more we were pushed around by the government in office, the more firmly did we stick together. Woe to anyone who attempted to divide us—or betray us!

Since the government was forced to deny the existence of these volunteer Corps, the authorities were unable to enquire into or punish offences committed by their members in the cause of their duties, offences such as the theft of weapons, the betrayal of military secrets, high treason and so on. The Freikorps and their successor organisations therefore administered justice themselves, after the ancient Germanic pattern of the *Vehmgericht*[1] of olden times. Treachery was punished with death, and there were many traitors so executed.

Only a few of these incidents became known, however, and even then it was only very rarely the ' executioners ' were caught and

[1] Medieval courts that sat, and passed sentence, in secret.

brought to trial before the State Court for the Defence of the Republic, a court especially created for this purpose.[1]

But that was what happened in *my* case. There was a *Vehmgericht* murder trial in which I was involved and as a result of which I, as the alleged ringleader and the person most concerned, was sentenced to ten years' hard labour. We had killed the man who had betrayed Schlageter to the French. One of us who was present when we carried out the execution gave an account of it to *Vorwärts*, the leading social-democratic newspaper, ostensibly out of feelings of remorse but actually, as was afterwards established, in order to make money. What really happened was never made clear. The witnesses for the prosecution were not sufficiently sober at the time of the incident to be able to remember the exact details. Those who really knew what had taken place remained silent.

I was certainly there myself, but I was neither the ringleader nor the person chiefly concerned. When I saw, during interrogation, that the comrade who actually did the deed could only be incriminated by my testimony, I took the blame on myself, and he was released while the investigation was still going on. I need not emphasise that, for the reasons given above, I was in complete agreement with sentence of death being carried out on the traitor. In addition, Schlageter was an old comrade of mine. I had fought beside him in many a bitter scrap in the Baltic and in the Ruhr, and had worked with him behind the enemy lines in Upper Silesia. We had also done a lot of illicit gun-running together.

---

[1] The State Court for the Defence of the Republic was established in connection with the Law for the Defence of the Republic, enacted 26 June, 1922. It is incorrect to say that it was 'specially' created to deal with Vehm murders. Paragraph 7 of the Law in question shows that this Court was competent to judge cases in which the accused were tried for crimes directed against the Republic (as a State form) and against members of the government. This Law was passed, and the Court in question established, consequent on the murder of the Foreign Minister, Rathenau, on 24 June, 1922. (For an interesting though not always reliable description of this murder by one of the murderers, see *The Answers of Ernst von Salomon*, Putnam, 1945.) The Court was not concerned with Vehm murders as such. The reason why the Parchim trial was held in this Court, at Leipzig, and not in the normal district court at Schwerin, was that the Schwerin State Attorney had declared that Hoess and almost all his accomplices in the crime belonged to the 'Union for Agricultural Professional Training', an illegal successor-organisation to the banned 'Rossbach Labour Community', which itself had been the Freikorps Rossbach, also declared illegal, under another name: since this organisation was hostile to the republican form of government, political crimes committed by its members as such made them subject to the jurisdiction of this special Court.

I was at the time, and remain to this day, completely convinced that this traitor deserved to be put to death. In all probability no German court would have convicted him, so it was left to us to pass sentence in accordance with an unwritten law which we ourselves, owing to the exigencies of the times, had laid down.[1]

This can, perhaps, only be fully understood by those who lived, or can imagine themselves living, in the chaotic conditions existing at that time.

During the nine months that I spent awaiting trial, and also during the trial itself, I was far from appreciating the seriousness of my position. I firmly believed that my trial would probably never take place and that even if it did I would certainly be acquitted. The political crisis in the Reich during 1923 was so acute that the overthrow of the government by one side or the other seemed inevitable. I confidently anticipated that in due course we would be set free by our comrades. Hitler's abortive *putsch* on 9 November, 1923, should have made me think again. I still pinned my hopes, however, on a favourable turn of events.[2]

My two defence lawyers took great pains to point out the gravity of my position and were of the opinion that I must expect at least a lengthy term of imprisonment, if not the death sentence itself, as a result of the new political composition of the tribunal and the more stringent measures that were being enforced against all nationalist

[1] Hoess's description of the Parchim murder is coloured in his favour, and contains inaccuracies. Evidence given before the Court which sat in Leipzig from 12 to 15 March, 1924, shows this to have been a particularly brutal murder. It had been decided that a former elementary schoolteacher by the name of Kadow was a Communist spy who had infiltrated the Rossbach organisation. Hoess and others—Martin Bormann was indirectly implicated—spent the night of 31 May-1 June, 1922, drinking, and then abducted Kadow into the woods, where he was beaten almost to death with clubs and branches, after which his throat was cut and he was finally finished off with two revolver bullets. There is not the slightest scrap of evidence to show that Kadow was in any way connected with the Schlageter affair. However, since Schlageter had been condemned to death by the French authorities in the Ruhr only a few days before the Kadow murder, it is possible that Hoess had been confused by remarks that Kadow was a traitor 'like the man who betrayed Schlageter to the French'. Nor is there any reason to believe that the man who gave evidence against Hoess and the others sold his story to *Vorwärts*. He was named Jurisch, and the Court for the Defence of the Republic decided that he told his story, thus implicating himself, because he feared lest he himself be murdered by members of the Rossbach organisation for knowing too much.

[2] Hoess was arrested on 28 June, 1923. On 15 March, 1924, he was sentenced to ten years imprisonment, six months of this sentence to count as already served.

organisations. I could not bring myself to believe this. While in prison awaiting trial, we received every possible consideration, for the great majority of us were, politically speaking, from the left, mostly communists; comparatively few belonged, like myself, to the right. Even Zeigner, the Minister of Justice for Saxony, sat in his own prison accused of profiteering and of perverting the course of justice.[1] We could write a lot and were allowed to receive both letters and parcels. We could get the newspapers and so were at all times aware of what was happening outside. We were, however, kept strictly isolated from one another, and we were always blindfolded when we were taken from our cells. Contact with our friends was confined to a few, occasional words shouted through the windows.

During the trial we found that the conversations that we were able to have amongst ourselves during the intervals and during our journeys to and from the court, and the renewed contact with our comrades, were far more important and interesting than the trial itself. Even the pronouncement of sentence made little impression on myself or my comrades. We left the court in boisterous mood, shouting and singing our old songs of battle and defiance. Was this just a grim sort of humour? For my part I do not think so. I was simply unable to believe that I would have to serve my sentence.

The bitter awakening came only too soon, after I had been transferred to the prison where I was to begin my term of hard labour.

A new, and up to then unknown, world now opened before me. Serving a sentence in a Prussian prison in those days was no rest-cure.

Every aspect of life was strictly regulated down to the smallest details. Discipline was on severe, military lines. The greatest emphasis was placed on the punctilious discharge and most careful execution of the exactly calculated task that was alloted each day. Every offence was severely punished, and the effect of these ' house punishments ' was increased by the fact that they entailed a refusal of any possible reduction of sentence.

---

[1] Dr Erich Zeigner had attempted to set up a Communist Government in Saxony, and was deprived of his functions as Prime Minister and Minister of Justice for Saxony by a decree of the President of the Reich dated 29 October, 1923. He was later tried on a charge of abuse of public office, specifically for destroying public documents and subverting public funds for party political ends. On 29 March, 1924, he was sentenced to three years in prison.

As a political prisoner, found guilty of a ' crime of conviction ', I was kept in solitary confinement. At first I was not at all happy about this, for I had just had nine months solitary in Leipzig, but later I was only too thankful, in spite of the many small amenities that life in the large communal cells offered. In my cell I had only myself to consider. Once I had completed my allotted task, I could arrange my day as I wished without regard to any fellow-prisoner, and I escaped the hideous bullying practised by the real criminals in the larger cells. I had learnt, though at secondhand, a little about such bullying which is directed mercilessly against all who do not belong to the criminal fraternity or who fail to hide their views. Even the strict supervision of a Prussian prison was unable to prevent this terrorism.

At that time I believed I knew all about human nature. I had seen all sorts and types of men of many different nations and classes, and had observed their habits, both the good and even more so the bad. For though I was still young, I had had considerable experience of the world, and had been through a lot.

The criminals who shared my prison made me realise how little I really knew. Even though I lived alone in my cell, I yet came into daily contact with my fellow-prisoners during exercise in the court-yard, or on the way to one or other of the prison administration offices, in the wash-houses, through contact with the cleaners, or at the barber's, or with the prisoners who brought or collected the work materials or in many other ways. Above all, I listened to their talk every evening from my window. From all this I got a fairly good insight into the minds and souls of these people and an abyss of human aberrations, depravities and passions was opened before my eyes.

I had hardly begun to serve my sentence before I overheard a prisoner in a neighbouring cell tell another about a robbery he had committed at a forester's house. He had first made sure that the forester was sitting happily in the inn and had then, with an axe, killed first the servant girl and then the man's wife, who was far advanced in pregnancy. The forester's four small children began to cry and he seized each of them in turn and dashed their heads against the wall to stop their ' hollering '. The filthy, insolent language that he used when recounting the details of this appalling crime made me long to fly at his throat. I could not sleep all that night. Later I was to hear far more terrible stories, but nothing was ever again to disturb me as much as what I heard on that day. The man who told this story was a murderer who had been condemned to death many times, but had always been reprieved. Even while I was serving my sentence, he broke out of the dormitory one evening, attacked with a length of iron, a warder who was barring his way and escaped over the prison wall. He was arrested by the police after he had knocked down an innocent pedestrian in order to steal his clothes, and he then furiously attacked his captors, who immediately shot him dead.

The Brandenburg prison also held the cream of Berlin's professional criminals. They ranged from international pick-pockets to well-known safe-breakers, gangsters, card-sharpers, skilled confidence tricksters and men convicted of all kinds of disgusting sexual offences.

The place was a regular school for criminals. The younger ones, the learners, were enthusiastically initiated into the secrets of their craft, although their instructors kept their personal tricks of the trade a close secret. The old lags naturally saw to it that they were well paid for their services. Payment was often made in tobacco, which was the most usual form of prison currency. Smoking was strictly forbidden, but every smoker managed to procure tobacco for himself by going fifty-fifty with the junior warders. The provision of services of a sexual nature was also a customary form of payment. Sometimes, too, binding agreements were made for a share in a criminal undertaking planned to take place after release from prison. Many sensational crimes owed their origin to schemes hatched while their perpetrators were serving prison sentences. Homosexuality was widespread. The younger, good-looking prisoners were greatly in demand and were the cause of much bitter rivalry and intrigue. The more crafty of these made a good business out of their popularity.

In my opinion, based on years of experience and observation, the widespread homosexuality found in these prisons is rarely congenital, or in the nature of a disease, but is rather the result of strong sexual desires which cannot be satisfied in any other way. It arises primarily from a search for a stimulating or exciting activity that promises to give the men something out of life, in surroundings where absolutely no form of moral restraint applies.

Amongst this mass of criminals, who had become so from inclination or propensity, there were to be found a great many who had been driven to swindling and thieving through misery and want during the bad, post-war years and the inflation period: men whose character was not sufficiently strong to enable them to withstand the temptation of getting-rich-quick by illegal means: men who by some unlucky chance had been dragged into a whirlpool of crime. Many of these struggled honourably and bravely to break away from the a-social influence of this criminal atmosphere, so that they might start a decent life once more, after they had served their sentences.

Many, however, were too weak to fight against this interminable, a-social pressure and the incessant terrorisation, and they were soon condemned to a lifetime of crime.

In this respect, the prison cell became a confessional box. When I was in Leipzig gaol being interrogated before my trial, I heard many window-conversations: conversations in which men and women expressed their deeper anxieties and sought consolation from one another; conversations in which accomplices bitterly complained of betrayal, and in which the public prosecutor's office would have shown great interest, since they threw light on many an unsolved crime.

I used to be amazed at the free and easy way in which prisoners would give utterance through the window to their darkest and best-kept secrets. Was this urge to confide born of the misery of solitary confinement or did it spring from the universal need of all human beings to talk to one another? While we were awaiting trial, these window-conversations were extremely brief and were constantly threatened by the permanent watch which the warders kept on the cells. In the prison where we served our sentences, however, the warders only bothered about them if the voices became too loud. There were three types of prisoner in solitary confinement in the Brandenburg prison: 1. Political prisoners found guilty of a ' crime of conviction '; these young first-offenders were treated with consideration. 2. Violent criminals and trouble-makers, who had become intolerable in the large, communal cells. 3. Prisoners who had made themselves disliked because of their refusal to acquiesce in the terrorism practised by their fellow-criminals, or stool-pigeons who had betrayed their friends in some way and now feared revenge. For these it was a kind of protective custody.

Evening after evening I would listen to their conversations. I thus obtained a deep insight into the psyche of these condemned men.

Later, during the final year of my imprisonment, when my job as chief clerk in the general store brought me into daily, personal contact with them, I got to know them even more intimately and I found my previous knowledge of them abundantly confirmed.

The real, professional criminal who has become so either by choice or by reason of his inherent nature, has cut himself off from the society of his fellow-citizens. He combats that society by means of his criminal activities. He no longer wants to lead an honest life, for he has become wedded to his life of crime and has made it his profession.

Comradeship for him is based solely on expediency, though he also can slip into a sort of bondage-relationship, similar to that between a prostitute and her pimp, which endures however badly he may treat her. Moral concepts such as sincerity and honesty are as laughable to him as is the notion of private property. He regards his conviction and sentence as a bit of commercial bad luck, a business loss, a hitch, nothing more. He attempts to make his prison sentence as tolerable and even as pleasant as possible. He knows the insides of many prisons, their peculiarities and the influence wielded by their officials, and he makes every effort to be transferred to the one he prefers. He is no longer capable of any generous feelings. Every effort, by education or kindness, to lead him back into the right path, is rebuffed. Now and again, for tactical reasons, he will play the part of the repentant sinner in order to have part of his sentence remitted. He is generally rough and common, and it affords him great satisfaction to trample upon everything that others regard as sacred.

One incident will serve as an illustration. During the years 1926 and 1927 humane and progressive methods of punishment were introduced into the prison. Amongst other innovations a concert was held each Sunday morning in the prison church, in which some of Berlin's foremost performers took part. At one of these a famous Berlin singer sang Gounod's *Ave Maria* with a virtuosity and a tenderness such as I have seldom heard. Most of the prisoners were enraptured by this performance, and even the most callous may well have been stirred by the music. But not all. Hardly had the last notes died away, when I heard one old lag say to his neighbour: ' What wouldn't I do to get my hands on those sparklers, mate! ' Such was the effect of a deeply moving performance on criminals. A-social, in the true meaning of the word.

Amongst this mass of typical professional criminals was a great number of prisoners who could not be included in quite the same class. They were borderline cases. Some were already treading the slippery path that leads to the tempting and exciting world of crime, while others were fighting with all their strength against being enmeshed in its will-o'-the-wisp attractions. Others, led astray for the first time but weak by nature, found themselves in a constant state of vacillation between the external pressures of prison life and their own inner feelings.

The mentality of this group was made up of diverse characteristics and ranged through the whole scale of human sensibility. They often rushed between one extreme and the other.

Prison had no effect at all on men of a light-hearted and frivolous nature. Their souls lacked ballast and they lived gaily from day to day. They gave no thought to the future and would continue to amble easily through life as they had done before, until some new trouble overtook them.

It was quite different with those whose minds were of a serious bent. They tried to avoid the poisonous atmosphere of the communal cells. Most of them, however, found that they were unable to endure the rigours of solitary confinement; they were frightened by loneliness and the perpetual self-examination that it entailed, and they soon returned to the squalor of the crowded cells.

There was, indeed, the possibility of sharing a cell with two other men. But it was rare to find three men who could, for any length of time, endure living together at such close quarters. These little groups had repeatedly to be broken up. I knew of none that lasted long. A lengthy term of imprisonment makes even the best man irritable, unsociable, and lacking in consideration. In such close quarters, consideration for one's companions is an essential.

It was not only the imprisonment itself, the monotonous sameness of the daily round, the perpetual discipline imposed by countless orders and regulations, the endless bawling and cursing of the warders over trifles, that crushed these serious-minded prisoners, but even more it was the prospect of the future and of what they were to do with their lives after they had served their sentences. Their conversation usually revolved about this. Would they be able to fit into normal life again, or would they find themselves outcasts?

If they were married as well, their families were a further cause of gnawing anxieties. Would their wives remain faithful during such a long separation? Such considerations had a deeply depressing effect on men of this kind, which not even the daily work or the serious literature which they read in their spare time could dispel.

Often their minds became deranged, or they committed suicide for no real reason. By ' real reasons ' I mean such as bad news from home, divorce, the death of near relatives, refusal of a petition for mitigation of sentence and so on.

Nor was imprisonment easy for the irresolute types, the ones who could never make up their minds. They were too impressionable and easily influenced by the others. A few tempting words from some old lag, or a wad of tobacco, could be sufficient to scatter their best intentions to the winds.

On the other hand, a good book or a serious conversation would induce such men to peaceful self-contemplation and meditation.

In my opinion many of the inmates could have been brought back to the right path if the senior officials had been more human, and less conscious of their official positions. Especially was this so with regard to the priests of both confessions, who through their functions as censors of correspondence as well as through their official duties were well aware of the condition and frame of mind of the men who composed their flocks.

All these officials, however, had grown dull and grey in the perpetual monotony of their work. Their eyes were blind to the needs of a man struggling earnestly to re-make his life. Should such a prisoner manage to summon enough courage to ask his priest or clergyman for advice in his troubles, he was immediately greeted with the standard assumption: that he was feigning repentance in order to obtain a remission of sentence.

It is true that the officials had become accustomed to such deceptions, practised by men unworthy of pity or understanding. Even the most cynical criminal became devout when the time drew near for his petition for remission of sentence to be examined, though there might be only the smallest prospect of its success.

On countless occasions I heard prisoners complaining to one another how grievously they felt the lack of help from the prison administration in their worries and anxieties.

The psychological effect of their punishment on these serious-minded prisoners, who genuinely wished to be better men, was far greater than that caused by physical hardship. In comparison with their more irresponsible comrades, they were punished twice over.

After the consolidation of the political and economic situation following the inflation, a broadly democratic outlook prevailed in

Germany. Amongst many other government innovations in those years was the introduction of a humane and progressive attitude towards the purpose of prison sentences. It was believed that those who had broken the law of the State could be made into good citizens again by means of education and kindness. The theory was that every man is the product of his environment. If one gave the law-breaker who had served his sentence an economically adequate and secure existence, this would provide him with an incentive for social advancement, and he would be saved from going astray once more. Suitable social trust would enable him to forget his a-social attitude and would prevent him from slipping back into a life of crime.

The cultural standards of the penal establishments were to be raised by educational means such as musical performances, which would enliven the spirit, and well-chosen lectures on the basic moral laws governing human society and on the fundamental principles of ethics and other such themes.

The senior prison officials were to devote more attention to the individual prisoners and to their psychological troubles. The prisoner himself, owing to a three-degree system offering many kinds of contractual privileges hitherto unknown, could gradually advance, by means of good behaviour, diligent work and proof of a change of heart, to the IIIrd degree and thus obtain an early release on probation. In optimum cases he could obtain a remission of half his sentence.

I myself was the first of approximately 800 prisoners to reach the IIIrd degree. Up to the time of my release there were not more than a dozen who, in the opinion of the authorities, were worthy of wearing the three stripes on their sleeve. In my case all the afore-mentioned qualifications were present. I had never been given any kind of house punishment or even a reprimand; I had always completed more than my daily work-task; I was a first offender who had not been deprived of civil rights, and I was classified as guilty of a ' crime of conviction '. Since, however, I had been condemned by the political tribunal, I could only be released before completing my sentence as the result of an Act of Grace on the part of the President of the Reich, or of an amnesty.

Almost as soon as I had begun to serve my sentence, I finally realised the full nature of my predicament. I came to my senses. There could be no doubt that I was faced with the almost certain prospect of serving a sentence of ten years' hard labour. A letter from one of my defending lawyers on the matter at last confirmed what I now knew to be the case. And I accepted the reality of this ten-year sentence. Up to then I had enjoyed each day as it came, had taken the good with the bad, and had never given a serious thought to my future. Now I had leisure enough to reflect on my past life, to recognise my mistakes and my weaknesses, and to train myself for a richer and more rewarding life in the future.

I had indeed found, in the periods between my Freikorps activities, a profession that I enjoyed and loved and in which I could do well. I had developed a passion for farming and had done well as a farmer; witnesses who gave evidence at my trial confirmed this.

But the real essence of life, that which makes living a true fulfilment, was still unknown to me at the time. I began to seek for it, absurd as this may sound, behind my prison walls, and found it, later!

I had been taught since childhood to be absolutely obedient and meticulously tidy and clean; so in these matters I did not find it difficult to conform to the strict discipline of prison.

I conscientiously carried out my well-defined duties. I completed the work allotted me, and usually more, to the satisfaction of the foreman. My cell was a model of neatness and cleanliness, and even the most malicious eyes could see nothing there with which to find fault.

I even became accustomed to the perpetual monotony of my daily existence, which was rarely broken by any unusual event, although this acceptance was quite contrary to my restless nature. My former life had been extremely hectic and lively.

An outstanding event during the first two years was the arrival of the letter which we were allowed to receive every three months. I would think about it for days before it came, imagining and envisaging everything it might possibly contain. The letter was from my fiancée. At least she was my fiancée as far as the prison administration was concerned. She was the sister of a friend of mine and I had never seen her or heard of her before. Since I was only allowed to correspond with relatives, my friends, when I was in Leipzig gaol, had produced a ' fiancée ' for me. This girl wrote to me faithfully throughout all the long years of my imprisonment. She did everything I asked of her, kept me informed of all that went on in my circle of friends outside, and passed on all my own news.

Yet I never became accustomed to the petty chicanery of the junior officials. This always had an extremely disturbing effect on me, especially when it was deliberate and malicious. The senior officials, up to the prison governor himself, always treated me correctly. So too did the majority of the junior officials with whom I came in contact during the course of the years. But there were three of these who, for political reasons, being Social Democrats, bullied me whenever they could. This bullying usually consisted of mere pin-pricks, but they nevertheless managed to wound me severely. In fact they hurt me much more in this way than if I had been physically beaten.

Every prisoner who lives a sensitive inner life suffers far more from unjustified, malicious and deliberate acts of spite, in a word, from acts of mental cruelty, than ever he does from the physical equivalent. Such acts produce a far more ignominious and oppressive effect than does corporal maltreatment.

I often tried to make myself indifferent to this, but I never succeeded.

I grew accustomed to the crude language of the junior warders, whose delight in the power they wielded increased in proportion to the lowness of their mentality. I also got used to the senseless orders which these same narrow-minded officials would give, and I would carry them out without demur, and even with an inward chuckle.

I became acccustomed, too, to the disgusting language used by the prisoners when they met.

But though it happened every day, I could never accustom myself to the common, cynical and filthy way in which the prisoners treated everything good and beautiful, everything which many men regard as sacred. They became especially vicious when they noticed that a fellow-prisoner could be hurt by such talk. This kind of behaviour has always affected me strongly.

I have ever regarded a good book as a good friend. Up to then my restless life had given me little time or leisure for reading. But in the loneliness of my cell books became my all, and this was especially so during the first two years of my sentence. They were my one relaxation, and they enabled me entirely to forget my situation.

Towards the end of the first two years, which had passed monotonously and without any special incident, I was overcome by a most peculiar state of mind. I became very irritable, nervous and excited. I felt a disinclination to work, although I was in the tailoring shop at the time and had hitherto thoroughly enjoyed this work. I could no longer eat and I brought up every mouthful that I forced myself to swallow. I could not read any more, and became completely unable to concentrate. I paced up and down my cell like a wild animal. I lay awake all night, although I had up to then always fallen at once into a deep and almost dreamless sleep. I had to get out of bed and walk round and round my cell, and was unable to lie still. Then I would sink exhausted on to the bed and fall asleep, only to wake again after a short time bathed in sweat from my nightmares. In these confused dreams I was always being pursued and killed, or falling over a precipice. The hours of darkness became a torment. Night after night I heard the clocks strike the hour. As morning approached, my dread increased. I feared the light of day and the people I should have to see once more. I felt incapable of seeing them again. I tried with all my strength to pull myself together, but without success. I wanted to pray, but my prayers dissolved into a distressed stammering. I had forgotten how to pray, and had lost the way to God. In my misery I believed that God had no wish to help me, since I had forsaken Him. I was tormented by the memory of my definite secession from the Church in 1922. Yet this had been the ratification of a state of affairs that had existed since the end of the war. In my heart I was already leaving the Church during the last years of the war. I reproached myself bitterly for not having followed the wishes of my parents, for my lack of piety. It was strange how all this worried me while I was in this plight.

My nervous agitation increased day to day, even from hour to hour. I nearly went raving mad. My health gave way. My foreman noticed my unaccustomed absent-mindedness and the mess I made of even the simplest tasks, and although I worked furiously I could not finish my daily task.

For several days I had fasted, thinking that after this I would be able to eat once more. The warder in charge of my section caught me in the act of throwing my dinner into the garbage pail. Although he usually did his job in a weary and indifferent manner, and hardly bothered about the prisoners, yet even he had noticed my behaviour and appearance, and on this account had been keeping a sharp watch over me, as he later told me. I was taken immediately to the doctor. He was an elderly man who had been attached to the prison staff for a great many years. He listened patiently to my story, thumbed through the pages of my file and then said with the greatest nonchalance: ' Prison psychosis. You'll get over it. It's not serious! '

I was taken to the sick-room and placed in an observation cell. Then I was given an injection, wrapped in cold sheets, and immediately I fell into a deep sleep. During the following days I was given sedatives and put on an invalid diet. My general nervous condition subsided and I began to pick up. At my own wish I was returned to my cell. It was first intended that I be put in a cell with other prisoners, but I had requested to be left on my own.

At this time I was informed by the prison governor that on account of my good behaviour and industriousness I was to be promoted to the IInd degree and as a result would receive various alleviations of my prison existence. I might now write letters once a month, and could receive as much mail as I liked. I might also have books and instructional literature sent in to me. I might grow flowers in my window, and keep my light on until ten o'clock at night. If I wished, I could spend an hour or two with the other prisoners on Sundays and holidays.

The gleam of light provided by these facilities did far more to help me out of my depression than any sedatives. Nevertheless, it was to be a long time before I could entirely shake off the deeper effects of my neurosis. There are things between heaven and earth which are outside the daily run of man's experience, but to which he can devote serious thought when he is completely alone. Is it possible to communicate with the dead? Often, during those hours of extreme mental agitation, yet before my mind became altogether bewildered, I saw my parents standing before me in the flesh. I spoke with them, and it seemed as though they were still watching over me. I still cannot find any explanation for this, nor have I, during all these years, ever spoken about it to anyone.

During the subsequent years of my imprisonment I was often able to observe this prison psychosis in others. Many cases ended in the padded cell; several in complete mental derangement. Those prisoners whom I knew, who had suffered from and overcome this psychosis, remained timid and depressed and pessimistic for a very long time afterwards. Some of them were never able to shake off this deep feeling of depression.

Most of the suicides which occurred while I was there could, in my opinion, be traced back to this prison psychosis. The conditions in which they lived deprived the men of all those sensible reflections and restraints which in normal life often stay the suicide's hand. The tremendous agitation which rages through a man so afflicted drives him to the final extremity—to put an end to his torment and find peace!

In my experience there were very few attempts by the prisoners to feign madness or delirium in order to escape from prison life, for the sentence was regarded as suspended from the moment of a man's removal to a mental asylum until he was sent back to prison, unless it was decided that he must remain in an asylum for the rest of his life.

Also, curiously enough, most prisoners have an almost superstitious fear of going mad!

After I had risen from the depths and had recovered from my nervous breakdown, my life in prison continued without any particular incident. My peace of mind and detachment increased daily.

During my free time I eagerly studied the English language, and had books of instruction in it sent to me. Later I arranged for a continuous supply of English books and periodicals, and consequently I was able, in about a year, to learn this language without any outside assistance. I found this a tremendous mental corrective.

My friends, and families of my acquaintances, were constantly sending me good and valuable books on all manner of topics. Those on ethnology, racial research and heredity interested me most of all, and I was happiest when studying these subjects. On Sundays I played chess with those prisoners whom I found congenial. This game, better described as a serious intellectual duel, is particularly well suited for maintaining and refreshing one's elasticity of mind, which is perpetually threatened by the sheer monotony of life behind bars.

Because of my many varied contacts with the outside world through letters and newspapers and periodicals, I was now constantly receiving fresh and welcome mental stimulus. Should I become dejected or weary or utterly fed up, the memory of my previous 'black days' acted like a scourge to drive such clouds away. The fear of a repetition of my illness was far too strong.

In the fourth year of my sentence I was promoted to the IIIrd degree, and this brought me fresh alleviations of my prison life.

Every fortnight I could write a letter, as long as I wished, on plain paper. Work was no longer compulsory, but voluntary, and I was allowed to choose my work and received better pay for what I did.

Up till then the 'reward for work', as it was called, amounted to eight pfennigs for each daily shift completed, out of which four pfennigs might be spent on the purchase of additional food, and that, if circumstances were favourable during the month, meant fat.

In the IIIrd degree a day's work was worth fifty pfennigs and a prisoner could spend the whole of this as he wished. Moreover he was allowed to spend up to twenty marks a month of his own money. Another privilege for men in the IIIrd degree was that they might listen to the radio and smoke at certain hours of the day.

At this time, too, the post of clerk in the prison stores fell vacant, and I was given it. I now had plenty of varied work to keep me busy all day long, and I heard items of news from the prisoners of every sort who came daily to the store for a change of clothing, or for their laundry or tools. The officials in charge also told me all the prison gossip.

The stores were a collecting-point for all prison news and rumours. It was there that I learnt how quickly rumours of all kinds are started and spread, and was able to see their effect. News and rumours, whispered from man to man in the greatest possible secrecy, are the prisoners' elixir of life. The more a prisoner was isolated, the more effective was the rumour that reached his ears. The really naïve prisoners were ready to believe absolutely anything they were told.

One of my companions who, like me, was employed in the stores, and who for over ten years had kept the inventories, took a satanic delight in inventing and spreading baseless rumours, and in observing their effect. He did this so cunningly, however, that it was never possible to put the blame on him for the serious results that sometimes flowed from his efforts.

I too was once the victim of one of these rumours. It got about that it was now possible, through the influence of friends amongst the senior officials, for me to receive women in my cell at night. A prisoner smuggled this piece of information out of the prison, in the form of a complaint, and it eventually reached the ears of the prison Board of Control.

One night the president of the Prison Commission, accompanied by several other high officials, and by the prison governor who had been got out of bed, suddenly appeared in my cell, in order to convince themselves with their own eyes of the truth of this accusation. In spite of an exhaustive investigation neither the informant nor the man who had spread the rumour was ever found. On my eventual release my colleague in the stores, to whom I have referred, told me that he had invented the rumour, that the prisoner in the cell next to mine had written the complaint and had smuggled the letter out in order to get his own back on the prison governor, who had refused him a reprieve. Cause and effect! A malicious person could create a great deal of harm in this way.

Especially interesting to me in my job were the newcomers. The professional criminal was cheeky, self-confident and insolent, and even the most severe sentence could not get him down. He was an optimist, who relied on luck turning in his favour sooner or later. Often he had been only a few weeks 'outside', on leave as it were. Prison had gradually become his real home. The first offender, or one who through an adverse stroke of fate was being punished for the second or third time, would be depressed, timid, often miserable, taciturn and anxious. Unhappiness, distress, desolation and despair could be read on his face. Material in plenty there for the psychoanalyst or the sociologist!

I was always glad, after a day of varied sights and sounds, to find refuge in the solitude of my cell. In peaceful meditation I reviewed the happenings of the day and formed my conclusions about them. I buried myself in my books and magazines, or read the letters sent me by my kind and dear friends. I read of the plans they had for me on my release, and smiled at their good intentions in offering me consolation and courage. I no longer needed such solace and had gradually, after five years, become inured and indifferent to my imprisonment.

A further five years lay ahead of me, without any prospect of the slightest remission. Several petitions for clemency from influential people, and even a personal request from someone who was very close to President von Hindenburg, had all been refused on political grounds. I no longer expected to be released before my full term had expired, but I now confidently hoped to be able to remain physically and mentally fit till the end. I had also made plans for keeping myself usefully occupied, for learning languages and for educating myself further in my chosen profession. I thought of everything, but I never anticipated an early release.

Then it came overnight! In the Reichstag a sudden and unexpected majority was created by a coalition of the extreme right wing and the extreme left, both of which had a great interest in having their political prisoners set free. A political amnesty was granted almost on the spur of the moment, and along with many others I was set free.[1]

After six years of imprisonment, I was restored to freedom and to life!

I can see myself today, standing on the steps of the Potsdamer station in Berlin and gazing with interest at the milling crowds in the Potsdamer Platz. I stood there for a long time, until at last a gentleman spoke to me and asked me where I wanted to go. I must have seemed very stupid and my reply half-witted, for he at once turned and hurried away. All this bustle and activity were completely unreal to me. It was like watching a film. My release had been too sudden and unexpected, and everything appeared too improbable and strange.

A friendly Berlin family had invited me, by telegram, to stay with them. Although I knew Berlin well, and their house was within easy reach, it took me a very long time to get there. At first someone always accompanied me when I dared to go into the street, for I paid no attention to the traffic signs or to the frenzied streams of cars that filled the metropolis. I wandered about as though in a dream, and it was some days before I became reconciled to harsh reality.

People showed me every kindness. They dragged me to films and theatres and parties and to every possible place of entertainment, in fact to all those functions that a city-dweller regards as a necessity of existence. It was all too much for me.

I was bewildered, and I began to long for peace. I wanted to get away as quickly as possible from the noise and rush and bustle of the big city. Away, and into the country. After ten days I left Berlin to take a job as an agricultural official. Many more people had indeed invited me to stay with them for rest and recuperation, but my desire was to work. I had rested long enough.

Many different plans were put forward by thoughtful families and friends interested in my well-being. All were eager to help me to earn a living and to make it easy for me to resume a normal life once more. I should go to East Africa, to Mexico, to Brazil, to Paraguay

[1] The Amnesty Act in question was passed on 14 July, 1928.

E

or to the United States. All this was done with the honourable intention of getting me away from Germany, so that I would not become involved once more in the political struggles of the extreme right.

Others again, especially my old comrades, insisted that I take up a prominent position in the front rank of the fighting organisation of the NSDAP (National Socialist German Workers Party).

I refused both these propositions. Although I had been a Party member since 1922[1] and was in firm agreement with the Party's aims, I had nevertheless emphatically objected to their use of mass propaganda, their bargaining for the goodwill of the people, the way they appealed to the lowest instincts of the masses, and indeed their tone. I had become acquainted with ' the masses ' during the years 1918 to 1923! I certainly wished to remain a member of the Party, but I wanted neither any official position nor to join any of the subsidiary organisations. I had other ideas.

Nor did I want to go abroad. I wished to stay in Germany and help in its rebuilding. Building with a far-sighted goal in view. I wanted to settle on the land!

During the long years of seclusion in my cell I had come to this conclusion: there was for me only one object for which it was worth working and fighting, namely, a farm run by myself, on which I should live with a large and healthy family. That was to be the content and aim of my life!

Immediately after my release I established contact with the *Artamanen*.

I had learned about this organisation and its objects through reading its literature during my imprisonment, and I had investigated it thoroughly. It was a community of young people of both sexes, who had the interests of their country at heart. They came from the youth movements of all the nationalist-inclined parties and were people who all, at one time or another, had wanted to escape from the unhealthy, dissolute and superficial life of the towns and especially of the large cities, and to discover for themselves a healthy and tough but natural way of life on the land. They did not drink or smoke, and forswore everything that did not contribute to the healthy development of their minds and bodies. They wanted,

[1] Rossbach was responsible for Hoess visiting Munich, where he joined the NSDAP in November 1922 with Party number 3240.

furthermore, to return to the soil from which their forefathers had sprung, and to settle on the land which had given birth to the nation.

That was also my desire, and the goal for which I had searched so long.

I relinquished my post as an agricultural official and joined this community of people who held the same ideas as myself. I broke off all contact with my former comrades and the kind families I had met. They were too conventional to understand my disagreement with their preconceived ideas. I wanted to be left completely alone to start my life afresh.

I very soon met the girl who was to be my wife. She had the same ideals as myself, and with her brother had found her way to the *Artamanen*.

From the very first moment it was plain to us both that we were completely suited to one another. Our mutual trust and understanding were such that it seemed as though we had lived together all our lives. We were complementary to each other in every respect and we shared the same outlook on life. I had found the very woman for whom, during all the tedious years of loneliness, I had longed.

This inner harmony has remained with us throughout all our married life, undisturbed by all the accidents of daily life, through bad times as through good, unaffected by the outside world.

Yet there was one matter that caused her perpetual sorrow. I could never talk to her about those things that most deeply moved me, but was always forced to ponder them over in my own mind, alone.

We got married as soon as possible,[1] so that we might share the hardships of the life which we had willingly chosen. We were under no illusions concerning the difficulties that lay ahead, but we were determined that nothing should stand in our way. Our life during the next five years was certainly not an easy one, but we never let ourselves be disheartened by any hardships. We were happy and satisfied when we were able, by our example and training, to win new adherents to our beliefs.

Three of our children had already been born; they were ready to take their place in the bright future we were planning. Soon our land would be allotted to us.

But it was not to be!

In June 1934 came Himmler's call to join the ranks of the active

[1] In 1929.

SS. This was to take me away from the life which had hitherto seemed so secure and with so well-defined a purpose.[1]

I was unable to come to a decision for a long, long time. This was quite unlike my usual self.

The temptation of being a soldier again was, however, too strong. Stronger than my wife's expressed doubts as to whether this profession would really give me complete fulfilment and inner satisfaction. But when she saw how deeply I was drawn to a soldier's life, she finally agreed with my wishes.

Because of the reasonably certain prospect of rapid promotion and the financial emoluments that went with it, I became convinced that I must take this step. But at the same time I felt that I could still keep to my aim of ultimately settling down as a farmer.

This aim in life, a farmstead home for ourselves and our children, was one which we never lost sight of. Even in the years to come I never changed my mind about this. It was my intention to go back to farming immediately I was retired from active service after the war.

It was only after many doubts and hesitations that I finally decided to join the active SS.

Today I deeply regret having abandoned my previous way of life.

My life and that of my family would have taken a different turn. Even though today we would be equally without a home and without a farm, yet we would in the meantime have had several years of soul-satisfying work.

Yet who is able to foresee the intricate course of a man's destiny? What is right? And what is wrong?

When I read Himmler's invitation to join the ranks of the active

---

[1] This statement requires amplification. According to his SS record file, Hoess joined the SS as 'candidate' (*Anwärter*) on 20 September, 1933. On 1 April, 1934, he was accepted as SS-Mann, and promoted on 20 April SS-Sturmmann (private first class). In the affidavit that he signed in British custody on 14 March, 1946, he described his career between leaving prison and going to the Dachau concentration camp as follows: 'Period 1929–1934, with various agricultural organisations in Brandenburg and Pomerania. Heinrich Himmler was also a member of the League of Artamanen (Gau leader, Bavaria). . . . In 1933 on the Sallentin estate in Pomerania I formed a troop of Mounted-SS. As a former cavalryman I was asked to do this by the Party and the estate owners. . . . While he was reviewing the SS in Stettin, Himmler's attention was drawn to me—we already knew one another from the Artamanen League—and he urged me to join a concentration camp administration. That is how I came to Dachau in November 1934.'

SS as a member of the unit guarding a concentration camp, I gave no thought to the reference to concentration camps. The whole idea was too strange to me. It was quite beyond my powers of imagination. In the seclusion of our country existence in Pomerania we had hardly heard of concentration camps.

To me it was just a question of being an active soldier once again, of resuming my military career.

I went to Dachau.

Once more I was a recruit, with all the joys and sorrows that that entails, and soon I was myself training other recruits. The soldier's life held me in thrall.[1]

During our training, we were told about the ' enemies of the State ' (as Eicke, the Inspector of Concentration Camps, called them), that is to say the prisoners behind the wire. We were given instruction concerning our relations with them, and their custody, and the use of our arms. It was impressed on us how dangerous these prisoners were.

I observed them at work, and as they marched in and out of the camp, and I heard a lot about them from those of my comrades who had served in this camp since 1933.

I can clearly remember the first flogging that I witnessed. Eicke had issued orders that a minimum of one company of troops must be present during the infliction of these corporal punishments.

Two prisoners who had stolen cigarettes from the canteen were sentenced to twenty-five strokes each, with the lash.

The troops, bearing arms, were formed up in an open square, in the middle of which stood the whipping block.

The two prisoners were led forward by their block leaders. Then

[1] The SS unit that Hoess joined as SS-Unterscharführer (corporal) on 1 December, 1934, had been formed earlier that year by Theodor Eicke under the name of Guard Unit Upper Bavaria as part of the General-SS. From the end of June 1933 Eicke had been Commandant of Dachau. In that same year Eicke drafted the Disciplinary and Punishment Regulations for use in concentration camps, and also the regulations for the guard units in the camps. In May 1934 Eicke was given the job of rationalising the concentration camps, some of which, such as Oranienburg near Berlin, had been set up by the SA, while others, such as Dachau, were run by the SS. Eicke played a very prominent part in the murder of Roehm and his followers and the elimination of the SA as a political force on 30 June, 1934, and in the following month was appointed Inspector of Concentration Camps and of the Death's Head Formations, into which the Guard Unit Upper Bavaria was now incorporated. For Hoess's views on Eicke, see Appendix 8.

the commandant arrived.[1] The commander of the protective custody camp and the senior company commander reported to him.

The Rapportführer read out the sentence and the first prisoner, a small, impenitent malingerer, was made to lie across the block. Two soldiers held his head and hands and two block leaders carried out the punishment, delivering alternate strokes. The prisoner uttered no sound. The other prisoner, a professional politician of strong physique, behaved quite otherwise. He cried out at the very first stroke, and tried to break free. He went on screaming to the end, although the commandant shouted at him several times to be quiet. I was stationed in the front rank and was thus compelled to watch the whole procedure. I say compelled, because if I had been in the rear of the company I would not have looked. When the man began to scream, I went hot and cold all over. In fact the whole thing, even the beating of the first prisoner, made me shudder. Later on, at the beginning of the war, I attended my first execution, but it did not affect me nearly so much as witnessing this corporal punishment. I am unable to give an explanation of this.

Corporal punishment was standard practice in the prisons up to the 1918 revolution, but was then abolished.

The warder who had always carried out this punishment was still in the prison service and was nicknamed 'the bone-breaker'. He was a rough, dissolute fellow, always reeking of alcohol, who regarded prisoners as no more than numbers. He was just the man for the job. When under arrest I had seen the block and the whips in the punishment cellar, and I felt my flesh creep as I pictured the 'bone-breaker' at work.

After this first experience I always took care to be in the rear rank when, as a private soldier, I had to attend these whippings.

Later, as block leader,[2] I avoided them as best I could or at least

---

[1] The commandant was responsible for the concentration camp as a whole. The SS officer responsible for the camp in which the prisoners were kept was called the *Schutzhaftlagerführer* (commander of the protective custody camp), whose chief assistant—and the SS official with whom the prisoners came most directly in contact—was called the *Rapportführer*. Under him were the SS non-commissioned officers responsible for the various blocks, originally called companies.

[2] On 1 March, 1935, Hoess was made block leader at Dachau, being promoted SS-Scharführer (sergeant) on 1 April and SS-Oberscharführer (staff-sergeant) on 1 July, 1935, and SS-Hauptscharführer (sergeant-major) on 1 March, 1936. From 1 April, 1936, until September of that year he was *Rapportführer* at Dachau.

always left the parade before the actual whipping began. I found it easy to do this, for some of the block leaders were only too eager to attend.

As Rapportführer, and later as commander of the protective custody camp, I was forced to be present, much as I disliked it.

When I became commandant and therefore responsible for ordering corporal punishment, I rarely attended in person.

I certainly never ordered it without first giving the matter very careful consideration.

Why did I have such an aversion to this form of punishment? With the best will in the world I am unable to answer this question.

There was another block leader at this time who was affected in the same way and who always tried to avoid attending these affairs. This was Schwarzhuber, who later commanded the protective custody camps at Birkenau and Ravensbrück.

The block leaders who hastened to these whippings, and whose taste for these spectacles I learned to know, were almost without exception sly, rough, violent and often common creatures, whose behaviour towards their comrades and their families was in character with their natures.

They did not regard prisoners as human beings at all.

Three of them later hanged themselves while under arrest, after they had been held responsible for brutally mistreating prisoners in other camps.

There were also plenty of SS-men amongst the troops who regarded the sight of corporal punishment being inflicted as an excellent spectacle, a kind of peasant merry-making.

I was certainly not one of these.

The following incident occurred while I was still a recruit at Dachau. It was discovered that an immense racket had been organised in the butcher's shop by the prisoners and by non-commissioned officers of the SS. Four members of the SS were sentenced by a

---

In June 1936 Himmler and Bormann visited the camp, and Hoess was specially recommended for promotion both by the commandant, Loritz, and by his predecessor, Eicke. Himmler and Bormann both being aware of his 'past services', he was promoted SS-Untersturmführer (2nd lieutenant) on 13 September, 1936, thus becoming a member of the SS officer corps. From September 1936 until May 1938, when he was transferred to Sachsenhausen concentration camp, he was *Effektenverwalter*, that is to say, the officer responsible for the administration of stores and of prisoners' property, at Dachau.

Munich court—SS courts were not then in existence—to long terms of imprisonment.

These four men were then paraded in front of the entire guard unit, personally degraded by Eicke, and discharged with ignominy from the ranks of the SS. Eicke himself tore off their national emblems, their badges of rank and SS insignia, had them marched past each company in turn, and then handed them over to the prison authorities to serve their sentences. Afterwards he took this opportunity to deliver a long, admonitory speech. He said that he would have dearly liked to have seen these four men dressed in concentration camp clothes, flogged and put behind the wire with their associates. The Reichsführer of the SS, however, had not allowed him to do this.

A similar fate would overtake anyone who was caught having dealings with the prisoners, whether with criminal intent or from pity. Both motives were equally reprehensible. Any show of sympathy would be regarded by the ' enemies of the State ' as weakness, which they would immediately exploit. Furthermore, it was unworthy of an SS-man to feel pity for 'enemies of the State'. He had no room for weaklings in his ranks, and if any man felt that way he should withdraw to a monastery as quickly as possible. Only tough and determined men were of any use to him. It was not for nothing that they wore the death's head badge and always kept their weapons loaded!

They were the only soldiers who, even in peacetime, faced the enemy every hour of the day and night—the enemy behind the wire.

The degradation and dismissal of these men were painful events that affected every soldier and especially myself, for I was witnessing such a scene for the first time. But Eicke's address gave me even more to think about. I was still, however, not able to understand clearly what he meant by ' enemies of the State ' and the ' enemy behind the wire '. I did not know enough about them, although I was not to be left in ignorance for long!

After I had served six months with my unit, Eicke suddenly gave orders that all the older officers and non-commissioned officers were to leave their units and be given official positions in the camp. I was one of these.

I was made block leader in the protective custody camp. That was a position that I had no desire whatever to hold. Shortly afterwards, Eicke visited the camp and I submitted a formal request for an interview. I asked him if he would make an exception in my case, and let me rejoin my unit. I explained that soldiering was in my blood, and that it was entirely because of my longing to be a soldier once more that I had applied for active service with the SS.

He was well aware of my past history and considered that my personal experiences of prison life made me eminently suitable for taking charge of prisoners myself. In fact there was no one better qualified than I for duty in the protective custody camp.

In any case he was not prepared to make any exceptions. His order had been drafted on basic principles and would not be altered in any way. I must obey, since I was a soldier.

Yes, I had wanted to be a soldier. Yet at that moment I yearned for the rich soil, and longed to return to the hard but free life I had left behind.

But there was no returning now!

With strange feelings I entered upon my new round of duties. It was an unknown world, and one to which I was to remain bound and fettered for the next ten years.

It is true that I had myself been a prisoner for six long years and therefore knew by heart the prisoner's life and habits, his lighter and even more his darker moments, all his emotions and all his needs.

But the concentration camp was something new. I had first to learn the enormous difference between life in one of these and life in a prison or penitentiary. And I was to learn it, in every detail and often in more detail than I cared for.

With two other newcomers, Schwarzhuber and Remmele, later Commandant of Eintrachthütte, I was let loose amongst the prisoners, without very much instruction from the commander of the protective custody camp or the Rapportführer.

I felt quite embarrassed as I stood in front of the prisoners committed to forced labour who had been entrusted to my care, and noticed the curiosity with which they eyed their new company leader, as block leaders were then called. Only later was I to understand the searching expression on their faces.

My sergeant-major, as the block senior was then called, had got the company, later called block, into good shape.

He and his five corporals, the room seniors, were political prisoners, dyed-in-the-wool communists, but they had also been soldiers and loved retelling tales of their experiences in the army. Without a word from me, they imposed order and cleanliness upon the forced labour prisoners, most of whom had arrived in the camp in a thoroughly disreputable and slovenly condition. The prisoners themselves endeavoured not to fall short of the standards set, since it depended on their conduct and industry whether they were released after six months or whether they were then required to do a further three or six months' corrective training.

I soon got to know each of the two hundred and seventy men in my company well, and I could judge their fitness for release. There were only a very few, during the time I was block leader, whom I had to have transferred to prison on account of their incorrigibly a-social character. These men stole like magpies, shirked any kind of work, and were in every respect thorough slackers. Most of the men showed improvement by the end of their stipulated term of training. There were hardly any who later relapsed.

Provided they had not served numerous previous sentences or in some other way acquired a-social tendencies, imprisonment weighed heavily on these people. They were ashamed of being where they were, particularly the older men who had not previously come into conflict with the law. Now all of a sudden they found themselves punished because, out of pigheadedness or Bavarian stubbornness, they had consistently shirked their work or had shown an exaggerated fondness for beer. Or perhaps they had become idle for some other reason, and the Labour Office had sent them to the camp for training.

But all of them managed to remain more or less unaffected by the worse aspects of camp life, for they knew with reasonable certainty that after completing their sentence they would be set free.

It was quite another story, however, with the remaining nine-tenths of the camp. This consisted of one company containing Jews, emigrants, homosexuals, and Jehovah's Witnesses, one company of a-socials, and seven companies of political prisoners, mostly communists.

The political prisoners had no idea how long their detention would last. This depended on factors that were incalculable. They knew this and the uncertainty made their captivity very hard to bear. On this account alone their life in camp was a torment. I have discussed this with many sensible and discerning political prisoners. All were unanimous that they could put up with all the inconveniences of camp life, such as the arbitrary powers of the SS-men or of the prisoners' leaders, the harsh camp discipline, the years of living as a member of a crowd, and the monotony of the daily routine; but the uncertainty of the duration of their confinement was something with which they could never come to terms.

It was this that wore them down and broke the strongest wills.

According to my experience and observation, it was this uncertainty, often dependent on the whim of some quite junior official, that had the gravest and strongest psychological effect on the prisoners.

A professional criminal, who might have been sentenced to fifteen years' hard labour, always knew that he would at least regain his freedom at the end of this period, and probably much sooner.

A political prisoner, however, who had in many cases been taken into custody merely because of a vague accusation brought against him by some personal enemy, was sent to a concentration camp for an indefinite period. It might be for a year, or it might be ten. The quarterly review of prison sentences, as laid down for all German prisoners, was a mere formality. The final word lay with the office that had sent the man to the camp, and the last thing such an office wished to do was to admit to a mistake. The victim of mistake was inevitably the prisoner, who for good or ill had been handed over by the ' sending office '. He could make no appeal or complaint. Favourable circumstances might in exceptional cases lead to a ' re-check ' and result in an unexpected release. But these were invariably exceptions. As a general rule the period of detention remained in the lap of the gods!

The guards who have the duty of supervising prisoners can be divided into three distinct categories, and this applies equally to remand prisons, penitentiaries and concentration camps. They can make life hell for the prisoner, but they can also make his wretched existence easier and even tolerable.

Malicious, evil-minded, basically bad, brutal, inferior, common creatures regard the prisoner as an unresisting object on which they can exercise their unrestrained and often perverted desires and whims and so find relief for their inferiority complexes. They do not know the meaning of pity or of any kind of warm fellow-feeling. They seize every opportunity to terrorise the prisoners entrusted to their care, especially those against whom they have a personal grudge. The odious machinations of these creatures range over the whole scale from the smallest trickery to the most brutal ill-treatment, according to the individual's temperament and talents. The spiritual anguish of their victims gives them particular satisfaction. No regulations, however strict, will restrain them in their evil ways. Only supervision can limit the torments they inflict. They spend their time thinking up new methods of physical and mental torture. Woe to the prisoners under their charge when these perverted creatures have as their superiors men who acquiesce in their evil propensities, or even share in their inclinations and encourage them!

The second category, comprising the overwhelming majority, consists of those who are uninterested or indifferent. They carry out their tasks stolidly and discharge their duties, so far as they must, in a competent or indolent fashion.

To them, too, the prisoners are mere objects that they have to supervise and guard. They scarcely regard them as human beings with lives of their own.

For convenience they keep to the regulations, which they obey to the letter. It is too much of a strain for them to attempt to interpret those regulations sensibly. They are in general men of limited abilities.

They have no deliberate wish to do the prisoners harm. But because of their indifference and narrow-mindedness and their desire for an easy life, they do cause a lot of harm and inflict much physical and mental anguish upon the prisoners quite unintentionally.

It is primarily they, however, who enable some prisoners to obtain a domination over their fellows that is so often evil.

The third category consists of men who are kindly by nature, good-hearted, compassionate and able to sympathise with a fellow-human's troubles.

Within this category the individual guards vary considerably.

First there are those who stick firmly and conscientiously to the regulations and will overlook no departure from them on the part of the prisoners, but who, out of kindness of heart and good nature, construe the regulations in favour of the prisoners and endeavour, so far as this is possible, to alleviate their situation, or at any rate not to make it unnecessarily hard.

There are others who are simply good-hearted, and whose naïvety borders on the miraculous. They will try to gratify a prisoner's every wish, and out of sheer good nature and boundless sympathy will attempt to help him in every way. They are unable to believe that evil men exist amongst prisoners, too.

Generally speaking, strictness, combined with goodwill and

understanding, give a prisoner a certain reassurance, for he is perpetually on the look-out for human comprehension, and the worse his position the greater his need of it. A kind glance, a friendly nod or a pleasant word will often work wonders, especially on sensitive minds. To find that some consideration, however slight, is being given to his situation and position produces an unexpected effect upon a prisoner. Even the most desperate man, who has already given up all hope, will find new courage if he sees or feels the slightest sign of human fellow-feeling.

Every prisoner tries to improve his lot and to make his conditions of life more tolerable. He will exploit kindness and human understanding. Unscrupulous prisoners will go the limit and will try, by evoking sympathy, to get the better of their guards.

Since the prisoner is, generally speaking, mentally superior to the junior guards and supervisory staff, he is quick to find the weak spot in those who are kind or merely stupid.

And this is the disadvantage of showing too much kindness and goodwill towards the prisoners. A single gesture of human understanding towards a strong-minded prisoner will often inaugurate a series of lapses from discipline on the part of the guard that can only end in the most severe punishment. Such lapses may begin with the harmless smuggling out of a letter, but may lead to actual assistance in escaping.

Examples will show the different effects, in the same circumstances, produced by the three characteristic types of guard mentioned above.

To take the remand prison first. The prisoner asks the guard to increase the steam-heating in his cell because he has a bad cold and is freezing. A malicious-minded warder will immediately turn the heating off altogether and watch with amusement while the prisoner runs round and round his cell or tries to keep warm by doing endless gymnastic exercises. In the evening another guard comes on duty. He is one of the indifferent type. Once again the prisoner asks for more heat. The guard turns it full on, and forgets all about it for the rest of the night. Within an hour the cell is so over-heated that the prisoner has to leave the window open all night, with the result that his cold becomes far worse.

Now take the penitentiary. There is a stipulated time for bathing. A sadistic guard marches the prisoners to the baths. He throws the window in the dressing-room wide open, in mid-winter, because the place is full of steam. With much shouting to hurry them on, he drives the prisoners under the showers and turns the hot water full on so that no man can stay underneath it for more than a second. Then he turns on the cold water, and makes them stand under it for a long time, shivering. With a mocking grin he then watches the prisoners, who are now so cold that they can hardly dress themselves.

On another occasion they are taken to the baths by a guard of the indifferent type. It is also winter. The prisoners undress and the guards sits down and reads a newspaper, After a long time he manages to tear himself away from his paper and switches on the water. He turns the hot full on and returns to his paper. No one can go under the shower, which is almost boiling. He pays no attention to the prisoners' shouts. Only when he has finished his reading does he stand up, and then immediately turns the water off altogether. The prisoners dress themselves again without having washed at all. He looks at his watch, sees that the time is right, and feels he has done his duty.

Then the concentration camp. The scene is the gravel pit. A good-natured guard takes care to see that the trucks are not overloaded, that extra men are there to push them up the slope, that the tracks are firmly laid and that the points are oiled. Without any shouting the day goes by and the stipulated amount of gravel is duly shifted.

The malicious guard has the trucks overloaded, allows no extra hands to help push them up the slope, and insists on their being pushed the whole way at the double. He even does without the prisoner whose job it is to look after the tracks and see that the points are oiled. The result of all this is that the trucks are constantly derailed, the Capos[1] are given reason for bullying, and a large proportion of the prisoners are incapable of work by midday because of their cut and bruised feet. All day long the air is filled with deafening shouts of command from all sides. By evening it is found that barely half of the stipulated work has been accomplished.

The indifferent guard does not worry in the least about his work party. He lets the Capos do the work, which they carry out as the fancy takes them. Their favourites amongst the prisoners have a lazy day and the rest have to work all the harder. The sentries see nothing. The guard himself is continually absent.

I have taken these three examples from innumerable incidents that I myself have seen. I could fill several books with them. They are

---

[1] Prisoners who acted as supervisors of the prison barrack-rooms, the other prisoners work, etc.

intended only to emphasise the extent to which a prisoner's life is dependent on the behaviour and attitude of mind of the individual guards and supervisors. In spite of all the rules and regulations, and however good the intentions behind them, the fact remains that it is not the physical hardships which make the prisoner's life so unbearable, but the indelible mental suffering caused by the tyranny and wickedness and meanness of indifferent or malicious individuals among the guards and supervisors. The prisoner can cope with stern but impartial severity, however harsh it may be, but tyranny and manifestly unjust treatment affect his soul like a blow with a club. He is powerless against it, and can only suffer in silence.

To put it crudely, guards and prisoners constitute two hostile and opposing worlds. The prisoner is usually on the defensive: first because of the fact that he is a prisoner, and secondly because of the behaviour of the guards. If he wants to fit into the scheme of things, then he has to look after number one. Since he cannot fight back with the same weapons, he must find other means of self-protection. According to his nature he either allows his enemy to vent his spite against an armour of indifference, and continues to carry on more or less as before: or he becomes cunning, furtive and deceitful, and hoodwinks his opponent in order to obtain alleviations and privileges: or he goes over to the enemy and becomes a trusty, a Capo, a block senior and so on, and manages thus to make his own life bearable at the expense of his fellow-prisoners: or he stakes everything on one throw and breaks out: or he abandons hope, goes to pieces and ends up by committing suicide.

All this sounds harsh and may seem improbable, and yet it is true. I feel that I am a fair judge of these matters, owing to the life I have lived, and to my own experiences and observation.

Work plays a very large part in a prisoner's life. It can serve to make his existence more bearable, but it can also lead to his destruction.

To every healthy prisoner, in normal circumstances, work is a necessity, and satisfies an inner need. This does not apply to notorious idlers and loafers and other types of a-social spongers; they can vegetate quite happily without work, and without thereby doing any harm to their souls.

Work helps a prisoner to get over the emptiness of imprisonment. It pushes the wretchedness of the daily round in prison into the background if it occupies his mind sufficiently; and if he does it willingly, by which I mean with an inner readiness, he will derive satisfaction from it.

If he can go further, and find an occupation connected with his own profession, or work that corresponds to his abilities and which appeals to him, he has managed to achieve for himself a psychological basis that will not easily be shaken, however inimical his surroundings.

It is true that work in the prisons and concentration camps is compulsory. But generally speaking every prisoner employed on the right kind of work does it willingly. The inner satisfaction that it gives him affects his whole state of mind. On the other hand, dissatisfaction with his work can make his life a burden.

How much pain and discomfort, and frustration too, could have been avoided if the work inspectors and the foremen had had regard for these facts, and had kept their eyes open when they went through the workshops and places of employment!

All my life I have thoroughly enjoyed working. I have done plenty of hard, physical work, under the severest conditions, in the coal mines, in oil refineries and in brickyards. I have felled timber, cut sleepers and stacked peat. I have, with my own hands, done every principal sort of agricultural work. Not only have I done such work myself, but wherever I have worked I have carefully observed the behaviour, habits and conditions of life of the men working with me.

I can justly maintain that I know what work means, and that I am fully qualified to judge another man's working efficiency.

I myself derive no real satisfaction from my labours unless I have completed a good job of work thoroughly.

I have never asked my subordinates to undertake any task in excess of what I could have done myself. Even in prison in Leipzig where I had plenty to occupy my mind, such as the investigation and the trial itself, not to mention the many letters and newspapers and visitors I received, I missed my work. Finally I asked for work, and I was given the job of pasting paper bags. Although this was an extremely monotonous job, it nevertheless occupied the greater part of the day and gave me a regular occupation. I voluntarily assigned to myself a definite task to be performed daily, and that was the essential.

During my subsequent imprisonment, where choice was possible, I chose work that required a certain amount of attention and was not purely mechanical.

Such employment spared me hours of useless and enervating self-pity. In the evening I had the satisfactory feeling that not only had I put another day behind me, but also that I had done a useful job of work.

The worst punishment for me would have been if my work had been taken away.

In my present imprisonment I feel the lack of any physical work very much, and I am so thankful that I can do this writing, which I find completely absorbing and satisfying.

I have discussed this question of work with many of my fellow-prisoners in the penitentiary and also with many of those detained in the concentration camps, especially at Dachau. All of them were convinced that in the long run life behind bars or behind wire would be unbearable without work, and that to be without work would be the worst imaginable punishment.

Work in prison is not merely an efficient corrective, in the best sense of the word, in that it encourages the prisoners to discipline themselves and thus makes them better able to withstand the demoralising effect of their confinement. It is also a means of training for those prisoners who are fundamentally unstable and who need to learn the meaning of endurance and perseverance. The beneficent influence of work can draw many prisoners away from a life of crime.

The above statements, however, only apply where the conditions are normal.

Only thus can the slogan 'Work Brings Freedom'[1] be understood. It was Eicke's firm intention that no matter what category, those prisoners whose steady and zealous work marked them out from the others should in due course be released, regardless of what the Gestapo and the Criminal Police Office might think to the contrary. Indeed this occasionally happened, until the war put an end to all such good intentions.

I have written exhaustively on the subject of work, because I have myself had such ample opportunity of appreciating its psychological value, and because I wished to show the beneficial effect it always has on a prisoner's mind, as I know from first-hand experience.

I shall write later about what was afterwards done in this matter of work and the planned use of camp labour.

[1] *Arbeit macht frei* was the slogan which Hoess placed above the main gate of Auschwitz concentration camp.

F

In Dachau, as block leader, I now came into direct contact with the individual prisoners, and not only with those of my own block.

As block leaders we had at that time to censor the prisoners' outgoing mail. Any man who has spent a considerable time reading a prisoner's letters, and who possesses adequate knowledge of human nature, will obtain a clear picture from them of the prisoner's psyche. Each prisoner tries in his letters to his wife and mother, to describe his needs and his troubles and, depending on his disposition, will be more or less outspoken. In the long run no prisoner can disguise his true thoughts. He can, in the final analysis, deceive neither himself nor the practised eye of the experienced observer. And it is the same with the letters he writes.

Eicke had drummed the notion of ' dangerous enemies of the State ' so firmly and persuasively into the heads of his SS-men, and had been preaching this for so many years, that any man who knew no better believed in it. I also believed. I now sought to study these ' dangerous enemies of the State ', and to find out why they appeared so dangerous.

What did I find ? A small number of dyed-in-the-wool communists and social-democrats, who, if they had been given their freedom, would have stirred up unrest amongst the people and would have stopped at nothing to make their illegal work effective. They quite openly admitted this.

But the great mass of them, although they had indeed been communist or social-democrat officials, who had also struggled and fought for their ideals, and who had in some cases done considerable harm to the nationalist concepts of the NSDAP, appeared at closer glance, and after daily contact, harmless and peaceable men who, having seen their world destroyed, wished only to find some quiet job and to be able to go home to their families, I am certain that during the period 1935 and 1936 three-quarters of the political prisoners in Dachau could have been released without any resultant harm whatsoever to the Third Reich.

There remained, nevertheless, that quarter who were fanatically convinced that their world would rise again. These people had to be kept shut up and it was they who were the ' dangerous enemies of the State '. They were, however, easily recognisable, even though they did not openly express their views but on the contrary tried skilfully to disguise them.

Far more dangerous to the State and the people as a whole were the professional criminals, a-socials with more than twenty or thirty convictions behind them.

It was Eicke's intention that his SS-men, by means of continuous instruction and suitable orders concerning the dangerous criminality of the inmates, should be made basically ill-disposed towards the prisoners. They were to ' treat them rough ', and to root out once and for all any sympathy they might feel for them. By such means, he succeeded in engendering in simple-natured men a hatred and antipathy for the prisoners which an outsider will find hard to imagine. This influence spread through all the concentration camps and affected all the SS-men and the SS leaders who served in them, and indeed it continued for many years after Eicke had relinquished his post as Inspector.[1]

All the torture and ill-treatment inflicted upon the prisoners in the concentration camps can be explained by this ' hate indoctrination '.

This basic attitude towards the prisoners was exacerbated by the influence of the senior commandants such as Loritz and Koch, who did not regard the prisoners as men, but as ' Russians ' or ' Kanakas '.

The prisoners were of course not unaware of this artificial hatred that had been whipped up against them.

The more fanatical and stubborn amongst them were only reinforced thereby in their attitudes of mind. The men of goodwill, on the other hand, were hurt and repelled.

It was easy to tell when a new Eicke instruction had been issued to the concentration camp guards. Morale sank at once. Every action of the SS-men was watched with fearful alarm. Rumours of new measures came thick and fast. A general feeling of uneasiness filled the camp. It was not that the prisoners feared that some new form of ill-treatment would be meted out to them. Rather it was that the hostile attitude of the greater proportion of the guards and supervisory personnel towards the prisoners became more strongly felt.

I must emphasise again that prisoners, and especially those in concentration camps, are oppressed and tormented, and brought to the verge of despair, far, far more by the psychological than by the physical effects and impressions of the life.

To most prisoners it is not a matter of indifference whether their guards are hostile, or neutral, or sympathetic. Even though the guard never comes near the prisoner, his hostile attitude and his

[1] See also Hoess's description of Eicke as given in Appendix 8.

scowling, hate-filled glance are alone sufficient to frighten, depress and torment him.

Time and again in Dachau I used to hear prisoners say:

'Why do the SS hate us so? After all, we are men like them.'

This alone makes clear the general relationship between the SS-men and the prisoners.

I do not believe that Eicke personally hated and despised the 'dangerous enemies of the State', as he constantly described them to the men. I am rather of the opinion that his perpetual 'cult of severity' had the sole purpose of keeping the SS-men at all times on their toes. But thought of the results of this policy, of the far-reaching effects of this deliberate 'baiting', never entered his mind.

It was in this atmosphere fostered by Eicke that I was trained, and that I *had* to carry out my concentration camp duties as block leader, as Rapportführer and as stores administrator. And here I must make a statement: I always carried out my duties carefully and conscientiously to everyone's satisfaction. I never indulged the prisoners, and I was firm and often severe. But I had been a prisoner myself for too long not to perceive their needs. It was not without an inner feeling of concern that I observed the 'goings-on' in the camp.

Outwardly cold and even stony, but with most deeply disturbed inner feelings, I attended the enquiries and examined the bodies of those prisoners who had committed suicide, or had been shot while attempting to escape—and I was well able to recognise whether such cases were genuine or not, or had been accidentally killed at work, or had 'run into the wire', or had been legally executed and now lay in the dissecting-room.

It was the same with the floggings and other punitive measures ordered by Loritz, most of which he supervised himself. These were 'his' punishment fatigues, 'his' executions of sentence.

My stony mask convinced him that there was no need to 'toughen me up', as he loved to do with those SS-men who seemed to him too weak.

And it is here that my guilt actually begins.

It was clear to me that I was not suited to this sort of service, since in my heart I disagreed with Eicke's insistence that life in the concentration camp be organised in this particular way. My sympathies lay too much with the prisoners, for I had myself lived their life for too long and had personal experience of their needs.

I should have gone to Eicke or to the Reichsführer SS[1] then, and explained that I was not suited to concentration camp service, because I felt too much sympathy for the prisoners.

I was unable to find the courage to do this.

I did not want to make a laughing-stock of myself. I did not wish to reveal my weakness. I was too obstinate to admit that I had made a mistake when I abandoned my original intention of settling on the land.

I had voluntarily joined the ranks of the active SS and I had become too fond of the black uniform to relinquish it in this way.

My admission that I was too soft for a job assigned to the SS would unquestionably have led to my being cashiered, or at least immediately discharged.

And this I could not face.

For a long time I wrestled with this dilemma, the choice between my inner convictions on the one hand and my oath of loyalty to the SS, and my vow of fidelity to the Führer on the other. Should I become a deserter? Even my wife knows nothing about my mental struggle on this issue. I have kept it to myself until this very moment.

As a National Socialist of long standing, I was convinced of the need for a concentration camp.

True opponents of the State had to be securely locked up; and a-socials and professional criminals, who under the law as it then stood could not be imprisoned, must be deprived of their freedom in order to safeguard the rest of the people from their evil deeds.

I was also convinced that this task could only be carried out by the SS in their capacity as the guardians of the new State.

But I was not in agreement with Eicke's attitude towards the inmates of these camps. I disagreed with the way he whipped up the vilest emotions of hatred amongst the SS guards, and with his policy of putting incompetent men in charge of the prisoners and of allowing these unsuitable, indeed intolerable, persons to keep their jobs.

Nor did I agree with the arbitrary method of fixing the term of imprisonment.

Nevertheless, by remaining in the concentration camps I accepted the ideas and the rules and regulations that there prevailed.

I became reconciled to my lot, which I had brought upon myself quite freely. Silently I continued to hope that one day I might find another form of service.

[1] National SS Leader: Heinrich Himmler: abbreviated RFSS.

But for the time being there was no prospect of this. In Eicke's opinion I was pre-eminently suitable for the job of looking after prisoners.

Although I became accustomed to all that was unalterable in the camps, I never grew indifferent to human suffering. I have always seen it and felt for it. Yet because I might not show weakness, I wished to appear hard, lest I be regarded as weak, and had to disregard such feelings.

I was then given the post of adjutant at Sachsenhausen.[1]

I now got to know the Concentration Camp Inspectorate, its work and its usages. I became more closely acquainted with Eicke, and with the effects of his influence upon the camp and the troops.

I came into contact with the Gestapo.

From the mass of official correspondence I learned to understand the relationships within the higher reaches of the SS. In short, I acquired a broader view.

I heard a lot about what went on in the Führer's immediate circle, from a friend on Hess's liaison staff. Another of my old friends held an important post at the headquarters of the Reich Youth Organisation, while yet a third was a public relations officer on Rosenberg's staff and a fourth was with the Reich Chamber of Medicine. In Berlin I often saw these old comrades of mine from Freikorps days, and became increasingly knowledgeable concerning the ideals and intentions of the Party, since I enjoyed their confidence. During these years a powerful upsurge could be felt throughout Germany. Industry and trade flourished as never before. Hitler's foreign policy successes were plain enough to silence all doubters and opponents.

The Party ruled the State. Its successes could not be denied. The means and the ends of the NSDAP were right. I believed this implicitly and without the slightest reservation.

My inner scruples about remaining in the concentration camp, despite my unsuitability for such work, receded into the background now that I no longer came into such direct contact with the prisoners as I had done in Dachau.

Also, in Sachsenhausen there was not the same atmosphere of hatred that existed in Dachau. And this in spite of the fact that Eicke's own offices were located in the camp.

[1] According to SS records he was transferred to Sachsenhausen on 1 August, 1938.

The troops were of a different type. There were many young recruits and many junior SS officers from the Junker school.

'Old Dachauites' were only to be met with now and then.

The commandant,[1] too, was a different sort of man. Strict and severe, it is true, but with a meticulous desire for justice and a fanatical sense of duty. He was for me the prototype of the original SS leader and National Socialist. I always regarded him as a much enlarged reflection of myself. He, too, had moments when his good nature and kind heart were in evidence, yet he was hard and mercilessly severe in all matters appertaining to the service. He was a perpetual example to me of how, in the SS, 'hard necessity' must stifle all softer emotions.

The war came, and with it the great turning point in the history of the concentration camps. But who could then have foreseen the horrifying tasks to be assigned them as the war went on?

On the very first day of the war, Eicke delivered an address to the officers of the reserve formations which had relieved the regular SS units in the camps.

In it he emphasised that the harsh laws of war now prevailed. Each SS-man was committed body and soul, regardless of the life he had hitherto led. Every order received must be regarded as sacrosanct and even those which appeared most harsh and severe must be carried out without hesitation. The Reichsführer SS demanded that every SS-man should exhibit an exemplary sense of duty and should be prepared to devote himself to his people and his fatherland even unto death.

The main task of the SS in this war was to protect Adolf Hitler's State from every kind of peril and especially against internal dangers. A revolution, as in 1918, or a munition workers' strike, such as that of 1917,[2] was out of the question. Anyone identifiable as an enemy of the State, and any saboteur of the war effort, must be destroyed.

The Führer demanded of the SS that they protect the homeland against all hostile intrigues.

He, Eicke, therefore demanded that they, the men now serving with the reserve formations in the camps, should display an inflexible harshness towards the prisoners. They would have most difficult

---

[1] SS-Standartenführer Hermann Baranowski. From 1936 to early 1938 he had been commander of the protective custody camp at Dachau, under Loritz, where he got to know Hoess, whose transfer to Sachsenhausen he requested.

[2] The reference is presumably to the strike of January 1918.

tasks to perform and the hardest orders to obey. That, however, was the reason for their being there. The SS had now to show that the intensive training they had received in peacetime was justified. Only the SS were capable of protecting the National Socialist State from all internal danger. All other organisations lacked the necessary toughness.

On this same evening the first execution of the war was carried out in Sachsenhausen.

It was of a communist who had refused to carry out ARP work at the Junkers factory in Dessau. The responsible factory authority had reported him, and he was arrested by the local police and taken to Gestapo headquarters in Berlin, where he was interrogated. A report of the proceedings was laid before the Reichsführer SS, who ordered that he be shot forthwith.

According to a secret mobilisation order, all executions ordered by the Reichsführer SS or by the Gestapo were to be carried out in the nearest concentration camp.

At ten o'clock that night, Müller of the Gestapo[1] telephoned to say that a courier was on the way with orders. These orders were to be carried out at once. Almost at once a truck arrived with two police officials and a handcuffed civilian. The commandant opened and read the orders, which said, quite briefly: ' By command of the Reichsführer SS the prisoner is to be shot. He is to be informed of this while in custody, and the sentence is to be carried out one hour later.'

The commandant immediately informed the condemned man of the orders he had received. The man was completely resigned to his fate, although, as he later said, he had not expected to be executed. He was allowed to write to his family, and was given cigarettes for which he had asked.

Eicke had been informed by the commandant and arrived in the course of the hour before the sentence was to be carried out.

As adjutant, I was head of the commandant's staff and, in accordance with the secret mobilisation order, had to carry out the execution. When, on the morning that war was declared, the commandant opened the sealed mobilisation order, neither of us thought that we should have occasion to follow the instructions in it regarding executions on that very same day.

I quickly got together three of my older and more imperturbable junior staff officers, told them what had to be done, and instructed them in matters of procedure.

[1] See Appendix 4.

A post was rapidly erected in a sandpit adjoining the workshops, and almost at once the trucks arrived. The commandant told the condemned man to stand by the post. I led him there. He calmly made himself ready. I stepped back and gave the order to fire. He collapsed and I gave him the *coup de grâce*. The doctor established that he had received three bullets through the heart. In addition to Eicke, a few officers of the reserve formations were also present at the execution.

None of us who had listened to Eicke's instructions that morning had imagined that his words would so quickly become harsh reality. Nor indeed had Eicke, as he himself told us after the execution.

I had been so busy with the preparations for the execution that it was not until it was over that I began to realise what had happened. All the officers who had been present at the shooting assembled for a while in our mess. Oddly enough, no real conversation took place, and each of us just sat, wrapped in his own thoughts. We all remembered Eicke's speech. We had just been given a clear picture of war with which we would be faced. Apart from myself, all those present were elderly men who had already served as officers during the First World War. They were veteran leaders of the SS, who had held their own in street battles during the NSDAP's early struggle for existence. All of us, however, were deeply affected by what had just happened, not least myself.

Yet in the days to come we were to have plenty of experiences of this kind. Almost every day I had to parade with my execution squad.

Most of those we executed were men who refused to do their war service, or saboteurs. The reasons for execution could only be learnt from the police officials who accompanied them. They were not given on the execution order itself.

One incident affected me very closely. An SS leader, a police official with whom I had had many dealings, since he frequently accompanied notable prisoners or came to the camp to deliver important secret documents to the commandant, was himself suddenly brought in one night for immediate execution. Only the day before, we had been sitting together in our officers' mess discussing the executions. Now a similar fate was to overtake him, and it was I who had to carry out the order! This was too much even for my commandant. After the execution, we went for a long, silent walk together through the camp, trying to calm our feelings.

We learned from the officials who had accompanied him that this

SS officer had been ordered to arrest and bring to the camp a man who had formerly been an official of the Communist Party. The SS officer had known the man well and for a long time, since he had had to keep him under supervision. The communist had always behaved with complete good faith. Out of kindness the SS officer had let him pay a last visit to his home, to change his clothes and say goodbye to his wife. While the SS official and his colleagues were talking with the wife in the sitting-room, the husband escaped out of the back. By the time they realised he had fled, it was too late. The SS officer was actually arrested inside the Gestapo building, while reporting the escape, and the Reichsführer SS ordered him court-martialled immediately. One hour later he was sentenced to death. The men who had accompanied him were given long terms of imprisonment. Even attempts by Heydrich and Müller to intercede on his behalf were sharply dismissed by the Reichsführer SS. This first grave dereliction of duty on the part of an SS officer since the start of the war must be punished with terrifying and exemplary severity. The condemned was a respectable man in his middle thirties, married and with three children, who had hitherto carried out his duties faithfully and conscientiously. Now he had fallen victim to his own good nature and trustfulness.

He met his death with calm and resignation.

I cannot understand to this day how I was able, quite calmly, to give the order to fire. The three men of the firing squad did not know the identity of their victim, and this was just as well, for their hands might well have trembled. I was so agitated that I could hardly hold the pistol to his head when giving him the *coup de grâce*. But I was able to pull myself together sufficiently to prevent those present from being aware of anything unusual. I know this, because I asked one of the three junior officers in the execution squad about it a few days later.

This execution was always before my eyes to remind me of the demand that had been made upon us to exercise perpetual self-mastery and unbending severity.

At the time I believed that this was asking too much of human nature, and yet Eicke was insisting on ever greater harshness. An SS-man must be able to destroy even his closest dependants should they commit an offence against the State or the ideals of Adolf Hitler. ' There is only one thing that is valid: Orders! ' That was the motto which he used as his letter-head.

What this motto implied, and what Eicke meant by it, I was to learn in these first few weeks of the war, and not only I, but also many of the other old SS leaders. Some of these, enjoying very senior rank in the General SS and with very low SS serial numbers, dared to express their opinion in the mess that such hangman's work soiled the black uniform of the SS. This was reported to Eicke. He sent for them and also summoned all SS officers in his Oranienburg district, and he addressed them more or less as follows: The remarks about hangman's work and the SS show that the men concerned, despite their long service with the SS, have not yet understood what the function of the SS is. The most important task assigned to the SS is to protect the new State by any and every means. Every opponent of the State, according to the danger he represents, must either be kept in custody or be destroyed. In either case it is the responsibility of the SS to see that this is done. Only thus can the security of the State be guaranteed, until a new code of laws has been created which will give true protection to the State and the people. The destruction of internal enemies of the State is just as much a duty as is the destruction of the enemy from beyond the frontiers, and such action can therefore never be regarded as dishonourable.

The reported remarks show adherence to the ideology of an out-of-date bourgeois world which, thanks to Hitler's revolution, has long ceased to exist. They are a sign of weakness and sentimentality, emotions which are not only unworthy of an SS leader, but which might become dangerous.

For this reason it was his duty to report the persons concerned to the Reichsführer SS, with a view to punishment.

So far as the district under his control was concerned, he forbade once and for all any such weak-kneed attitude.

He only had use for men who were unconditionally tough, and who also understood the meaning of the death's head, which they wore as a special badge of honour.

The Reichsführer SS did not punish the men concerned directly. But he personally warned and lectured them. They were, however, given no further promotion and roamed around for the rest of the war as *Ober* or *Hauptsturmführer*.[1] They also remained subordinated to the Inspector of Concentration Camps until the end of the war. Theirs was a heavy fate to bear, but they had learnt at least to hold their tongues and to do their duty regardless.

[1] Equivalent army ranks: captain or lieutenant.

At the beginning of the war those prisoners in the concentration camps who were considered worthy to bear arms were examined by recruiting officers from the various sub-districts. The names of those passed as fit for service were submitted to the Gestapo or to the Criminal Police, and those offices decided whether the men should be set free for military service, or should be further detained.

There were many Jehovah's Witnesses in Sachsenhausen. A great number of them refused to undertake military service and because of this the Reichsführer SS condemned them to death. They were shot in the presence of all the inmates of the camp duly assembled. The other Jehovah's Witnesses were placed in the front rank so that they must watch the proceedings.

I have met many religious fanatics in my time; on pilgrimages, in monasteries, in Palestine, on the Hejaz road in Iraq, and in Armenia. They were Catholics, both Roman and Orthodox, Moslems, Shiites and Semites. But the Witnesses in Sachsenhausen, and particularly two of them, surpassed anything that I had previously seen. These two especially fanatical Witnesses refused to do any work that had any connection whatever with military matters. They would not stand at attention, or drill in time with the rest, or lay their hands along the seam of their trousers, or remove their caps. They said that such marks of respect were due only to Jehovah and not to man. They recognised only one lord and master, Jehovah. Both of them had to be taken from the block set aside for Jehovah's Witnesses and put in the cells, since they constantly urged on the other Witnesses to behave in a similar manner.

Eicke had frequently sentenced them to be flogged because of their anti-disciplinarian behaviour. They underwent this punishment with a joyous fervour that amounted almost to a perversion. They begged the commandant to increase their punishment, so that they might the better be able to testify to Jehovah. After they had been ordered to report for military service, which, needless to say, they flatly refused, indeed they refused even to put their signature to a military document, they too were condemned to death by the Reichsführer SS. When told of this in their cells, they went almost mad for joy and ecstasy, and could hardly wait for the day of execution. They wrung their hands, gazed enraptured up at the sky, and constantly cried: ' Soon we shall be with Jehovah! How happy we are to have been chosen! ' A few days earlier they had witnessed the execution of some of their fellow-believers and they could hardly be kept under control, so great was their desire to be shot with them. Their frenzy was painful to watch. They had to be taken back to their cells by force. When their time came, they almost ran to the place of execution. They wished on no account to be bound, for they desired to be able to raise their hands to Jehovah. Transformed by ecstasy, they stood in front of the wooden wall of the rifle-range, seemingly no longer of this world. Thus do I imagine that the first Christian martyrs must have appeared as they waited in the circus for the wild beasts to tear them in pieces. Their faces completely transformed, their eyes raised to heaven, and their hands clasped and lifted in prayer, they went to their death.[1]

All who saw them die were deeply moved, and even the execution squad itself was affected.

These Jehovah's Witnesses became even more fanatical in their faith as a result of the martydom of their comrades. Several of them who had already signed a declaration that they would cease to proselytise, a declaration which helped them to obtain their freedom, now withdrew it, since they were anxious to suffer even more for Jehovah.

As people, Jehovah's Witnesses were quiet, industrious and sociable men and women, who were always ready to help their fellow-creatures. Most of them were craftsmen, though many were peasants from East Prussia. In peacetime, so long as they confined their activities to prayer and the service of God and their fraternal gatherings, they were of no danger to the State and indeed quite harmless generally. From 1937 onwards, however, the increased proselytising by the sect attracted the attention of the authorities, and investigations were made. These investigations showed that our enemies were zealously fostering the propagation of the beliefs of Jehovah's Witnesses in order to undermine by religious means the military morale of our people. So proselytising by Jehovah's Witnesses was forbidden. It became only too evident, at the outbreak of the war, what a danger would have arisen if the more energetic and fanatical of the Witnesses had not been taken into custody during the previous couple of years, and a stop put to their active proselytising. In the camp the Witnesses were industrious and reliable workers, who could well have been sent out to work

[1] For further information about Jehovah's Witnesses in the concentration camps, see Eugen Kogan, *The Theory and Practice of Hell*, and also Nuremberg doct. NG-190.

without guards. It was indeed their wish to suffer imprisonment for Jehovah's sake. They stubbornly refused to do work that had any connection whatever with the war. The women Witnesses in Ravensbrück, for example, refused to roll bandages for military field-dressings. Some of these fanatical women refused to line up for roll-call and would only parade as a disorderly crowd.

The Witnesses under arrest were members of the International Association of Jehovah's Witnesses, but they knew virtually nothing about its organisation. They only knew the officials who distributed the literature and who organised the meetings and the Bible studies. They were completely ignorant of the political use which was being made of their fanatical beliefs. If this was pointed out to them they laughed, and could not understand. Their duty was simply to follow the call of Jehovah and be true to him. Jehovah spoke to them through inspiration, through visions, through the Bible when properly read, through the preachers and the writings of their sect. That was the plain truth, and it allowed of no argument. To suffer and even to die for Jehovah was their coveted aim. They believed that in this way they would be among the first to ascend and to join Jehovah's elect. It was in this light that they regarded their imprisonment and detention in the concentration camp. They willingly submitted to all hardships. It was touching to observe the brotherly care they bestowed on each other, giving help and comfort whenever this was in any way possible.

There were, however, many cases of Witnesses voluntarily 'abjuring', as they called it. This meant signing a declaration in which they dissociated themselves from the International Association of Jehovah's Witnesses, undertook to recognise and obey all the laws and regulations of the State, and promised not to enrol any new Witnesses for Jehovah. On this basis of swearing to break their allegiance to the International Association of Jehovah's Witnesses, they were eventually—later in the war, immediately—set free. In the early days, however, when their release did not at once follow upon their signature of the document of abjuration, they often wondered whether in fact the Reichsführer SS was to be trusted, and whether they would really be released. The abjurers were berated by their brother and sister Witnesses for their disloyalty to Jehovah. Many of the abjurers, especially among the women, later felt remorse and repudiated their signatures. The constant moral pressure was too great. It was quite impossible to shake their faith, and even those who had abjured still wished to remain completely loyal to their beliefs, even though they had broken away from their spiritual community. If their attention was drawn to contradictions in their doctrine or in the Bible, they would simply declare that this might appear so to human eyes, but with Jehovah there were no contradictions, that He and His doctrine were infallible.

On many occasions Himmler, as well as Eicke, used the fanatical faith of Jehovah's Witnesses as an example.

SS-men must have the same fanatical and unshakeable faith in the National Socialist ideal and in Adolf Hitler that the Witnesses had in Jehovah. Only when all SS-men believed as fanatically in their own philosophy would Adolf Hitler's State be permanently secure.

A *Weltanschauung*[1] could only be established and permanently maintained by fanatics utterly prepared to sacrifice their egos for their ideals.

I must refer once more to the executions which took place in Sachsenhausen at the beginning of the war.

How diverse were the ways in which men went to their death!

Jevohah's Witnesses were filled with a strangely contented, one might almost say radiant, exaltation, firm in the knowledge that they were about to be permitted to enter Jehovah's kingdom.

The men who refused to do their military service and the political saboteurs were generally composed, steadfast and calm, resigned to the inevitability of their fate.

The professional criminals, the real a-social types, were quite different: these were either cynical, brazen, feigning indifference, yet inwardly trembling before the Great Unknown. Or raving and struggling. Or whining for spiritual support.

Here are two striking examples. Two brothers by the name of Sass had been arrested in Denmark after a police raid and, in accordance with international law, had been extradited to Germany. Both were internationally notorious thieves, who specialised in safebreaking. They had many previous convictions, but had never served a complete sentence, since they had always managed to break out of prison. In spite of every safety precaution, they invariably found a way of escape. Their latest spectacular 'job' had been to break into the very up-to-date strong-room of a big Berlin bank. They had dug a tunnel under the street, starting from a tomb in a graveyard across the way. After carefully dealing with the various alarm mechanisms,

---

[1] *Weltanschauung:* literally, 'attitude towards the world'.

they entered the strong-room, where they were able to work in peace. They succeeded in removing a vast amount of gold, bills of exchange and jewellery. They buried their loot securely in several graves, and helped themselves from their ' bank ' until they were caught.

After being extradited, these two big-time crooks were sentenced by a Berlin court to twelve and ten years' imprisonment; these were the maximum sentences that could be imposed under German law.

Two days after they had been sentenced, the Reichsführer SS, by virtue of his special powers, ordered them to be removed from prison and brought to Sachsenhausen for execution. They were to be shot at once.

They were taken by truck straight to the sandpit. The officials who accompanied them said that they had been impertinent and demanding during the journey, and had wished to know where they were being taken.

At the place of execution I read out to them the sentence of death. They at once began to shout: ' That's impossible. You've got it all wrong. We must first see a priest,' and so on and so forth. They absolutely refused to stand at the post and I had to have them bound to it. They struggled furiously. I was extremely relieved when I could give the order to fire.

A man who had many previous convictions for indecent assault had enticed an eight-year-old girl into a doorway in Berlin, and there assaulted and strangled her. He was sentenced by the court to fifteen years' imprisonment. On the same day he was brought to Sachsenhausen for execution.

I can see him now as he stepped out of the truck at the place of execution. Grinning cynically, he was an evil and vicious-looking, middle-aged individual, a typical a-social. The Reichsführer SS had ordered that this professional criminal be shot straight away. When I informed him of his fate, his face turned a sickly yellow and he began whining and praying. Then he screamed for mercy, a repulsive sight. I had to have him bound to the post. Were these immoral creatures frightened of what they might find on ' the other side '? I can see no other explanation for their behaviour.

During the Olympic Games the beggars and tramps were cleared off the streets and put in work-houses and concentration camps, and at the same time the many prostitutes and homosexuals were rounded up in the towns and at the bathing-places. They were to be trained to do more useful work in the camps.

The homosexuals in Dachau had already presented a problem, although there were not nearly so many of them there as in Sachsenhausen. The commandant and the commander of the protective custody camp believed that it would be best to distribute them throughout the camp, one or more in each room. I was against this, for I had learnt to know them well during my own years in prison.

It was not long before a constant stream of reports of homosexual activities began to flow in from every block. Punishment had no effect whatever.

The epidemic spread. I now proposed that all homosexuals be kept together. They were given a block senior who understood how to deal with them. They were also kept away from the other prisoners at work. They were given the job of pushing the heavy rollers used to level the camp streets. Some prisoners from the other categories, also afflicted with this vice, were sent to join them.

In this way the epidemic was at once stopped from spreading. Thereafter only isolated cases of this unnatural intercourse occurred, since a strict watch was kept on these men.

In this connection an extraordinary case comes to mind. A Rumanian prince, who lived with his mother in Munich, had become a public scandal owing to his unnatural behaviour. Despite all political and social considerations, the publicity which he had brought on himself had become intolerable and he was brought to Dachau. The police thought that his excessive debaucheries had wearied him of women, and that he had taken to homosexuality as a pastime in order to get a new thrill. The Reichsführer SS believed that hard work and the strict life of a concentration camp would soon effect a cure.

The moment he arrived, it was obvious to me what was wrong with him. His roaming eyes, the way he started at the slightest noise, his weak and dancer-like movements, all made me suspect the true homosexual at once. When the commandant harshly ordered him to go through the customary routine for new entrants, he began to weep. Then he did not want to have a bath, because he was shy. We saw the reason when he undressed. The whole of his body, from neck to wrists and ankles, was tattooed with obscene pictures. Curiously enough, these pictures not only depicted every form of perversion that the human brain can invent, but also normal intercourse between man and woman. Students of sexology would certainly have obtained some new and unusual material for their researches from this living picture-book. On being interrogated, he said that he had acquired these tattooings in every sort of seaport, both in the old world and the new.

When his sexual picture-book was photographed by the police, for all tattoo marks had to be recorded for the purposes of the State Criminal Police Office, he became sexually excited, particularly when touched. I told his room senior that he was directly responsible for him and that he was never to let him out of his sight. After a few hours I went to see how this rare plant was thriving, and I was met by the room senior who begged me to release him at once from his charge. It was, he said, rapidly 'getting him down'. The prince stood the whole time in front of the stove, staring before him. Whenever anyone came near him, or touched him in order to move him away, he became sexually excited and began to masturbate. I took him to the doctor. No sooner had the doctor started to ask him questions about his condition than he began to get excited again. He said that since his earliest youth he had suffered from strong sexual impulses, for which he had never been able to find any means of complete satisfaction. He was perpetually seeking new ways to satisfy these impulses.

The doctor prepared a report for the Reichsführer SS, which concluded by saying that the prisoner ought to be in a nursing-home and not in a concentration camp. Any attempt to cure him by hard work was doomed to failure from the start.

The report was sent off and while we were awaiting a reply the newcomer was given work, as had been ordered. His job was to cart sand. He could scarcely lift a shovel. He fell over while pushing an empty wheel-barrow. I had him taken back to his room, and informed the commandant. The commandant wished to see this performance with his own eyes on the following day. The man must work, for the Reichsführer SS has ordered it. On the next day he was staggering so that he could hardly get to the sandpit, although it was not far away. Work was out of the question; even Loritz realised this. He was taken back to his room and put to bed. That too was wrong, for he masturbated constantly. The doctor talked to him as to a sick child. It was all quite useless. They tried tying his hands, but that was not effective for long. He was given sedatives and kept cool. All in vain. He became weaker and weaker. Nevertheless he crawled out of bed in an attempt to reach the other prisoners. He was put under arrest, pending the decision of the Reichsführer SS. Two days later he was dead. He died while masturbating. Altogether he had been five weeks in the camp. The Reichsführer SS ordered a post-mortem examination to be carried out and a detailed report sent to him. The examination, at which I was present, showed a complete physical debilitation but no abnormality. The professor at the Munich Institute of Pathology, who performed the post-mortem, had never before come across a similar case in all his experience covering a great many years.

I was present when the commandant showed the man's corpse to his mother. The mother said that his death was a blessing, both for himself and for her. His uncontrollable sexual life had made him impossible to everyone. She had consulted the most famous medical specialists throughout Europe, but without success. He had run away from every sanatorium. He had spent some time in a monastery. But he could not stay there either. She had even, in her despair, suggested to him he take his own life, but he lacked the courage to do so. Now he would at least be at peace with himself. It makes me shiver even now when I remember this case.

In Sachsenhausen the homosexuals, from the very beginning, were kept in a special block. They were also kept away from the other prisoners at work. They were employed in the clay pit of a large brick works. It was hard work, and each of them had to complete a definite amount of work per day. They were exposed to all kinds of weather, since a stipulated number of truck-loads of clay had to be filled daily. The process of baking the clay could not be held up through lack of raw material. For this reason they were forced to work in all weathers, summer and winter.

The effect of hard work, which was supposed to make them ' normal ' again, varied greatly according to the different types of homosexuals.

It had its most salutary effect on the *Strichjungen*. This was Berlin slang for the male prostitutes who thought to make a comfortable living and shirked any work, however easy. They could not be classified as true homosexuals: prostitution was just their trade.

Youths of this sort were soon brought to their senses by hard work and the strict discipline of camp life. Most of them worked hard and took great care not to get into trouble, so that they might be released as soon as possible. They avoided association either with the genuine or with the viciously depraved type of homosexual. They hoped thus to show that they really had nothing at all in common with homosexuals.

Many could be trained in this fashion and then released without any danger of their relapsing into their old ways of life. One lesson was effective enough, especially since most of them were young boys.

A proportion, too, of those who had become homosexual out of inclination, men who through over-indulgence had grown weary of women and sought fresh excitements to enliven their parasitical existence, could also be cured of their vice.

This was not the case with those who had begun by dabbling in homosexuality for such reasons but had later become deeply addicted to their vice. They were comparable to the genuine homosexuals, of whom there were only a few examples. Neither the hardest work nor the strictest supervision was of any help in these cases. Whenever they found an opportunity they would fall into one another's arms. Even when physically in a very bad way, they would continue to indulge in their vice. They were easy enough to pick out. Their soft and girlish affectations and fastidiousness, their sickly-sweet manner of speech and their altogether too affectionate deportment towards their fellows distinguished them from those who had put their vice behind them and wished to be free of it, and whose steps on the road to recovery were visible to any acute observer.

Those who really wanted to renounce their vice, and were sufficiently strong-minded to do so, were able to stand up to the hardest work, but the others, each according to his constitution, graduallly broke down physically. Because they could not or would not give up their vice, they knew that they would never be set free. The effect of this psychological burden, on men whose natures were for the most part delicate and sensitive, was to accelerate their physical collapse.

Should one of these lose his ' friend ' through sickness, or perhaps death, then the end could be at once foreseen. Many would commit suicide. To such natures, in such circumstances, the ' friend ' meant everything. There were many instances of ' friends ' committing suicide together.

In 1944 the Reichsführer SS had ' renunciation ' tests carried out in Ravensbrück. Homosexuals, whose recovery was still in doubt, would be unobtrusively set to work in company with whores, and their behaviour carefully observed. The whores were ordered to approach the homosexuals inconspicuously and attempt to excite them sexually. Those who were cured at once took advantage of this opportunity, and scarcely required any encouragement. The incurable ones took no notice whatever of these women, and if approached in too obvious a manner would turn away, trembling with disgust. The procedure then was for those who appeared fit for release to be given an opportunity of intercourse with their own sex. Almost all of them spurned the opportunity thus offered and firmly rejected the advances of the real homosexuals. There were border-line cases, individuals who took advantage of both opportunities. Whether these men could be described as bi-sexual, I do not know.

I can only add that I found the habits and mentality of the various kinds of homosexuals, and the study of their psyches under prison conditions, extremely instructive.

In Sachsenhausen there were quite a number of prominent prisoners and also a number of special prisoners.

'Prominents' was the term given to those who had formerly played a part in public life. Most of them were treated as political prisoners and lived with others of their sort in the camp without any special privileges. At the beginning of the war their numbers were considerably increased by the re-arrest of former officials of the KPD, the German Communist Party, and the SPD, the German Social-Democratic Party.

Special prisoners were those who, for reasons of State policy, were accommodated separately in or near a concentration camp. They were not allowed to mix with other prisoners. No one except those directly concerned was allowed to know the place of their imprisonment, or indeed that they were under arrest at all. Before the war there were only a few of them, but as the war went on their numbers increased considerably. Later I shall return to this subject.

In 1939 a number of Czechoslovak professors and students and also some Polish professors from Cracow were imprisoned in Sachsenhausen. They were put in a special block in the camp. So far as I can remember they were not made to work, but neither were they given any special treatment. After a few weeks the professors from Cracow were released, because many German professors had spoken to Göring on their behalf and he had intervened with the Führer to have them set free.

According to my recollection they amounted in all to about a hundred teachers. I myself only saw them on their arrival, and I heard nothing of them during their imprisonment.

I must, however, give a more detailed account of one special prisoner, because of his unique behaviour in prison and because I was in a position to know all the facts of the case.

He was the evangelical pastor, Niemöller. He had been a famous U-boat commander in the First World War. He became a pastor after that war. The German evangelical church was split up into numerous separate groups. One of the most important of these groups, the *Bekenntniskirche* or Confessional Church, was led by Niemöller. The Führer wished to see the evangelical church reunited into one, and with this aim in view he appointed an Evangelic State Bishop. But many of the groups refused to recognise him, and indeed were bitterly opposed to him. Niemöller was of their number. His parish was in Dalhem, a Berlin suburb. The whole of the Berlin and Potsdam reactionary evangelical opposition joined his congregation, all the old imperial nobility and others dissatisfied with the National Socialist régime. Niemöller preached resistance, and it was this which led to his arrest. He was accommodated in the cell building in Sachsenhausen, where his detention was made as light and pleasant as possible. He could write to his wife as often as he wished. His wife was allowed to visit him every month and to bring him whatever he wanted in the way of books and tobacco and food. He could, if he wished, go for walks in the courtyard of the cell building. His cell, too, was made as comfortable as possible. In short, everything was done for him that was in any way feasible. The commandant had been instructed to keep him constantly in mind and to enquire after his wishes.

The Führer had an interest in persuading Niemöller to abandon the stand he had taken. Well-known people came to Sachsenhausen in order to reason with him, including Admiral Lanz, who was for many years his superior officer in the navy and who was also a member of the Confessional Church. But in vain. Niemöller firmly maintained his attitude that no State had the right to interfere with canon law or to promulgate new laws concerning the Church. These were entirely and solely the concern of the congregation of each church. The *Bekenntniskirche* flourished. Niemöller became its martyr. His wife was active in furthering his beliefs. I knew all about it, because I read all his mail and also listened to the conversations he had with visitors in the commandant's quarters. In 1938 he wrote to the commander-in-chief of the navy, Grand Admiral Raeder, renouncing his right to wear the uniform of a naval officer since he was not in agreement with the State which that navy served. On the outbreak of war he volunteered for service, and requested to be given command of a U-boat. Now it was Hitler's turn to refuse, on the grounds that Niemöller had declined to wear the uniform of the National Socialist State. As time went by, Niemöller began to flirt with the idea of going over to the Catholic Church. He produced the most curious arguments in support of this, even maintaining that in important matters the Catholic Church and his own were in agreement. His wife vigorously dissuaded him. In my opinion he believed that conversion to the Catholic Church would result in his obtaining his freedom. His followers, however, would never have gone over with him. I had many and searching discussions with Niemöller. He would discuss almost anything, and was interested in subjects far removed from his sphere, but as soon as the conversation turned on church matters, it was as though an iron curtain had been rung down. He stubbornly maintained his standpoint, and would brook no criticism of his obstinacy, however reasonable. Nevertheless his readiness to embrace the Catholic faith must have involved his willingness to recognise the State, since the Catholic Church had done so by virtue of the Concordat.[1] In 1941 the Reichsführer SS ordered all clerics to be transferred to Dachau, and Niemöller was among them. I saw him there in 1944, in the cell building. He was given even more freedom there, and had the former Evangelical Bishop of Posen, Wurm, to keep him company. He was in good health, despite his long years in prison. His physical needs were always most carefully catered for, and it is certain that nothing was ever done to offend his sensibilities. He was at all times treated with courtesy.[2]

[1] There follows a brief description of an incident in Pastor Niemöller's family life, concerning his daughter's engagement. Since this is of no interest to the public and in no way concerns the subject-matter of this book, it is omitted.

[2] The following note is taken from the German edition of this book. Pastor Wilhelm Niemöller, brother of Martin Niemöller and author of the book *Kampf und Zeugnis der Bekennenden Kirche* (Bielefeld, 1948), after a conversation with his brother, submitted the following comments on the above passage in a letter to the *Institut für Zeitgeschichte* dated 8 March, 1958.

1. The statement that 'the whole of the reactionary opposition' joined his Dahlem congregation is, of course, incorrect. Owing to prevailing circumstances the number of educated persons attending divine service at Dahlem was greater than in most Berlin parishes. The fact that the Dahlem congregation was very much alive cannot be minimised by the use of such words as 'reactionary' and 'dissatisfied'. For the life of that congregation has lasted far longer than did National Socialism. See my book, page 197.

2. Niemöller never preached 'resistance'. The National Socialists failed to understand what his preaching was really about. The Confessional Church attempted to preach that men are men, even if their name is Hitler, but that God is God. That a Jew is also human, Niemöller clearly stated.

3. Niemöller was not permitted to write letters as often as he wished. Usually he might send his wife two letters per month. But at various periods he was not permitted to write at all, and this frequently for months on end. It is doubtful whether Hoess ever read a letter of Niemöller's, since censorship was done by the 'political department'. Frau Niemöller was not allowed to bring her husband any books whatsoever in Sachsenhausen. He was permitted books, within limits, after his move to Dachau, though a very strict censorship was of course imposed. The time during which he was allowed out of his cell—initially twenty minutes, later one hour—was very strictly enforced. Only in Dachau was this somewhat relaxed.

4. Hoess implies that regular enquiries concerning the prisoner's wishes were the most characteristic aspect of Niemöller's imprisonment. I myself was allowed on one occasion to visit my brother in Sachsenhausen (29 September, 1938), and came away with a very different impression. The commandant had never then enquired concerning the 'wishes' of the prisoner. The prisoner can, indeed, not recall ever having seen the commandant. The statement that his cell was made 'comfortable' is pure invention on the part of Hoess.

5. Hitler had no interest in persuading Niemöller one way or the other. The visitor referred to was Admiral von Lans. He came on his own initiative, and attempted to persuade Niemöller that he state his intention to avoid touching on 'political questions' in future. The admiral did not belong to the Confessional Church.

6. Martin Niemöller's request for reinstatement in the Navy was dated 7 September, 1939. In it there is no reference to his possible employment as a U-boat commander. The sentence concerning Hitler's refusal, and particularly the alleged grounds for this, are pure invention. The truth is that on 29 September, 1939, Keitel wrote a letter, addressed to: 'The Rev. Senior Lieut. (retd.) Niemöller, Oranienburg, near Berlin, Concentration Camp Sachsenhausen.' This letter, written in his own hand, ran as follows: 'In reply to your request of 7 September, 1938, I regret that I must inform you that your recall to active service with the armed forces is not envisaged. Heil Hitler! Keitel, Col.-Gen.' To the best of my recollection it was only after this that he renounced the right to wear uniform.

7. That Niemöller hoped to obtain his freedom by conversion to Catholicism is nonsense. It is well known that many devout Catholics were in Dachau. From 1941 on he was with three of these (Neuhäusler and others). He studied the doctrines of the Catholic Church in great detail, and for years on end. But this was purely in connection with matters of the faith, of which Hoess can have no comprehension.

8. The statement that the Provincial Bishop D. Wurm was in Dachau is a strange invention. This Bishop of Wurttemberg was never either in Dachau or in Posen. He was once under house arrest, in Stuttgart in 1934. In the Dachau cell block Martin Niemöller was the only evangelical cleric. The other pastors were in Barrack 26 of the 'Priests' Block'. The confusion can doubtless be traced to the fact that General Superintendent D. Bursche, head of the Polish Evangelical Church, was in Sachsenhausen, where, indeed he died, during Martin Niemöller's time there. The commander of the Sachsenhausen protective custody camp should surely have been aware of this.

Whereas Dachau was predominantly red because the majority of the prisoners were politicals, Sachsenhausen was green.[1] The atmosphere in the camps varied accordingly, even though in both of them politicals had the most important jobs. In Dachau there was a certain *esprit de corps* amongst the prisoners; this was completely lacking in Sachsenhausen.

The two main colours fought each other fiercely, and it was easy for the camp authorities to use this rivalry for their own ends, and to play the one off against the other.

Escapes were relatively more numerous than in Dachau. Their preparation and execution were also far more subtle and elaborate.

Although an escape in Dachau was regarded as a most unusual event, much more fuss was made in Sachsenhausen, because of the presence there of Eicke. As soon as the sirens went, Eicke, if he happened to be in Oranienburg, would hurry to the camp. He wanted to know every detail of the escape, and he systematically hunted out the culprits whose inattention or negligence had made it possible. The chain of sentry posts often had to stand to for three or four days, if there were reasons to believe that the missing man was still within their circle. For days and nights on end everything connected with the escape was subjected to the closest scrutiny. The officers and especially the commandant, the commander of the protective custody camp and the officer of the day were given no respite. Eicke was perpetually asking for information as to the progress of the search. In his view no escape ought to be able to succeed. As a result of his keeping the chain of sentry posts standing to, the escaping prisoner, who had hidden himself somewhere or gone to earth, was usually found. But what a strain it was for the camp! The men often had to stand to for sixteen or twenty hours at a stretch. The prisoners had to stay where they were until the sentry posts were stood down. As long as the search continued they were not marched out to work, and only the most essential services maintained. If an escaped prisoner had managed to break through the line of sentry posts, or if he had escaped from a working squad outside the camp, an immense operation was set in motion for his recovery. All the resources of the SS and the police were called into play. The

[1] The concentration camp prisoners wore triangles of cloth upon their pyjama-like camp uniform, the colour of the triangle indicating the category to which they belonged, viz.: red—political, green—professional criminal, black—a-social, yellow—Jew, mauve—homosexual, etc.

roads and railways were watched. Motorised police squads, equipped with radio apparatus, combed roads and highways. A guard was placed on all bridges over the numerous streams in the Oranienburg district. The occupants of remote houses were warned of the escape, although most of them already knew what had happened, since they had heard the sirens. Prisoners were often recaptured thanks to the help given by the civilian population. Those who lived in the neighbourhood were aware that the camp contained mostly professional criminals, and the idea of such men being on the run frightened them. They would immediately report anything they saw to the camp or to the search parties.

When an escaped prisoner was recaptured, he was led past the assembled prisoners, in Eicke's presence if possible, wearing a large placard on which was written: ' I am back.' In addition he was made to beat a large drum hung round his neck. After this parade he was given twenty-five strokes of the lash and assigned to the penal company.

The SS-man who had found or recaptured him would be commended in daily orders and given special leave. Police employed outside the camp or civilians received a monetary award. If an SS-man managed, by care and vigilance, to prevent an escape, Eicke gave him special leave and promotion.

Eicke insisted that absolutely everything be done to prevent escapes.

If a prisoner did succeed in escaping, he insisted that every possible measure be taken for his recapture.

Severe punishment was meted out to any SS-man whose conduct had contributed to the escape, however slight the blame that could be attached to him.

Prisoners who had helped another to escape were punished even more severely.

I would like to give a description here of some unusual escapes.

Seven professional criminals, all of them tough young men, managed to tunnel under the wire which ran beside their barracks, and one night they escaped into the woods. They had put the waste earth from the tunnel under the barracks, which was raised on piles; the entrance to the tunnel was under a bed. They had worked at the tunnel for several nights without being noticed by their fellow-prisoners. A week later one of the escaped men was recognised by a block leader in a Berlin street, and arrested. Under interrogation he revealed where his comrades were hidden, with the result that they were all recaptured.

One of the homosexuals succeeded in escaping from the clay pit, despite the open nature of the country and the many sentry posts and wire entanglements. No clue could be found as to how the escape had been made. The outgoing trucks, filled with clay, were all checked personally by two SS-men and the commanding officer of the work party. The search organisation was set in motion and for days the nearby forests were combed, but without result. Just ten days later a teleprinter message was received from the frontier post at Warnemünde saying that the man had been brought in by fishermen. He was brought back to the camp and made to describe his escape. He had spent weeks preparing his flight, and had carefully considered all the possibilities. The only feasible one was the train that took the clay away from the pit. He worked hard and his industry was noticed. He was given the job of greasing the trucks and looking after the tracks. For days on end he observed how the outgoing trains were controlled. Each truck was searched from top to bottom. The diesel engine was examined as well, but he noticed that no one looked underneath it, for the guard plates reached almost to the rails. At the same time he noticed the rear guard plate hung quite loose. One day when the train stopped at the control point prior to its departure, he quickly crept under the engine and, hanging on between the two wheels, went off with it. At the first sharp curve, when the train reduced speed, he dropped between the rails. The train passed on over him. Then he vanished into the forest. He knew that he would have to head north. His escape had been rapidly discovered and the commanding officer of the work-party had telephoned the alarm to the camp. The first action taken in such cases was to have the bridges guarded by motorised squads. When the prisoner reached the great Berlin-Stettin ship canal, he saw that the bridge was already guarded. He hid in a hollow tree from which he could keep a watch on the canal and the bridge. I myself had occasionally walked past this willow tree. When night fell, he swam the canal. He continued in a northerly direction, always avoiding roads and villages. He obtained civilian clothes from a workman's hut in a sandpit. He lived on wild fruit and he milked the cows he found grazing in the meadows. Thus he managed to reach the Baltic by way of Mecklenburg. He had no difficulty in stealing a sailboat in a fishing village, and in this he sailed off towards Denmark.

Shortly before reaching Danish territorial waters, he ran into a party of fishermen who recognised the boat. They at once suspected him as a runaway, detained him, and handed him over in Warnemünde.

A professional criminal from Berlin, a decorator by trade, worked in the houses occupied by the SS inside the ring of sentry posts. He had formed a liaison with a servant girl employed by a doctor and he repeatedly came to the doctor's house where there was always work to be done. Neither the doctor nor his wife was aware of the intimate relationship between their maid and the prisoner. The doctor and his wife went away from time to time and, while they were away, the girl was given a holiday. This was the prisoner's opportunity. The girl had left a window open in the cellar, and through this he climbed in after he had observed the departure of her employers. He removed a plank from one wall on the top floor and made a hiding place for himself in the attic. He bored a hole through the wooden outside wall and was thus able to observe most of the sentry posts and the SS encampment. He laid in a stock of food and drink, and a pistol against emergencies. When the alarm went, he crept into his hiding-place, pulled a heavy piece of furniture against the place where the plank had been, and waited. When an escape was made, the houses in the SS encampment were also searched. I myself searched this very house on the day of the escape, for the fact that it was unoccupied had made me suspicious. I saw nothing unusual, however, even though I stood in the very room where the fugitive was crouched behind the wall with his pistol cocked. He said later that he would certainly have fired if he had been discovered. He was determined to gain his freedom at all costs, since an investigation was under way into his complicity in a robbery with murder that had happened some years before, and he had been betrayed out of homosexual jealousy by an accomplice in the camp. The sentries stood to for four days. On the fifth day he took the early morning train to Berlin. He had quite calmly taken his choice of the doctor's wardrobe, and had made free with the contents of the larder and cellar, as the many empty liqueur and wine bottles showed. He had filled two large suitcases with silver, linen, cameras and other valuable articles. He took his time in deciding what he wanted. He was arrested a few days later in an obscure gin-shop where, quite by chance, he was arrested by a police patrol in the act of converting the contents of his last suitcase into cash.

He had arranged to meet the servant girl, and she was sent to Ravensbrück.

The doctor was certainly surprised when he came back to his house. Eicke wanted to call him to account because of the pistol, but he let it pass when the doctor offered a large sum of money in compensation.

These are just three incidents that I can recall off-hand, a small cross-section of the richly varied life of a concentration camp.

If I remember correctly I became commander of the protective custody camp in Sachsenhausen round about Christmas 1939.

In January 1940 a surprise visit from the Reichsführer SS resulted in a change of commandant.

Loritz arrived. He let it be understood that he intended to bring the camp, which according to the Reichsführer SS had become undisciplined, 'back into line'. Loritz was well able to do this. As *Rapportführer* at Dachau in 1936, I had already taken part in a similar operation of his.

This was a bad time for me. Loritz was forever treading on my heels. The more so because my departure in 1938, to become adjutant to his most hated rival, had caused him considerable irritation. He assumed that I had organised my transfer behind his back. This was not so. The commandant of Sachsenhausen had asked for me because he had seen that I was being pushed into a dead-end job at Dachau, owing to my excessive loyalty to himself when he had been commander of the protective custody camp there.

Loritz was very resentful of this and made me only too clearly aware of his dislike.

In his opinion everyone in Sachsenhausen was treated much too softly, SS-men and prisoners alike.

In the meantime Commandant Baranowski, who was an old man, had died and Eicke, who had enough on his hands with the formation of his new division, let Loritz do much as he liked.

Glücks had never cared much for Baranowski. Loritz's return to the concentration camp suited him very well. In him he saw one of the 'old guard' commandants, who would give him full support in his new post of Inspector of Concentration Camps.

When the question of building a new camp at Auschwitz became urgent, the authorities had not far to go for a commandant. Loritz was glad to let me go, so that he could find a commander of the protective custody camp more to his liking. This was Suhren, later to be commandant of Ravensbrück, who had been Loritz's adjutant in the General SS.

I therefore became commandant of the quarantine camp which was to be built at Auschwitz.

It was far away, in the back of beyond, in Poland. There the inconvenient Hoess could exercise his passion for work to his heart's content. That was what Glücks, the Inspector of Concentration Camps, had intended. It was in these circumstances that I took up my new task.

I had never anticipated being made a commandant so quickly, especially as some very senior protective custody camp commanders had been waiting a long time for a commandant's post to fall vacant.

My task was not an easy one. In the shortest possible time I had to construct a transit camp for ten thousand prisoners, using the existing complex of buildings which, though well-constructed, had been completely neglected, and were swarming with vermin. From the point of view of hygiene, practically everything was lacking. I had been told in Oranienburg, before setting off, that I could not expect much help, and that I would have to rely largely on my own resources. In Poland I would find everything that had been unobtainable in Germany for years!

It is much easier to build a completely new concentration camp than to construct one quickly out of a conglomeration of buildings and barracks which require a large amount of constructional alteration. I had hardly arrived in Auschwitz before the Inspector of the Security Police and of the Security Service in Breslau was enquiring when the first transports could be sent to me!

It was clear to me from the very beginning that Auschwitz could be made into a useful camp only through the hard and untiring efforts of everyone, from the commandant down to the lowest prisoner.

But in order to harness all the available manpower to this task, I had to ignore all concentration camp tradition and customs. If I was to get the maximum effort out of my officers and men, I had to set them a good example. When reveille sounded for the SS rankers, I too must get out of bed. Before they had started their day's work, I had already begun mine. It was late at night before I had finished. There were very few nights in Auschwitz when I could sleep undisturbed by urgent telephone calls.

If I wanted to get good and useful work out of the prisoners then, contrary to the usual and universal practice in concentration camps, they must be given better treatment. I assumed that I would succeed in both housing and feeding them better than in the other camps.

Everything that, from my point of view, seemed wrong in the other camps, I wished to handle differently here.

I believed that in such conditions I could obtain the willing co-operation of the prisoners in the constructional work that had to be done. I also felt that I could then demand the maximum effort from them.

I had complete confidence in these assumptions. Nevertheless, within a few months, I might even say during the first weeks, I became bitterly aware that all goodwill and all the best intentions were doomed to be dashed to pieces against the human inadequacy and sheer stupidity of most of the officers and men posted to me.

I used every means at my disposal to make all my fellow-workers understand my wishes and intentions, and I attempted to make it clear to them that this was the only practicable way of getting everyone to co-operate fruitfully in completing the task assigned us.

My good intentions were in vain. Over the years the teaching of Eicke, Koch and Loritz had penetrated so deeply into the minds of the 'old hands', and had become so much a part of their flesh and blood, that even the best-willed of them simply could not behave otherwise than in the way to which they had become accustomed during long service in the concentration camps. The 'beginners' were quick to learn from the 'old hands', but the lessons they learnt were unfortunately not the best.

All my endeavours to obtain at least a few good and competent officers and non-commissioned officers for Auschwitz from the Inspector of Concentration Camps were of no avail. Glücks simply would not co-operate. It was the same with the prisoners who were to act as supervisors of the others. The *Rapportführer* Palitzsch was to find thirty useful professional criminals of all trades, since the RSHA[1] would not let me have politicals for this purpose at Auschwitz.

He brought back thirty of these, whom he considered the best among those offered to him at Sachsenhausen.

Less than ten of them were suited to my wishes and intentions.

[1] Reichssicherheitshauptamt: Reich Security Head Office, the supreme police and SS headquarters.

Palitzsch had selected these men according to his own opinions and his own ideas as to how prisoners should be treated, which he had already acquired and to which he had grown used. He was by disposition incapable of behaving in any other way.

So the whole backbone about which the camp was to be built was defective from the start. From the very beginning the camp was dominated by theories which were later to produce the most evil and sinister consequences.

Despite all that, it might have been possible to control these men, and indeed even to bring them round to my way of thinking, if the officer in charge of the prison camp[1] and the *Rapportführer* had followed my instructions and obeyed my wishes.

But this they neither could nor would do, owing to their intellectual limitations, their obstinacy and malice, and above all for reasons of convenience.

For these men the key-prisoners we had been sent were exactly right, right, that is, for the purposes which they envisaged, and for their attitude.

The real ruler of every concentration camp is the officer in charge of the prison camp. The commandant may set his stamp upon the outer form of communal camp life, and this will be more or less obvious according to the energy and enthusiasm he devotes to his job. It is he who directs policy, has final authority, and bears ultimate responsibility for all that happens. But the real master of the prisoners' whole life, and of the entire internal organisation, is the officer in charge of the prison camp or alternatively the *Rapportführer*, if that officer is strong-minded and more intelligent than his immediate superior. The commandant may decide the lines on which the camp is to be run and issue the necessary general orders and regulations concerning the life of the prisoners, as he thinks best. But the way in which his orders are carried out depends entirely on the officers in charge of the prison camp. The commandant is thus entirely dependent on their goodwill and intelligence.

It follows that if he does not trust them, or considers them incapable, he must take over their duties himself. Only thus can he be certain that his instructions and orders will be carried out in the way he intends. It is hard enough for a regimental commander to be sure

---

[1] Owing to the size of Auschwitz there were always a first and a second prison camp commander. The first two at Auschwitz were Karl Fritzsch and Hans Aumeier.

that his orders will be carried out correctly at section level in the manner he intends, particularly when they relate to matters other than mere routine. How much harder it is for the commander of a concentration camp to know that all his orders concerning the prisoners, orders which are often of the greatest consequence, will be correctly interpreted and carried out regardless! The Capos always prove particularly difficult to control. For reasons of prestige as well as for disciplinary reasons, the commandant can never interrogate the prisoners concerning the SS set over them: only in extreme cases, with a view to a criminal investigation, can this be done. Even then the prisoners, almost without exception, will say they know nothing or will give evasive replies, for they inevitably fear reprisals.

I had learned enough about all this at first hand in Dachau and Sachsenhausen, as block leader, *Rapportführer* and commander of the protective custody camp. I know very well how easy it is in a camp for unwelcome orders to be deliberately misinterpreted, and even to be given an entirely opposite construction, without the issuing authority ever being aware of this. In Auschwitz I was very soon quite sure that this was being done.

Such a state of affairs could only be radically altered by an immediate change of the entire protective custody camp staff. And the Inspector of Concentration Camps would never in any circumstances have permitted this.

It was impossible for me personally to see that my orders were carried out down to the smallest detail, since this would have meant diverting my attention from my main task, the building of a serviceable camp as rapidly as possible, and acting as officer in charge of the protective custody camp myself.

It was during the early period, when the prison camp was being got under way, that I should have spent my whole time in the camp, just because of this attitude of mind of the camp staff.

But it was precisely then that I was compelled to be almost always away from the camp owing to the inefficiency of most of the officials with whom I had to deal.

In order to get the camp started I had already had to negotiate with various economic offices, and with the local and district authorities. My executive officer was a complete halfwit and I was thus forced to take matters out of his hands and to organise the entire victualling of troops and prisoners myself.

Whether it was a question of bread or meat or potatoes, it was I

H

who had to go and find them. Yes, I even had to visit the farms in order to collect straw. Since I could expect no help of any kind from the Inspectorate, I had to make do as best I could on my own. I had to ' organise ' the trucks and lorries I needed, and the fuel for them. I had to drive as far as Zakopane and Rabka[1] to acquire cooking-pots for the prisoners' kitchen, and to the Sudetenland for bed-frames and palliasses.

Since my architect could not acquire the materials he needed most urgently, I had to drive out with him to look for them. In Berlin they were still quarrelling about the responsibility for the construction of Auschwitz, for it had been agreed that the whole project was an army affair and had only been handed over to the SS for the duration of the war.

The RSHA, the Commander of the Security Police in Cracow, and the Inspector of the Security Police and the Security Service in Breslau were repeatedly enquiring when ever-larger groups of prisoners could be accepted at the camp.[2]

Yet I still could not lay my hands on a hundred yards of barbed wire. There were mountains of it in the Engineer Depot at Gleiwitz. But I could not touch it without first getting authority to have it decontrolled from the Senior Engineer Staff in Berlin. The Inspectorate of Concentration Camps refused to help in this matter. So the urgently needed barbed wire just had to be pilfered. Wherever I found old field fortifications I ordered them to be dismantled and the pillboxes broken up, and thus I acquired the steel they contained. Whenever I came across installations containing material I urgently needed, I simply had it taken away at once without worrying about the formalities. I had to help myself.

Furthermore, the evacuation of the first zone of the area assigned to the camp was going on.[3] The second zone had also begun to be cleared. I had to work out how all this additional agricultural land was to be used.

[1] Both these places are on the Polish-Slovak border, some sixty miles from Auschwitz.

[2] The local regional representative of the RSHA (Reich Security Head Office) was the Inspector of the Security Police and the Security Service in Breslau. The Commander of the Security Police at Cracow, SS-Brigadeführer Bruno Streckenbach, was also responsible for the despatch of prisoners to Auschwitz from all the former Polish territories which, during the German occupation, constituted the *Général-Gouvernement*.

[3] An area of 40 sq. kilometres, containing three Polish villages, including Brzezinka (Birkenau).

At the end of November 1940 the first progress report was submitted to the Reichsführer SS, and an expansion of the whole camp area was begun as ordered.[1]

I thought that the construction and completion of the camp itself were more than enough to keep me occupied, but this first progress report served only to set in motion an endless and unbroken chain of fresh tasks and further projects.

From the very beginning I was so absorbed, I might say obsessed, with my task that every fresh difficulty only increased my zeal. I was determined that nothing should get me down. My pride would not allow it. I lived only for my work.

It will be understood that my many and diverse duties left me but little time for the camp and the prisoners themselves.

I had to leave them entirely in the hands of individuals such as Fritzsch, Meier, Seidler and Palitzsch, distasteful persons in every respect, and I had to do this even though I was well aware that they would not run the camp as I wished and intended.

But I could only dedicate myself completely and wholly to one task. Either I had to devote myself solely to the prisoners, or I had to use all my energies in the construction and completion of the camp. Either task required my entire and undivided attention. It was not possible to attempt both. But my job was, and always remained, to complete the construction and enlargement of the camp.

In the course of the years many other tasks occupied my attention, but the primary one remained the same throughout. All my thoughts and aspirations were directed towards this one end, and everything else had to take second place. I had to direct the whole undertaking from this standpoint alone. I therefore observed everything from this one point of view.

Glücks often told me that my greatest mistake was in doing everything myself instead of delegating the work to my responsible subordinates. The mistakes that they would make through incompetence, I should simply accept. I should become reconciled to that. Matters cannot be expected to run just as one wants, always.

He refused to accept the validity of my arguments when I objected that in Auschwitz I had certainly been given the worst type of human material to act as Capos and as junior officers: and that it was not only their incompetence, but far more their deliberate carelessness

[1] See Appendix 2.

and malice, that compelled me to handle all the more important and urgent tasks myself.

According to him, the commandant should direct and control the whole camp by telephone from his office desk. It should be quite enough if he took an occasional walk through the camp. What innocence! Glücks was only able to hold this view because he had never worked in a concentration camp. That was why he could never understand or appreciate my real needs.

This inability on the part of my superior to understand me brought me to the verge of despair. I put all my ability and my will into my work; I lived for it entirely; yet he regarded it as though this were a game or even a hobby of mine, in which I had become too absorbed and which prevented me from taking the broader view.

When, as a result of the visit of the Reichsführer SS in March 1941,[1] new and larger tasks were assigned me without any extra help in the most vital matters being forthcoming, my last hope of obtaining better and more reliable assistants vanished.

I had to resign myself to the 'bigwigs' and to my continuing quarrels with them. I had a very few good and reliable colleagues to support me, but unfortunately these were not in the most important and responsible positions. I was now forced to load and indeed to overload them with work, and I was often slow in appreciating that I was making the mistake of demanding too much of them.

Because of the general untrustworthiness that surrounded me, I became a different person in Auschwitz.

Up to then I had always been ready to see the best in my fellow-creatures, and especially in my comrades, until I was convinced of the contrary. I had often been badly let down by my credulity. But in Auschwitz, where I found my so-called colleagues constantly going behind my back, and where each day I suffered fresh disappointments, I began to change. I became distrustful and highly suspicious, and saw only the worst in everyone. I thus snubbed and hurt many honest and decent men. I had lost all my confidence and trust.

The sense of comradeship, which up to then I had regarded as something holy, now seemed to me to be a farce. The reason was that so many of my old comrades had deceived and double-crossed me.

Any form of friendly contact became repugnant to me. I repeatedly

[1] See Appendix 2.

refused to attend social gatherings, and was glad when I could find a plausible excuse for staying away. My comrades strongly and repeatedly reproached me for this. Even Glücks drew my attention more than once to the lack of that friendly comradeship which should have linked the commandant and his officers at Auschwitz. But I simply could not do it any more. I had been too deeply disillusioned.

I withdrew further and further into myself. I hedged myself in, became unapproachable, and visibly harder.

My family, and especially my wife, suffered on account of this, since my behaviour was often intolerable. I had eyes only for my work, my task.

All human emotions were forced into the background.

My wife was perpetually trying to draw me out of my seclusion. She invited old friends from outside the camp to visit us, as well as my comrades in the camp, hoping that I would be able to relax in their company. She arranged parties away from the camp with the same end in view. She did this in spite of the fact that she had never cared for this sort of social life any more than did I.

These efforts did succeed for a time in making me abandon my self-imposed seclusion occasionally, but new disillusionments quickly sent me back behind my glass wall.

Even people who hardly knew me felt sorry for me. But I no longer desired to change, for my disillusionment had, to a certain extent, made me into an unsociable being.

It often happened that when I was with friends whom I had invited, and who were close friends of ours, I would suddenly become tongue-tied and even rude. My only desire then was to run away, and be alone, and never see anyone again. With an effort I would pull myself together and try, with the help of alcohol, to put my ill-humour aside: I would then become talkative and merry and even boisterous. Alcohol, more than anything else, was able to put me in a happy and contented frame of mind. Drink has never made me quarrel with anyone. It has, however, made me admit to things that I would never have divulged when sober. I have never been a solitary drinker, nor have I ever had a craving for drink. I have never been drunk or given way to alcoholic excesses. When I had had enough, I would quietly disappear. There was no question of neglecting my duties through over-indulgence in alcohol. However late I returned home, I was always completely fresh for work and ready for duty next morning. I always expected my officers to behave in the same way. This was on disciplinary grounds. Nothing has a more demoralising effect on subordinates than the absence of their superior officers at the beginning of the day's work due to over-indulgence in alcoholic consumption on the previous night.

Nevertheless, I found little sympathy for my views.

They only obeyed because they knew that I was watching them, and they cursed 'the old man's bad temper'. If I wanted to carry out my task properly, I had to be the engine, tirelessly and ceaselessly pushing on the work of construction and constantly dragging everyone else along with me. Whether SS-man or prisoner, it made no difference.

Not only had I to struggle with all the tedious wartime difficulties in connection with constructional work, but also, daily and even hourly, with the indifference and sloppiness and lack of co-operation of my subordinates.

Active opposition is something that can be met head-on and dealt with, but against resistance a man is powerless; it eludes his grasp, even though its presence can be felt everywhere. I had to urge on the reluctant shirkers; when there was no alternative by force.

Before the war, the concentration camps had served the purpose of self-protection, but during the war according to the will of the Reichsführer SS, they became a means to an end. They were now primarily to serve the war effort, the munitions production. As many prisoners as possible were to become armaments workers. Every commandant had to run his camp ruthlessly with this end in view.

The intention of the Reichsführer SS was that Auschwitz should become one immense prison-cum-munitions-centre. What he said during his visit in March of 1941 made this perfectly plain. The camp for 100,000 prisoners of war, the enlargement of the old camp to hold 30,000 prisoners, the ear-marking of 10,000 prisoners for the synthetic rubber factory, all this emphasised his point. But the numbers envisaged were at this time something entirely new in the history of concentration camps.

At that time a camp containing 10,000 prisoners was considered exceptionally large.

The insistence of the Reichsführer SS that the constructional work must be pushed on regardless of all present or future difficulties, many of which were and would be well-nigh insuperable, gave me much food for thought even then.

The way in which he dismissed the very considerable objections raised by the Gauleiters and by the local authorities was itself enough to indicate that something unusual was afoot.

I was accustomed to the ways of the SS and of the Reichsführer SS. But his stern and implacable insistence on these orders being carried out as speedily as possible was new even in him. Glücks himself noticed this. And it was I and I alone who was to be responsible for it all. Out of nothing, and with nothing, something vaster than ever before had to be built in the shortest possible time; with these people to work with and, to judge by previous experience, without any help worth mentioning from higher authorities.

And what was the situation as regards my labour force? What had been happening to the protective custody camp in the meantime?

The officers of the camp had taken great care to observe the Eicke tradition in their treatment of the prisoners. Fritzsch from Dachau, Palitzsch from Sachsenhausen and Meier from Buchenwald had competed among themselves in the employment of ever-better ' methods ' of dealing with the prisoners along the lines laid down by Eicke.

My repeated instructions that Eicke's views could be abandoned as hopelessly out-of-date in view of the new functions of the concentration camps fell on deaf ears.

It was impossible for their limited minds to forget the principles that Eicke had taught them, for these were admirably suited to their mentality. All my orders and instructions were ' turned about ' if they ran contrary to these principles.

For it was not I, but they, who ran the camp. It was they who taught the Capos, from the chief block senior down to the last block clerk, how to behave.

They trained the block leaders and told them how to treat the prisoners.

But I have said and written enough on this subject. Against this passive resistance I was powerless.

This will only be comprehensible and credible to men who have themselves served for years in a protective custody camp.

I have already described the influence which the Capos generally exercised over the lives of their fellow-inmates. This influence was especially noticeable in this concentration camp. It was a factor of decisive importance in Auschwitz-Birkenau where the masses of prisoners could not be supervised. One would have thought a common fate and the miseries shared would have led to a steadfast and unshakeable feeling of comradeship and co-operation, but this was far from being the case.

Nowhere is crass egotism so nakedly self-evident as in prison. And for reasons of self-preservation the harder the life, the crasser that egotism.

Even people, who in ordinary life outside the camp were at all times considerate and good-natured, became capable, in the hard conditions of imprisonment, of bullying their fellow-prisoners mercilessly, if by so doing they could make their own lives a little bit easier.

More merciless yet was the behaviour of those who were naturally egotistical, cold and even criminally inclined, and who rode roughshod and without pity over the misery of their fellow-prisoners when they could thereby gain even the pettiest advantage for themselves. Quite apart from the physical effects of such mean and vile treatment, its psychological results were unspeakably worse for those of their fellow-prisoners whose sensibilities had not yet been blunted by the harshness of camp life. The treatment they received from the guards, however brutal, arbitrary and cruel, never affected them psychologically to the same extent as did this attitude on the part of their fellow-inmates.

The very fact of having to watch helplessly and without any power to intervene, while Capos of this sort tormented their fellows, had a thoroughly crushing effect on the prisoners' psyche. Woe betide the prisoner who tried to interfere, to stand up for the oppressed! The system of terrorisation that prevailed within the prison camp was far too great for any man to take such a risk.

Why do privileged prisoners and Capos treat their fellow-prisoners and fellow-sufferers in this fashion? Because they want to make a favourable impression on the guards and supervisors whose attitude is known to them, and to show how well-suited they are to the privileged positions that they hold. And also because of the advantages to be obtained in this way, and which will make their prison existence more pleasant. But such advantages are always obtainable only at the cost of their fellow-prisoners.

However, it is the guards and the supervisors who create the opportunity for such behaviour. They do so either out of indifference, since they are too lazy to stop such activities, or else, being themselves base and cruel by nature, they permit it because they enjoy the spectacle provided, and indeed even encourage the bullying, since they derive a satanic pleasure from watching the prisoners torment one another.

There were many Capos who needed no encouragement. Their mean, brutal and cowardly natures and their criminal tendencies led them to torment their fellow-prisoners both physically and mentally, and even to harass them to death out of pure sadism.

During my present imprisonment, I have had, and have now, ample opportunity of confirming, from a necessarily personal viewpoint, the truth of what I have just written.

In no place is the real 'Adam' so apparent as in prison. All the characteristics that a prisoner has acquired or affected are stripped from him, everything that is not an essential part of his real being. Prison in the long run compels him to discard all simulation and pretence. He stands naked, as he really is, for better or for worse.

How did the communal camp life of Auschwitz affect the various categories of prisoner?

For Germans from the Reich it was no problem, no matter what their category. Almost without exception they held 'high' positions, and were thus provided with all the physical necessities of life. Anything they could not obtain officially they would ' organise'. This skill in ' organisation ' was indeed shown by all the ' high ' Capos in Auschwitz, regardless of category or nationality. Their relative success varied only in accordance with their intelligence, daring and unscrupulousness. Opportunity was never lacking.

Once the Jewish Action was under way, there was practically no limit to what a man might obtain for himself. And the senior Capos also had the necessary freedom of movement for this.

Until early 1942 the largest single group of prisoners were Poles. They all knew that they would remain in the concentration camp at least for the duration of the war. Most of them believed that Germany would lose the war and, after Stalingrad, virtually all of them were convinced of this. They were kept fully informed about Germany's ' true position ' by the enemy news broadcasts. It was not difficult to listen to these enemy broadcasts, since there were plenty of wireless sets in Auschwitz. They were listened to even in my own house. Furthermore there was ample opportunity with the help of the civilian workers and even of the SS-men, for the extensive smuggling of letters. There were thus many sources of news. New arrivals also always brought in the latest information with them. Since, according to enemy propaganda, the collapse of the Axis powers was only a matter of time, the Polish prisoners felt in consequence that they had no cause for despair. The only question was: which prisoners would have the luck to survive their imprisonment? It was this uncertainty and fear which, psychologically speaking, made imprisonment so hard for the Pole. He lived in a perpetual state of anxiety as to what might befall him each day. He might at any time be swept away by an epidemic against which his weakened physical condition could offer no resistance. He might suddenly be shot or hanged as a hostage. He might also be unexpectedly brought before a drumhead court-martial in connection with a resistance movement, and condemned to death. He might be shot as a reprisal. He could meet with a fatal accident at work, brought about by someone who bore him a grudge. He could die as the result of ill-treatment. And there were many other similar fates perpetually hanging over his head.

The crucial question was whether he could physically survive in view of the steadily deteriorating diet, the increasingly crowded living quarters, the worsening of the already highly defective sanitary arrangements, and the hard work, which often had to be done in all weathers.

To this must be added perpetual worry about his family and dependants. Were they still living where he had left them? Had they also been arrested and sent to forced labour somewhere or other? Were they indeed still alive?

Many were tempted into flight in order to escape from such worries. Flight was not very difficult from Auschwitz, where opportunities for escape were innumerable. The necessary preparations were easily made, and it was a simple matter to avoid or outwit the guards.

A little courage and a bit of luck were all that was needed. When a man stakes everything on one throw, he must also of course reckon that if it goes wrong the result may be his death.

But these projects of escape always involved the prospect of reprisals, the arrest of family and relations, and the liquidation of ten or more fellow-sufferers.[1]

[1] On one occasion Hoess himself ordered the arrest of the parents of a man who had escaped from Auschwitz. Around their necks were hung placards announcing that they would remain in the camp until their son was brought back. Other and crueller reprisals for escape were also ordered, as for example by the protective custody camp commander Karl Fritzsch, who made indiscriminate arrests among the camp inmates and locked these people into the punishment cells, where they were left to starve.

Many of those who tried to escape cared little about reprisals, and were prepared to try their luck. Once beyond the ring of sentry posts, the local civilian population would help them on their way. The rest was no problem. If they had bad luck, then it was all up with them. One way or another, it was the solution of their problems.

The other prisoners had to parade past the corpses of those who had been shot while trying to escape, so that they would all see how such an attempt might end. Many were frightened by this spectacle, and abandoned their plans as a result.

But there were others who did not hesitate to make the attempt despite everything, hoping that they would be among the lucky ninety per cent who succeeded.

What can have passed through the minds of the prisoners as they marched past the corpse of a dead comrade? If I read their expression rightly, I saw horror at his fate, sympathy for the unlucky man, and a determination to exact revenge when the time came.

I saw the same expression on the faces of the prisoners when they were paraded to watch the hangings. Only terror, and a fear lest a similar fate overtake themselves, were here more in evidence.

I must refer here to the court-martial tribunal, and to the liquidation of hostages, since these solely affected the Polish prisoners.

Most of the hostages had been in the camp for a considerable time, and the fact that they were hostages was unknown both to them and to the camp authorities. Then one day a teleprinter message would arrive from the Security Police or from the Reich Security Head Office, stating that the prisoners named therein were to be shot or hanged as hostages.

A report that the executions had been carried out had to be forwarded within a few hours. The prisoners concerned would be taken away from their work or called out during the roll-call and placed in custody. Those who had been in the camp for some time usually knew what this meant, or had at least a very shrewd idea.

The order for their execution was made known to them after they had been arrested. At first, in 1940 and 1941, they were shot by a firing squad. Later they were either hanged or shot in the back of the neck with a small-calibre revolver. The bedridden were liquidated in the hospital building by means of an injection.

The Kattowitz military court visited Auschwitz every four or six weeks and sat in the punishment cell building.

The accused prisoners, most of whom were already camp inmates, although some had only recently been sent there for trial, were brought before the tribunal and interrogated through an interpreter concerning their statements and the admissions they had made. All the prisoners whom I saw tried admitted to their actions quite freely, openly and firmly.

In particular, some of the women answered bravely for what they had done. In most cases the death sentence was pronounced and carried out forthwith. Like the hostages, they all met their death with calm and resignation, convinced that they were sacrificing themselves for their country. I often saw in their eyes a fanaticism that reminded me of Jehovah's Witnesses when they went to their death.

But criminals condemned by the tribunal, men who had taken part in robberies with violence, gang crimes and so on, died in a very different way. They were either callous and sullen to the last, or else they whined and cried out for mercy.

The picture here was the same as it had been during the executions in Sachsenhausen: those who died for their ideals were brave, upstanding and calm, the a-socials stupefied or struggling against their fate.

Although the general conditions in Auschwitz were far from good, none of the Polish prisoners was willingly transferred to another camp. As soon as they heard that they were to be moved, they did everything in their power to be left out of the transport and kept in the camp. When, in 1943, a general order was issued that all Poles were to be taken to camps in Germany, I was overwhelmed by every works department with requests for the retention of prisoners described as indispensable. No one could spare his Poles. Finally the transfer had to be carried out compulsorily, a fixed percentage being moved.

I never heard of a Polish prisoner voluntarily requesting transfer to another camp. I have never understood the reason for this desire to hang on in Auschwitz.

There were three main political groups among the Polish prisoners, and the adherents of each fought violently against the others. The strongest was the chauvinistic-nationalist group. Each group competed with the others for the most influential posts. When one man managed to obtain an important position in the camp, he would quickly bring in other member of his own group and would remove his opponents from his domain. This was often accomplished by base intrigue. Indeed I dare day that many cases of spotted fever or typhus resulting in death, and other such incidents, could be accounted for by this struggle for power. I often heard from the doctors that this battle for supremacy was always waged most fiercely in the hospital building itself. It was the same story in regard to the control of work. That and the hospital building offered the most important positions of power in the entire life of the camp. Whoever controlled these, ruled the rest. And they did rule too, in no half-hearted fashion. A man who held one of these important positions could see to it that his friends were put wherever he wished them to be. He could also get rid of those he disliked, or even finish them off entirely. In Auschwitz everything was possible. These political struggles for power took place not only in Auschwitz and among the Poles, but in every camp and among all nationalities. Even among the Spanish communists in Mauthausen there were two violently opposed groups. In prison and in the penitentiary I myself had experienced how right and left wing would fight one another.

In the concentration camps these enmities were keenly encouraged and kept going by the authorities, in order to hinder any strong combination on the part of all the prisoners. Not only the political differences, but also the antagonisms between the various categories of prisoners, played a large part in this.

However strong the camp authorities might be, it would not have been possible to control or direct these thousands of prisoners without making use of their mutual antagonisms. The greater the number of antagonisms, and the more ferocious the struggle for power, the easier it was to control the camp. *Divide et impera!* This maxim has the same importance, which must never be underestimated in the conduct of a concentration camp as in high politics.

The next largest contingent consisted of the Russian prisoners of war, who were employed on building the prisoner-of-war camp at Birkenau.

They arrived from the military prisoner-of-war camp at Lamsdorf in Upper Silesia, and were in very poor condition. They reached the camp after many weeks' marching. They had been given hardly any food on the march, during halts on the way being simply turned out into the nearest fields and there told to ' graze ' like cattle on anything edible they could find. In the Lamsdorf camp there must have been about 200,000 Russian prisoners of war. This camp was simply a square area of ground on which most of them huddled as best they could in earth hovels they had built themselves. Feeding arrangements were completely inadequate and the distribution of food was irregular. They cooked for themselves in holes in the ground. Most of them—it could not be called eating—devoured their portion raw. The army was not prepared for the immense numbers of prisoners captured in 1941. The organisation of the army department responsible for prisoners of war was too rigid and inflexible, and could not improvise speedily. Incidentally, it was the same story with the German prisoners of war after the collapse, in May 1945. The Allies, too, were unable to cope with such massive numbers. The prisoners were simply herded on a convenient patch of ground, enclosed with a few strands of barbed wire, and left to their own devices. They were treated exactly as the Russians had been.

It was with these prisoners, many of whom could hardly stand, that I was now supposed to build the Birkenau prisoner-of-war camp. The Reichsführer SS ordered that only the strongest of the Russian prisoners, those who were particularly capable of hard work, were to be sent to me. The officers who accompanied them said these were the best available at Lamsdorf. They were willing to work, but were incapable of doing so because of their weakened condition. I remember very clearly how we were continually giving them food when first they arrived at the base camp, but in vain.[1] Their weakened bodies could no longer function. Their whole constitution was finished and done for. They died like flies from general physical exhaustion, or from the most trifling maladies which their debilitated constitutions could no longer resist. I saw countless Russians die while in the act of swallowing root vegetables or potatoes. For some time I employed 5,000 Russians almost daily unloading trainloads of swedes. The railway tracks were blocked, mountains of swedes lay on the lines, and there was nothing to be done about it. The Russians were physically all in. They wandered aimlessly about, crept into a safe corner to swallow something edible that they found —which was a great effort for them, or sought a quiet spot where they might die in peace. The worst time was during the mud-period

[1] Approximately 10,000 Russian prisoners of war were moved from Lamsdorf (Stalag VIII B) to Auschwitz early in the October of 1941. They were originally put into nine blocks, stone buildings and barracks, of Auschwitz I, which were separated by wire from the remainder of the base camp. By February 1942 most of the Russian prisoners of war had died of typhus, undernourishment and various ailments. Approximately 1,500 then remained alive, and these were moved to the new camp being built at Birkenau (Auschwitz II).

at the beginning and end of the winter of 1941–42. The Russians could endure the cold more or less, but not the damp and being constantly wet through. In the unfinished, simple stone barracks, hastily constructed in the early days of Birkenau, the death rate constantly rose. Even those who had hitherto shown some powers of resistance now declined rapidly in numbers day by day. Extra rations were of no avail; they swallowed everything they could lay their hands on, but their hunger was never satisfied.

On the road between Auschwitz and Birkenau I once saw an entire column of Russians, several hundred strong, suddenly make a rush for some nearby stacks of potatoes on the far side of the railway line. Their guards were taken by surprise, overrun, and could do nothing. I luckily happened to come along at this moment and was able to restore the situation. The Russians had thrown themselves on to the stacks, from which they could hardly be torn away. Some of them died in the confusion, while chewing, their hands full of potatoes. Overcome by the crudest instinct of self-preservation, they came to care nothing for one another, and in their selfishness now thought only of themselves. Cases of cannibalism were not rare in Birkenau. I myself came across a Russian lying between piles of bricks, whose body had been ripped open and the liver removed. They would beat each other to death for food. Once, riding past the camp, I saw a Russian hit another on the head with a tile, so as to snatch a piece of bread which the man had been secretly chewing behind a heap of stones. I happened to be outside the wire and by the time I found a gate and reached the spot the man was dead, his skull bashed in. I could not identify his assassin among the crowds of Russians swarming around. When the foundations for the first group of buildings were being dug, the men often found the bodies of Russians who had been killed by their fellows, partly eaten and then stuffed into a hole in the mud.

The mysterious disappearance of many Russians was explained in this way. I once saw, from a window of my house a Russian dragging a food-bucket behind the block next to the command building and scratching about inside it. Suddenly another Russian came around the corner, hesitated for a moment, and then hurled himself upon the one scrabbling in the bucket, and pushed him into the electrified wire before vanishing with the bucket. The guard in the watchtower had also seen this, but was not in a position to fire at the man who had run away. I at once telephoned the duty block leader and had the electric current cut off. I then went myself into the camp, to find the man who had done it. The one who had been thrown against the wire was dead, and the other was nowhere to be found.

They were no longer human beings. They had become animals, who sought only food.

Of more than 10,000 Russian prisoners of war who were to provide the main labour force for building the prisoner-of-war camp at Birkenau, only a few hundred were still alive by the summer of 1942.[1]

Those who did remain were the best. They were splendid workers and were used as mobile squads wherever something had to be finished quickly. But I never got over the feeling that those who had survived had done so only at the expense of their comrades, because they were more ferocious and unscrupulous, and generally ' tougher '.

It was, I believe, in the summer of 1942 that a mass break-out by the remaining Russians took place. A great part of them were shot, but many managed to get clear away. Those who were recaptured gave as reason for this mass escape their fear that they were to be gassed, for they had been told that they were to be transferred to a newly-built sector of the camp. They took it that this transfer was merely a deceptive measure. It was, however, never intended that these Russians should be gassed. But it is certain that they knew of the liquidation of the Russian *politruks* and commissars. They feared that they were to suffer the same fate.[2]

It is in this way that a mass psychosis develops and spreads.

The next largest contingent were the gypsies.

Long before the war gypsies were being rounded up and put into concentration camps as part of the campaign against a-socials. One department of the Reich Criminal Police Office was solely concerned with the supervision of gypsies. Repeated searches were made in the gypsy encampments for persons who were not true gypsies, and these were sent to concentration camps as shirkers or a-socials. In addition, the gypsy encampments were constantly being combed

[1] On 18 August, 1942—that is to say after the mass escape referred to below —only 163 Soviet prisoners of war were registered in Auschwitz. Of these, 96 survived until the end.

[2] Of the 10,000 Russian prisoners of war who came to Auschwitz, a Special Commission from the Gestapo Office, Kattowitz, in November 1941, pronounced some 300 to be commissars or fanatical communists. These were separated from the others and executed.

through for biological reasons. The Reichsführer SS wanted to ensure that the two main gypsy stocks be preserved: I cannot recall their names. In his view they were the direct descendants of the original Indo-Germanic race, and had preserved their ways and customs more or less pure and intact. He now wished to have them all collected together for research purposes. They were to be precisely registered and preserved as an historic monument.

Later they were to be collected from all over Europe, and allotted limited areas in which to dwell.

In 1937 and 1938 all itinerant gypsies were collected into so-called habitation camps near the larger towns, to facilitate supervision.

In 1942, however, an order was given that all gypsy-type persons on German territory, including gypsy half-castes, were to be arrested and transported to Auschwitz, irrespective of sex or age. The only exceptions were those who had been officially recognised as pure-blooded members of the two main tribes. These were to be settled in the Ödenburg district on the Neusiedlersee. Those transported to Auschwitz were to be kept there for the rest of the war in a family camp.

But the regulations governing their arrest were not drawn up with sufficient precision. Various offices of the Criminal Police inter-preted them in different ways, and as a result persons were arrested who could not possibly be regarded as belonging to the category that it was intended to intern.

Many men were arrested while on leave from the front, despite high decorations and several wounds, simply because their father or mother or grandfather had been a gypsy or a gypsy half-caste. Even a very senior Party member, whose gypsy grandfather had settled in Leipzig, was among them. He himself had a large business in Leipzig, and had been decorated more than once during the First World War. Another was a girl student who had been a leader in the Berlin League of German Girls.[1] There were many more such cases. I made a report to the Reich Criminal Police Office. As a result the gypsy camp was constantly under examination and many releases took place. But these were scarcely noticeable, so great was the number of those who remained.

I cannot say how many gypsies, including half-castes, were in Auschwitz. I only know that they completely filled one section of

---

[1] The feminine equivalent of the Hitler Youth, a Nazi organisation for young girls.

I

the camp designed to hold 10,000.[1] Conditions in Birkenau were utterly unsuitable for a family camp. Every pre-requisite was lacking, even if it was intended that the gypsies be kept there only for the duration of the war. It was quite impossible to provide proper food for the children, although by referring to the Reichsführer SS I managed for a time to bamboozle the food offices into giving me food for the very young ones. This was soon stopped, however, for the Food Ministry laid down that no special children's food might be issued to the concentration camps.

In July 1942 the Reichsführer SS visited the camp. I took him all over the gypsy camp. He made a most thorough inspection of everything, noting the overcrowded barrack-huts, the unhygienic conditions, the crammed hospital building. He saw those who were sick with infectious diseases, and the children suffering from Noma,[2] which always made me shudder, since it reminded me of leprosy and of the lepers I had seen in Palestine—their little bodies wasted away, with gaping holes in their cheeks big enough for a man to see through, a slow putrefaction of the living body.

He noted the mortality rate, which was relatively low in comparison with that of the camp as a whole. The child mortality rate, however, was extraordinarily high. I do not believe that many new-born babies survived more than a few weeks.

He saw it all, in detail, and as it really was—and he ordered me to destroy them. Those capable of work were first to be separated from the others, as with the Jews.

I pointed out to him that the personnel of the gypsy camp was not precisely what he had envisaged being sent to Auschwitz. He thereupon ordered that the Reich Criminal Police Office should carry out a sorting as quickly as possible. This in fact took two years. The gypsies capable of work were transferred to another camp. About 4,000 gypsies were left by August, 1944, and these had to go into the gas chambers. Up to that moment, they were unaware of what was in store for them. They first realised what was happening when they made their way, barrack-hut by barrack-hut towards Crematorium I.

---

[1] Lucie Adelsberger, in *Auschwitz Ein Tatsachenbericht*, Berlin, 1956, reckons that in the spring of 1943 there were some 16,000 gypsies in Birkenau camp. She also states that their huts were desperately overcrowded. 'Eight hundred, 1,000 or more people per block was normal.' These huts, it will be recalled, were supposed to house 300.

[2] A cancerous growth, usually fatal, which appears mostly on the face, as the result of starvation and physical debility.

It was not easy to drive them into the gas chambers. I myself did not see it, but Schwarzhuber[1] told me that it was more difficult than any previous mass destruction of Jews and it was particularly hard on him, because he knew almost every one of them individually, and had been on good terms with them. They were by their nature as trusting as children.[2]

Despite the unfavourable conditions the majority of the gypsies did not, so far as I could observe, suffer much psychologically as a result of imprisonment, apart from the fact that it restricted their roving habits.

The overcrowding, poor sanitary arrangements and even to a certain extent the food shortage were conditions to which they had become accustomed in their normal, primitive way of life. Nor did they regard the sickness and the high mortality rate as particularly tragic. Their whole attitude was really that of children, volatile in thought and deed. They loved to play, even at work, which they never took quite seriously. Even in bad times they always tried to look on the bright side. They were optimists.

I never saw a scowling, hateful expression on a gypsy's face. If one went into their camp, they would often run out of their barracks to play their musical instruments, or to let their children dance, or perform their usual tricks. There was a large playground where the children could run about to their heart's content and play with toys of every description. When spoken to they would reply openly and trustingly and would make all sorts of requests. It always seemed to me that they did not really understand about their imprisonment.

They fought fiercely among themselves. Their hot blood and pugnacious natures made this inevitable in view of the many different tribes and clans thrown together here. The members of each clan kept very much together and supported each other. When it came to sorting out the able-bodied, the resulting separations and dislocations within the clan gave rise to many touching scenes and to much pain and tears.

They were consoled and comforted to a certain extent when they were told later they would all be together again.

For a while we kept the gypsies who were capable of work in the

[1] Schwarzhuber was 1st Commander of the Protective Camp Birkenau (Auschwitz II) in 1944.
[2] This mass extermination took place during the night of 31 July–1 August, between 3,500 and 4,000 gypsies being murdered.

base camp at Auschwitz. They did their utmost to get a glimpse of their clan-mates from time to time, even if only from a distance. We often had to carry out a search after roll-call for homesick gypsies who had cunningly slipped back to join their clan.

Indeed, often, when I was in Oranienburg with the Inspectorate of Concentration Camps, I was approached by gypsies who had known me in Auschwitz, and asked for news of other members of their clan. Even when these had been gassed long ago. Just because of their complete trust, it was always hard for me to give them an evasive answer.

Although they were a source of great trouble to me at Auschwitz, they were nevertheless my best-loved prisoners—if I may put it that way. They never managed to keep at any job for long. They 'gypsied around' too much for that, whatever they did. Their greatest wish was to be in a transport company, where they could travel all over the place, and satisfy their endless curiosity, and have a chance of stealing. Stealing and vagrancy are in their blood and cannot be eradicated. Their moral attitude is also completely different from that of other people. They do not regard stealing as in any way wicked. They cannot understand why a man should be punished for it. I am here referring to the majority of those interned, the real wandering gypsies, as well as to those of mixed blood who had become akin to them. I do not refer to those who had settled in the towns. These had already learnt too much of civilisation, and what they learned was unfortunately not of the best.

I would have taken great interest in observing their customs and habits if I had not been aware of the impending horror, namely the Extermination Order, which until mid-1944 was known only to myself and the doctors in Auschwitz.

By command of the Reichsführer SS the doctors were to dispose of the sick, and especially the children, as inconspicuously as possible.

And it was precisely they who had such trust in the doctors.

Nothing surely is harder than to grit one's teeth and go through with such a thing, coldly, pitilessly and without mercy.

What effect did imprisonment have upon the Jews, who from 1942 on composed the greater part of the inmates of Auschwitz? How did they behave?

From the very beginning there were Jews in the concentration camps. I knew them well since Dachau days. But then the Jews still had the possibility of emigrating to any country in the world, provided only that they obtained the necessary entry permit. The duration of their stay in the camp was therefore only a question of time, or of money and foreign connections. Many obtained the necessary visa within a few weeks, and were set free. Only those who had been guilty of a racial offence,[1] or who had been particularly active politically during the 'system' period,[2] or who had been involved in one of the public scandals, were forced to remain in the camp.

Those with some prospect of emigrating did their best to ensure that their life in custody went as 'smoothly' as possible. They worked as diligently as they were capable of doing—the majority were unaccustomed to any sort of physical labour, behaved as unobtrusively as they could and carried out their duties quietly and steadily.

The Jews in Dachau did not have an easy time. They had to work in the gravel pit which, for them, was very strenuous physical labour. The guards, influenced by Eicke and by *Der Stürmer*,[3] which was on show everywhere in their barracks and the canteens, were particularly rough with them. They were sufficiently persecuted and tormented already as ' corrupters of the German people ', even by their fellow-prisoners. When a display case containing *Der Stürmer* was put up in the protective custody camp, its effect on those prisoners who had hitherto been not at all anti-semitic was immediately apparent. The Jews, of course, protected themselves in typically Jewish fashion by bribing their fellow-prisoners. They all had plenty of money, and could buy whatever they wanted in the canteen. It was therefore not hard for them to find penniless prisoners who were only too glad to render services in return for tobacco, sweets, sausage and such-like. In this way they were able to arrange for the Capos to give them easier work, or for the prisoner nursing staff to get them admitted to the camp hospital. On one occasion a Jew had the nails drawn from his big toes by one of the prisoner nurses in exchange for a packet of cigarettes, so that he might get into the hospital.

They were mainly persecuted by members of their own race, their foremen or room seniors. Eschen, their block senior, distinguished himself in this respect. He was to hang himself later, because he feared punishment on account of some homosexual affair in which

[1] By this Hoess means having sexual relations with a non-Jewish person, a crime in Nazi Germany.
[2] The Nazis referred to the Weimar Republic as the 'system'.
[3] A pornographic anti-semitic weekly publication, produced by Julius Streicher.

he had become involved. This block senior used every possible means, no matter how low, to terrorise the other prisoners, not only physically but above all mentally. He kept the screws on the whole time. He would entice them into disobeying the camp regulations, and then report them. He goaded them into acts of violence against one another, or against the Capos, so as to have an excuse to report them for punishment. He would not send his report in at once, however, but would keep it hanging over their heads as a means of blackmail. He was the ' Devil ' incarnate. He showed a repulsive zeal towards the members of the SS, but was ready to inflict any kind of iniquity on his fellow-prisoners and members of his own race.

I wanted to sack him more than once, but it was impossible. Eicke himself insisted on his retention.

Eicke invented a special form of collective punishment for the Jews. Each time an atrocity propaganda campaign about the concentration camps was inaugurated abroad, the Jews would be forced to lie in bed for anything from one to three months, and would be permitted to get up and leave their block only at meal times and for roll-call.

They were forbidden to ventilate their quarters and the windows were screwed down. This was a cruel punishment, with particularly severe psychological effects. As a result of this compulsory staying in bed for long periods, they became so nervous and overwrought that they could no longer bear the sight of each other, and could not stand one another's company. Many violent brawls broke out in consequence.

It was Eicke's opinion that responsibility for the atrocity propaganda campaigns must lie with those Jews who had emigrated after being in Dachau, and that it was therefore only right that the remaining Jews should suffer this distressing collective punishment.

In this connection, I must make the following statement. I was opposed to *Der Stürmer*, Streicher's anti-semitic weekly, because of the disgusting sensationalism with which it played on people's basest instincts. Then, too, there was its perpetual and often savagely pornographic emphasis on sex. This paper caused a lot of mischief and, far from serving serious anti-Semitism, it did it a great deal of harm. It is small wonder that after the collapse it was learnt that a Jew edited the paper and that he also wrote the worst of the inflammatory articles it contained.[1]

---

[1] It is not known on what grounds Hoess makes this assertion, for which no evidence can be found.

As a fanatical National-Socialist I was firmly convinced that our ideals would gradually be accepted and would prevail throughout the world, after having been suitably modified in conformity to the national characteristics of the other peoples concerned. Jewish supremacy would thus be abolished. There was nothing new in anti-semitism. It has always existed all over the world, but has only come into the limelight when the Jews have pushed themselves forward too much in their quest for power, and when their evil machinations have become too obvious for the general public to stomach.

But in my opinion the cause of anti-Semitism is ill-served by such frenzied persecution as was provided by *Der Stürmer*.

If one wished to combat Jewry spiritually, then better weapons must be used. I believed that our ideas would prevail because they were both better and stronger.

I had no hope that Eicke's collective punishments would have the slightest effect on the foreign newspaper atrocity campaigns. These would go on, though hundreds or even thousands were shot on that account. Nevertheless, I thought it right that the Jews we had in our power should be punished for the dissemination of these atrocity stories by their racial fellows.

Then came the 'Crystal Night', staged by Goebbels in November 1938, when, as a reprisal for the shooting of von Rath in Paris by a Jew, Jewish shops throughout the country were destroyed or at least had their windows smashed, and when fires broke out in all the synagogues and the fire-fighting services were deliberately prevented from putting them out. 'For their own protection, and to save them from the wrath of the people', all Jews who played any part in the trade or industry or business life of the country were arrested and brought into the concentration camps as 'protective custody Jews'.

Thus did I first learn to know them in the mass.

Up to then Sachsenhausen had been almost free of Jews,[1] but now came the Jewish invasion. Hitherto bribery had been almost unknown in Sachsenhausen. Now it was widespread, and took every form.

The 'green' prisoners welcomed the Jews with delight as objects to be plundered. Their money had to be taken away from them, since otherwise it would have been impossible to prevent the camp from falling into a state of chaos.

[1] The actual word is *Judenrein*, or 'Jew-pure', a term which the Nazis used when describing areas or cities in which all Jews had been exterminated.

They did their best to do each other in the eye whenever they could. Each tried to wangle a little position for himself and, with the tacit consent of the Capos they had won over, even invented new posts for themselves so as to avoid having to work. They did not hesitate to get rid of their fellow-prisoners by making false accusations against them, if this would enable them to obtain a nice, easy job. Once they had ' got somewhere ', they proceeded to harry and persecute their own people quite mercilessly. They far surpassed the ' green ' prisoners in every way.

Many Jews were driven to despair by this behaviour and in order to escape further persecution they ' ran into the wire ', or attempted flight, hoping to be shot, or hanged themselves.

The numerous incidents of this nature were duly reported to Eicke by the commandant. Eicke merely remarked: ' Let them carry on. The Jews can quietly devour each other.'

I must emphasise here that I have never personally hated the Jews. It is true that I looked upon them as the enemies of our people. But just because of this I saw no difference between them and the other prisoners, and I treated them all in the same way. I never drew any distinctions. In any event the emotion of hatred is foreign to my nature. But I know what hate is, and what it looks like. I have seen it and I have suffered it myself.

When the Reichsführer SS modified his original Extermination Order of 1941, by which all Jews without exception were to be destroyed, and ordered instead that those capable of work were to be separated from the rest and employed in the armaments industry, Auschwitz became a Jewish camp. It was a collecting place for Jews, exceeding in scale anything previously known.

Whereas the Jews who had been imprisoned in former years were able to count on being released one day and were thus far less affected psychologically by the hardships of captivity, the Jews in Auschwitz no longer had any such hope. They knew, without exception, that they were condemned to death, that they would live only so long as they could work.

Nor did the majority have any hope of a change in their sad lot. They were fatalists. Patiently and apathetically, they submitted to all the misery and distress and terror. The hopelessness with which they accepted their impending fate made them psychologically quite indifferent to their surroundings. This mental collapse accelerated its physical equivalent. They no longer had the will to live, everything had become a matter of indifference to them, and they would succumb to the slightest physical shock. Sooner or later, death was inevitable. I firmly maintain from what I have seen that the high mortality among the Jews was due not only to the hard work, to which most of them were unaccustomed, and to the insufficient food, the overcrowded quarters and all the severities and abuses of camp life, but principally and decisively to their psychological state.

For the mortality rate among the Jews was not much lower in other work places and other camps, where general conditions were far more favourable. It was always considerably higher with them than with other types of prisoner. I observed this again and again during my journeys of inspection as DI.[1]

This was even more noticeable in the case of the Jewish women. They deteriorated far more rapidly than the men, although from my observations they had in general far greater toughness and powers of endurance than the men, both physically and mentally. What I have just written applies to the bulk, the mass of the Jewish prisoners.

The more intelligent ones, psychologically stronger and with a keener desire for life, that is to say in most cases those from the western countries, reacted differently.

These people, especially if they were doctors, had no illusions concerning their fate. But they continued to hope, reckoning on a change of fortune that somehow or other would save their lives. They also reckoned on the collapse of Germany, for it was not difficult for them to listen to enemy propaganda.

For them the most important thing was to obtain a position which would lift them out of the mass and give them special privileges, a job that would protect them to a certain extent from accidental and mortal hazards, and improve the physical conditions in which they lived.

They employed all their ability and all their will to obtain what can truly be described as a ' living ' of this sort. The safer the position the more eagerly and fiercely it was fought for. No quarter was shown, for this was a struggle in which everything was at stake.

[1] In November 1943 Hoess was transferred from his post of commandant of Auschwitz to the Economic-Administration Head Office (WVHA) of the SS in Berlin. The Inspectorate of Concentration Camps had been subordinated to this quasi-ministry since April 1942, of which it formed Department D. From 10 November, 1943, Hoess was in charge of the political section (*Amt DI*) in this department.

They flinched from nothing, no matter how desperate, in their efforts to make such safe jobs fall vacant and then to acquire them for themselves. Victory usually went to the most unscrupulous man or woman. Time and again I heard of these struggles to oust a rival and win his job.

In the various camps I had become well acquainted with the struggles for supremacy waged between the different categories of prisoners and political groups, and with the intrigues that went on to secure the higher posts. But I found that the Jews in Auschwitz could still teach me a lot. 'Necessity is the mother of invention', and here it was an actual question of sheer survival.

Nevertheless, it frequently happened that persons who had acquired these safe positions would suddenly lose their grip, or would gradually fade away, when they learnt of the death of their closest relations. This would happen without any physical cause such as illness or bad living conditions. The Jews have always had very strong family feelings. The death of a near relative makes them feel that their own lives are no longer worth living, and are therefore not worth fighting for.

I have also seen quite the contrary, during the mass exterminations, but I shall refer to this later.

What I have written above applies particularly to the female inmates of all sorts.

But then everything was much more difficult, harsher and more depressing for the women, since general living conditions in the women's camp were incomparably worse. They were far more tightly packed in, and the sanitary and hygienic conditions were notably inferior. Furthermore the disastrous overcrowding and its consequences, which existed from the very beginning, prevented any proper order being established in the women's camp.[1]

The general congestion was far greater than in the men's camp. When the women had reached the bottom, they would let them-

[1] From mid-May 1942 the newly built Women's Camp at Birkenau was designated as the principal detention camp for German and non-German female prisoners. In July 1942 the Reich Security Head Office informed all senior police and security offices that henceforth all arrested females were to be sent to Auschwitz. In September of that year Himmler ordered that all the Jewish women in Ravensbrück Women's Concentration Camp were to be transferred to Auschwitz, and that Ravensbrück was to be made ' Jew-pure '. A number of non-Jewish inmates from Ravensbrück had already been moved to Auschwitz to act as female Capos in the new Women's Camp there; these were principally criminals and a-socials (see below).

1. Arrival of a transport train. To the left and right can be seen part of the barracks of the Birkenau camp, in the background the chimneys of crematoriums II and III

. The arrivals waiting for selection: men on one side, women on the other

3. An SS doctor examining the prisoners as to their fitness for work. Th white edge to his cap denotes an officer's rank

4. Women and children not fit for work sent to one side

5. Old men who failed the selection

6. Women and children waiting for further orders, often long delayed

7. Women and children walking along the road after receiving orders to proceed in the direction of the 'Baths'. They sometimes waited in nearby woods till the batch ahead had departed, then had to undress and go to the gas chambers

8. Men found capable of work waiting to enter the camp as prisoners

9. Entrance to the camp. The lettering over the gateway erected by the SS reads: 'Work Brings Freedom'. A guard tower and notice board warning about electric wires can be seen

10. Women prisoners after being undressed, shaved and given prison dress; their prison number was tattooed under their left arm

11. New women prisoners marching into the camp

12. Men prisoners after receiving their prison clothes. Men and women went to different camps

13. Inside the camp

selves go completely. They would then stumble about like ghosts, without any will of their own, and had to be pushed everywhere by the others, until the day came when they quietly passed away. These stumbling corpses were a terrible sight.

The ' green ' female prisoners were of a special sort. I believe that Ravensbrück was combed through to find the ' best ' for Auschwitz. They far surpassed their male equivalents in toughness, squalor, vindictiveness and depravity. Most were prostitutes with many convictions, and some were truly repulsive creatures. Needless to say, these dreadful women gave full vent to their evil desires on the prisoners under them, which was unavoidable. The Reichsführer SS regarded them as particularly well-suited to act as Capos over the Jewish women, when he visited Auschwitz in 1942. Not many of these women died, except from disease.

They were soulless and had no feelings whatsoever.

The Budy blood-bath is still before my eyes.[1] I find it incredible that human beings could ever turn into such beasts. The way the ' greens' knocked the French Jewesses about, tearing them to pieces, killing them with axes, and throttling them—it was simply gruesome.

Luckily not all the ' greens ' and ' blacks ' were such utter brutes. There were capable ones among them, who preserved a measure of sympathy for their fellow-prisoners. But such women were of course continually and cruelly persecuted by other members of their colour. Nor could the majority of female supervisors[2] understand this.

A welcome contrast were the female Jehovah's Witnesses, who were nicknamed ' bible-bees ' or ' bible-worms '.

Unfortunately there were too few of them. Despite their more or less fanatical attitude they were much in demand. They were employed as servants in the homes of SS-men with large families, the Waffen SS club-house, and even in the SS officers' mess. But they worked above all on the land.

They worked on the poultry farm at Harmense,[3] and on various

---

[1] Budy was a village some five miles from the Auschwitz base camp, where a punishment company of prisoners was stationed and employed on drainage work connected with the Vistula. This punishment unit was completely cut off from the rest of the camp and the Capos of both sexes, who were recruited from among the criminals, conducted a reign of terror over their prisoners.

[2] The female equivalent of the SS guards.

[3] One of the agricultural undertakings run from Auschwitz. There was also a fish-processing plant at Harmense.

other farms. They needed no supervision or guards. They were diligent and willing workers, for such was the will of Jehovah. Most of them were middle-aged German women but there were also a number of younger Dutch girls. I had two of the older women working for more than three years in my own household. My wife often said that she herself could not have seen to everything better than did these two women. The care that they bestowed on the children, both big and small, was particularly touching. The children loved them as though they were members of the family. At first we were afraid that they might try to save the children for Jehovah. But we were wrong. They never talked to the children about religion. This was really remarkable, considering their fanatical attitude. There were other wonderful beings among them. One of them worked for an SS officer, doing everything that had to be done without needing to be told, but she absolutely refused to clean his uniform, cap or boots or indeed even to touch anything that had any connection with the military life. On the whole they were contented with their lot. They hoped that, by suffering in captivity for Jehovah's sake, they would be given good positions in His kingdom, which they expected to enter very soon.

Strangely enough they were all convinced it was right that the Jews should now suffer and die, since their forefathers had betrayed Jehovah.

I have always regarded Jehovah's Witnesses as poor, misguided creatures, who were nevertheless happy in their own way.

The rest of the female prisoners, Poles, Czechs, Ukranians and Russians, were employed so far as possible on agricultural work. They thus escaped the congestion and the evil effects of camp life. They were far better off in their billets on the farms or in Raisko.[1] I have always found that the prisoners engaged on agricultural work and living away from the camp make a very different impression from the others. They were certainly not subjected to the same psychological strains as their fellows in the massive camps. They would not otherwise have been so willing to do the work demanded of them.

The women's camp, tightly crammed from the very beginning,

[1] The Raisko estate belonged to Auschwitz and was farmed for the SS. It had a plant-breeding establishment run by Dr Caesar, who in February 1942 was made responsible for all the agricultural work carried out by the Auschwitz prisoners.

meant psychological destruction for the mass of the female prisoners, and this led sooner or later to their physical collapse.

From every point of view, and at all times, the worst conditions prevailed in the women's camp. This was so even at the very beginning, when it still formed part of the base camp. Once the Jewish transports from Slovakia began to arrive, it was crammed to the roof within a matter of days. Wash-houses and latrines were sufficient, at the most, for a third of the number of inmates that the camp contained.

To have put these swarming ant-heaps into proper order would have required more than the few female supervisors allotted me from Ravensbrück. And I must emphasise once again that the women I was sent were not the best.

These supervisors had been thoroughly spoiled at Ravensbrück. Everything had been done for them, to persuade them to remain in the women's concentration camp, and by offering them extremely good living conditions it was hoped to attract new recruits. They were given the best of accommodation, and were paid a salary they could never have earned elsewhere. Their work was not particularly onerous. In short, the Reichsführer SS, and Pohl[1] in particular, wished to see the female supervisors treated with the utmost consideration.

Up to that time conditions in Ravensbrück had been normal, and there was no question of overcrowding.

These supervisors were now posted to Auschwitz—none came voluntarily, and had the job of getting the women's camp started in the most difficult conditions.

From the very beginning most of them wanted to run away and return to the quiet comforts and the easy life at Ravensbrück.

The chief female supervisor of the period, Frau Langefeldt, was in no way capable of coping with the situation, yet she refused to accept any instructions given her by the commander of the protective custody camp. Acting on my own initiative, I simply put the women's camp under his jurisdiction, since this seemed the only method of ending the disorderly way in which it was being run. Hardly a day passed without discrepancies appearing in the numbers of inmates shown on the strength-returns. The supervisors ran hither and thither in all this confusion like a lot of flustered hens, and had no idea what to do. The three or four good ones among them were driven crazy by the rest. The chief supervisor regarded herself as an

[1] See Appendix 5.

independent camp commander, and consequently objected to being placed under a man of the same rank as herself. In the end I actually had to cancel her subordination to him. When the Reichsführer SS visited the camp in July 1942 I reported all this to him, in the presence of the chief female supervisor, and I told him that Frau Lange-feldt was and always would be completely incapable of commanding and organising the women's camp at Auschwitz as this should be done. I requested that she be once again subordinated to the 1st commander of the protective custody camp.

The Reichsführer SS absolutely refused to allow this, despite the striking proofs he was given of the inadequacy of the chief supervisor and of the female supervisors in general. He wished a women's camp to be commanded by a woman, and I was to detail an SS officer to act as her assistant.

But which of my officers would be willing to take his orders from a woman? Every officer whom I had to appoint to this post begged to be released as soon as possible. When the really large numbers of prisoners began to arrive, I myself devoted as much time as I could to helping in the running of this camp.

Thus from the very beginning the women's camp was run by the prisoners themselves. The larger the camp became, the more difficult it was for the supervisors to exercise control, and self-rule by the prisoners became more and more apparent. Since it was the ' green ', who had the supremacy, and who therefore ran the camp by reason of their greater slyness and unscrupulousness, it was they who were the real masters in the women's camp, despite the fact that the camp senior and other key officials were ' red '. The women controllers, as the female Capos were called, were mostly ' green ' or ' black '. It was thus inevitable that the most wretched conditions prevailed in the women's camp.

The original female supervisors were, even so, far and away superior to those we got later. In spite of keen recruiting by the National-Socialist women's organisations, very few candidates volunteered for concentration camp service, and compulsion had to be used to obtain the ever-increasing numbers required.

Each armaments firm to which female prisoners were allotted for work had in exchange to surrender a certain percentage of their other female employees to act as supervisors. It will be understood that, in view of the general wartime shortage of efficient female labour, these firms did not give us their best workers.

These supervisors were now given a few weeks ' training ' in Ravensbrück and then let loose on the prisoners. Since the selection and allocation took place at Ravensbrück, Auschwitz was once again at the end of the queue. Obviously Ravensbrück kept what seemed to it the best ones for employment in the new women's labour camp which was being set up there.

Such was the position regarding the supervisory staff in the women's camp at Auschwitz.

As was only to be expected, the morals of these women were, almost without exception, extremely low. Many of them appeared before the SS tribunal charged with theft in connection with the Rheinhardt Action.[1] But these were only the few who happened to be caught. In spite of the most fearful punishments, stealing went on, and the supervisors continued to use the prisoners as go-betweens for this purpose.

I will give one very bad case as an illustration.

One of these female supervisors sank so low as to become intimate with some of the male prisoners, mostly ' green ' Capos. In return for sexual intercourse, in which she was only too anxious to take part, she received jewellery, gold and other valuable objects. As a cover for her shameless behaviour, she started an affair with a senior non-commissioned officer of the SS guard unit and used his house as a safe place in which to lock up her hard-earned winnings. This poor fool was completely unaware of what his sweetheart was up to, and was very surprised when all these pretty things were discovered in his house.

The supervisor was sentenced by the Reichsführer SS to life imprisonment in a concentration camp, and to twice twenty-five strokes of the lash.

Like homosexuality among the men, an epidemic of lesbianism was rampant in the women's camp. The most severe measures, including transfer to the punishment company, were inadequate to put a stop to this.

Time and again I received reports of intercourse of this sort between supervisors and female prisoners. This in itself indicates the low level of these supervisors.

Obviously they did not take their work or duties very seriously

[1] *Aktion Rheinhardt* was the code name given to the operation of collection and marketing the clothing, valuables and other belongings, including gold fillings from teeth, and women's hair, taken from the slaughtered Jews.

and most of them were inefficient as well. There were only a few punishments that could be inflicted for dereliction of duty. Confinement to their quarters was not looked on as a punishment at all, since it meant that they did not have to go out when the weather was bad. All punishments had first to be countersigned by the Inspector of Concentration Camps or Pohl. Punishment was to be kept to a minimum. 'Irregularities' were to be put right by careful training and good leadership. The female supervisors knew all about this, of course, and the majority of them reacted as might be expected.

I have always had a great respect for women in general. In Auschwitz, however, I learnt that I would have to modify my views, and that even a woman must be carefully examined before she is entitled to enjoy a full measure of respect.

What I have said certainly applied to the majority of the female supervisory staff. It is true that there were good, decent, reliable women among them, but they were very few. There is no need to emphasise that these suffered greatly from their surroundings and from the general conditions at Auschwitz. But they could not escape, being bound by their war service obligations. Many of them complained to me about their troubles, and even more so to my wife. We could only tell them to hope that the war would soon be over. This was indeed a poor means of consolation.

Attached to the women's camp, for the purpose of guarding the working parties employed outside the camp, were the dog-handlers.

Already at Ravensbrück the female supervisors in charge of outside working parties had dogs allotted them, so as to reduce the number of guards. These supervisors were of course armed with pistols, but the Reichsführer SS believed that a greater terror-effect would be produced by the use of dogs. For most women have a powerful respect for dogs, whereas men do not bother about them so much.

Because of the mass of prisoners at Auschwitz, how to guard the outside working parties effectively was a constant problem. There were never enough troops. Chains of sentry posts were useful, in that they could be used to enclose the larger working areas. But the constant moving of work-parties from one site to another, and the mobility necessitated by the nature of the work itself, made proper supervision impossible in the case of agricultural work, digging ditches and so on. Owing to the small number of female supervisors available, it was necessary to employ as many dog-handlers as possible.

Even our one-hundred-and-fifty-odd dogs were not enough. The Reichsführer SS calculated that one dog should be able to replace two sentries. This was probably so, as far as the female working parties were concerned, owing to the universal fear caused by the presence of the dogs.

The Auschwitz Dog-squad contained the most astonishing military material. Astonishing in the negative sense. When volunteers were sought for training as dog-handlers, half the SS regiment applied. They imagined that such work would be easier and less monotonous. Since it was impossible to take on all the volunteers, the companies hit upon a cunning solution, and gave up all their black sheep, so as to be rid of them. Someone else could have the headaches now. Most of these men had been punished for some offence or other. If the commander of the guard unit had looked at these men's conduct sheets a little more closely, he would never on any account have allowed them to be sent away for training.

At the Training and Experimental Establishment for Dog-handlers at Oranienburg some of the trainees were returned to their units before they had even finished their course, because of total unsuitability.

When those who had completed their training returned to Auschwitz they were formed into a unit, the *Hundestaffel*,[1] and it was not hard to see what a splendid new formation had here been created. And now it was time for them to be put to work. Either they played games with their dogs, or they found an easy hideout and went to sleep, their dogs waking them up on the approach of an 'enemy', or else passed the time in pleasant conversation with the female supervisors or the prisoners. A great many of them formed a regular liaison with the ' green ' controllers. Since the dog-handlers were always employed in the women's camp, it was not difficult for them to continue this liaison.

When they were bored, or wanted to have some fun, they would set their dogs on the prisoners. If they were caught doing this, they would maintain that the dog had done it of its own accord, owing to the peculiar behaviour of the prisoner, or that its lead had been lost, and so on. They always had an excuse. Every day, according to their regulations, they had to give their dog further training.

Because of the time and trouble it took to train fresh dog-handlers, they could only be relieved of their posts if they had been guilty of some grave offence, such as one that entailed punishment by SS

[1] Dog-squad.

K

court-martial, or alternatively if they had badly ill-treated or neglected their dogs. The kennelman, a former police sergeant, who had
looked after dogs for more than twenty-five years, was often driven
to despair by the behaviour of the dog-handlers. But they knew that
nothing much could happen to them, and that they were unlikely
actually to lose their jobs. A better commanding officer might have
been able to knock this gang into shape. But the gentleman concerned had far more important things to think about. I had much
trouble with the *Hundestaffel*, and many clashes with the commander
of the guard regiment, over this.[1] I had no understanding of what
was actually required of troops, at least according to Glücks's way
of thinking. Hence I was never able to get him to post away officers
as soon as they became intolerable at Auschwitz.

A very great deal of trouble could have been avoided if Glücks's
attitude towards me had been different.

As the war went on the Reichsführer SS was constantly insisting
on ever greater economies in the manpower employed on guard
duties. The men were to be replaced by devices such as movable
wire fencing, by encircling permanent places of work with electrified
wire, by minefields, and by ever larger numbers of dogs. Should a
commandant manage to devise a really efficient method of economising in the use of guards, he was given immediate promotion. But all
this achieved nothing at all.

The Reichsführer SS even imagined that dogs could be trained to
circle around the prisoners, as though they were sheep, and thus
prevent them from escaping. One sentry, aided by several dogs,
was supposed to be able to guard up to 100 prisoners with
safety. The attempt came to nothing. Men are not sheep. However
well-trained the dogs were in recognising the prisoners by their
uniforms and their smell and so on, and however accurately they
were taught to know how close prisoners might be allowed to
approach, they were all only dogs, and could not think like human
beings. If the prisoners purposely attracted them to one spot, the
dogs would then leave a wide section unguarded through which they
could escape.

Nor were the dogs any use in preventing a mass break-out. They
would of course savagely maul some of the escapers, but they would
be immediately slaughtered along with their 'shepherds'.

[1] The commander of the SS guard regiment at Auschwitz from 1942 on was
Friedrich Hartjenstein.

It was also proposed that dogs should replace the guards in the watchtowers. They were to be allowed to run loose between the double wire fencing that encircled the camp or the permanent places of work, each dog guarding a certain sector, and would give warning of the approach of a prisoner, thus preventing a break through the wire. This, too, came to nothing. The dogs either found a spot in which to go to sleep, or they let themselves be tricked. If the wind was in the wrong quarter the dog would notice nothing, or its barking would not be heard by the sentry.

The laying of mines was a two-edged weapon. They had to be accurately laid and their precise situation plotted on the plan of the minefield, since after three months at the most they became defective and had to be replaced. It was also necessary to walk through the minefield from time to time, and this gave the prisoners a chance to observe the lanes where no mines had been laid.

Globocnik[1] had used mines in this way at his extermination centres. But despite the carefully laid minefields at Sobibor, the Jews knew where the lanes through the minefield ran, and were able by force to achieve a major break-out during which almost all the guard personnel were wiped out.

Neither mechanical devices nor animals can replace human intelligence.

Even the double electrified fence can be neutralised in dry weather with a few simple tools, provided a man is sufficiently cold-blooded and gives the problem a little thought. This has frequently succeeded. Often too the sentries outside the wire have come too close to it, and have had to pay for their lack of caution with their lives.

I have referred several times to what I regarded as my main task; namely, to push on, with all the means at my disposal, with the construction of all the installations belonging to the SS in the Auschwitz camp area.

Sometimes, during a period of quiet, I used to think that I could see an end in sight to the constructional work resulting from the numerous schemes and plans that the Reichsführer SS had laid down for Auschwitz, but at that point new plans would arrive, involving further urgent action.

The perpetual rush in which I lived, brought about by the demands of the Reichsführer SS, by wartime difficulties, by almost daily problems in the camps and above all by the unending stream of

[1] See Appendix 7.

prisoners flowing into the whole camp area, left me no time to think of anything except my work. I concentrated exclusively on this.

Harassed thus by circumstances, I passed on my harassment in double measure to all who came under my jurisdiction, whether SS, civilians, officials, business firms or prisoners. I had only one end in view: to drive everything and everyone forward in my determination to improve the general conditions so that I could carry out the measures laid down. The Reichsführer SS required every man to do his duty and if necessary to sacrifice himself entirely in so doing. Every German had to commit himself heart and soul so that we might win the war.

In accordance with the will of the Reichsführer SS the concentration camps were to become armaments plants. Everything else was to be subordinated to this. All other considerations must be set aside.

His words made it quite clear that the unwarrantable general conditions in the camps were of secondary importance. Armaments came first, and every obstacle to this must be overcome. I dared not allow myself to think otherwise. I had to become harder, colder and even more merciless in my attitude towards the needs of the prisoners. I saw it all very clearly, often far too clearly, but I knew that I must not let it get me down. I dared not let my feelings get the better of me. Everything had to be sacrificed to one end, the winning of the war. This was how I looked on my work at that time. I could not be at the front, so I must do everything at home to support those who were fighting. I see now that all my driving and pushing could not have won the war for us. But at the time I had implicit faith in our final victory, and I knew I must stop at nothing in my work to help us achieve this.

By the will of the Reichsführer SS, Auschwitz became the greatest human extermination centre of all time.

When in the summer of 1941 he himself gave me the order to prepare installations at Auschwitz where mass exterminations could take place, and personally to carry out these exterminations, I did not have the slightest idea of their scale or consequences. It was certainly an extraordinary and monstrous order. Nevertheless the reasons behind the extermination programme seemed to me right. I did not reflect on it at the time: I had been given an order, and I had to carry it out. Whether this mass extermination of the Jews was necessary or not was something on which I could not allow myself to form an opinion, for I lacked the necessary breadth of view.

If the Führer had himself given the order for the 'final solution of the Jewish question', then, for a veteran National-Socialist and even more so for an SS officer, there could be no question of considering its merits. 'The Führer commands, we follow' was never a mere phrase or slogan. It was meant in bitter earnest.

Since my arrest it has been said to me repeatedly that I could have disobeyed this order, and that I might even have assassinated Himmler. I do not believe that of all the thousands of SS officers there could have been found a single one capable of such a thought. It was completely impossible. Certainly many SS officers grumbled and complained about some of the harsh orders that came from the Reichsführer SS, but they nevertheless always carried them out.

Many orders of the Reichsführer SS deeply offended a great number of his SS officers, but I am perfectly certain that not a single one of them would have dared to raise a hand against him, or would have even contemplated doing so in his most secret thoughts. As Reichsführer SS, his person was inviolable. His basic orders, issued in the name of the Führer, were sacred. They brooked no consideration, no argument, no interpretation. They were carried out ruthlessly and regardless of consequences, even though these might well mean the death of the officer concerned, as happened to not a few SS officers during the war.

It was not for nothing that during training the self-sacrifice of the Japanese for their country and their emperor, who was also their god, was held up as a shining example to the SS.

SS training was not comparable to a university course which can have as little lasting effect on the students as water on a duck's back. It was on the contrary something that was deeply engrained, and the Reichsführer SS knew very well what he could demand of his men.

But outsiders simply cannot understand that there was not a single SS officer who would disobey an order from the Reichsführer SS, far less consider getting rid of him because of the gruesomely hard nature of one such order.

What the Führer, or in our case his second-in-command, the Reichsführer SS, ordered was always right.

Democratic England also has a basic national concept: 'My country, right or wrong!' and this is adhered to by every nationally-conscious Englishman.

Before the mass extermination of the Jews began, the Russian *politruks* and political commissars were liquidated in almost all the concentration camps during 1941 and 1942.

In accordance with a secret order issued by Hitler, these Russian *politruks* and political commissars were combed out of all the prisoner-of-war camps by special detachments from the Gestapo.[1] When identified, they were transferred to the nearest concentration camp for liquidation. It was made known that these measures were taken because the Russians had been killing all German soldiers who were party members or belonged to special sections of the NSDAP, especially members of the SS, and also because the political officials of the Red Army had been ordered, if taken prisoner, to create every kind of disturbance in the prisoner-of-war camps and their places of employment and to carry out sabotage wherever possible.

The political officials of the Red Army thus identified were brought to Auschwitz for liquidation. The first, smaller transports of them were executed by firing squads.

While I was away on duty, my deputy, Fritzsch, the commander of the protective custody camp, first tried gas for these killings. It was a preparation of prussic acid, called Cyclon B,[2] which was used in the camp as an insecticide and of which there was always a stock on hand. On my return, Fritzsch reported this to me, and the gas was used again for the next transport.

The gassing was carried out in the detention cells of Block 11. Protected by a gas-mask, I watched the killing myself. In the crowded cells death came instantaneously the moment the Cyclon B was thrown in. A short, almost smothered cry, and it was all over. During this first experience of gassing people, I did not fully realise what was happening, perhaps because I was too impressed by the whole procedure. I have a clearer recollection of the gassing of nine hundred Russians which took place shortly afterwards in the old crematorium, since the use of Block 11 for this purpose caused too much trouble. While the transport was detraining, holes were pierced in the earth and concrete ceiling of the mortuary. The Russians were ordered to undress in an anteroom; they then quietly entered the mortuary, for they had been told they were to be deloused. The whole transport exactly filled the mortuary to capacity. The doors were then sealed and the gas shaken down through the

---

[1] The reference is doubtless to Hitler's notorious instructions, dated 30 March, 1941, and 6 June, 1941, ' On the Treatment of Political Commissars.'
[2] A crystalline powder.

holes in the roof. I do not know how long this killing took. For a little while a humming sound could be heard. When the powder was thrown in, there were cries of ' Gas! ', then a great bellowing, and the trapped prisoners hurled themselves against both the doors. But the doors held. They were opened several hours later, so that the place might be aired. It was then that I saw, for the first time, gassed bodies in the mass.

It made me feel uncomfortable and I shuddered, although I had imagined that death by gassing would be worse than it was. I had always thought that the victims would experience a terrible choking sensation. But the bodies, without exception, showed no signs of convulsion. The doctors explained to me that the prussic acid had a paralysing effect on the lungs, but its action was so quick and strong that death came before the convulsions could set in, and in this its effects differed from those produced by carbon monoxide or by a general oxygen deficiency.

The killing of these Russian prisoners-of-war did not cause me much concern at the time. The order had been given, and I had to carry it out. I must even admit that this gassing set my mind at rest, for the mass extermination of the Jews was to start soon and at that time neither Eichmann[1] nor I was certain how these mass killings were to be carried out. It would be by gas, but we did not know which gas or how it was to be used. Now we had the gas, and we had established a procedure. I always shuddered at the prospect of carrying out exterminations by shooting, when I thought of the vast numbers concerned, and of the women and children. The shooting of hostages, and the group executions ordered by the Reichsführer SS or by the Reich Security Head Office had been enough for me. I was therefore relieved to think that we were to be spared all these blood-baths, and that the victims too would be spared suffering until their last moment came. It was precisely this which had caused me the greatest concern when I had heard Eichmann's description of Jews being mown down by the Special Squads[2] armed with machine-guns and machine-pistols. Many gruesome scenes are said to have taken place, people running away after being shot, the finishing off of the wounded and particularly of the women

[1] See Appendix 3.

[2] The *Einsatzkommandos* which moved into Russia behind the advancing German armies and massacred the Russian Jews. See Poliakov and Reitlinger, *op. cit.*

and children. Many members of the *Einsatzkommandos,* unable to endure wading through blood any longer, had committed suicide. Some had even gone mad. Most of the members of these *Kommandos* had to rely on alcohol when carrying out their horrible work. According to Höfle's description, the men employed at Globocnik's[1] extermination centres consumed amazing quantities of alcohol.[2]

In the spring of 1942 the first transports of Jews, all earmarked for extermination, arrived from Upper Silesia.[3]

They were taken from the detraining platform to the ' Cottage '— to Bunker I—across the meadows where later Building Site II was located.[4] The transport was conducted by Aumeier and Palitzsch and some of the block leaders. They talked with the Jews about general topics, enquiring concerning their qualifications and trades, with a view to misleading them. On arrival at the 'Cottage', they were told to undress. At first they went calmly into the rooms where they were supposed to be disinfected. But some of them showed signs of alarm, and spoke of death by suffocation and of annihilation. A sort of panic set in at once. Immediately all the Jews still outside were pushed into the chambers, and the doors were screwed shut. With subsequent transports the difficult individuals were picked out early on and most carefully supervised. At the first signs of unrest, those responsible were unobtrusively led behind the building and killed with a small-calibre gun, that was inaudible to the others. The presence and calm behaviour of the Special Detachment[5] served to reassure those who were worried or who suspected what was about to happen. A further calming effect was obtained by members of the Special Detachment accompanying them into the rooms and remaining with them until the last moment, while an SS-man also stood in the doorway until the end.

It was most important that the whole business of arriving and undressing should take place in an atmosphere of the greatest possible calm. People reluctant to take off their clothes had to be helped by those of their companions who had already undressed, or by men of the Special Detachment.

[1] See Appendix 7.

[2] Hans Höfle was Globocnik's chief of staff at Lublin. He was later transferred to Oranienburg, where he and Hoess became friends.

[3] One of the first, if not the very first, of these was a transport of Jews from Beuthen on 15 February, 1942.

[4] See Appendix. 1

[5] This, the *Sonderkommando,* consisted of prisoners.

The refractory ones were calmed down and encouraged to undress. The prisoners of the Special Detachment also saw to it that the process of undressing was carried out quickly, so that the victims would have little time to wonder what was happening.

The eager help given by the Special Detachment in encouraging them to undress and in conducting them into the gas-chambers was most remarkable. I have never known, nor heard, of any of its members giving these people who were about to be gassed the slightest hint of what lay ahead of them. On the contrary, they did everything in their power to deceive them and particularly to pacify the suspicious ones. Though they might refuse to believe the SS-men, they had complete faith in these members of their own race, and to reassure them and keep them calm the Special Detachments therefore always consisted of Jews who themselves came from the same districts as did the people on whom a particular action was to be carried out.

They would talk about life in the camp, and most of them asked for news of friends or relations who had arrived in earlier transports. It was interesting to hear the lies that the Special Detachment told them with such conviction, and to see the emphatic gestures with which they underlined them.

Many of the women hid their babies among the piles of clothing. The men of the Special Detachment were particularly on the look-out for this, and would speak words of encouragement to the woman until they had persuaded her to take the child with her. The women believed that the disinfectant might be bad for their smaller children, hence their efforts to conceal them.

The smaller children usually cried because of the strangeness of being undressed in this fashion, but when their mothers or members of the Special Detachment comforted them, they became calm and entered the gas chambers, playing or joking with one another and carrying their toys.

I noticed that women who either guessed or knew what awaited them nevertheless found the courage to joke with the children to encourage them, despite the mortal terror visible in their own eyes.

One woman approached me as she walked past and, pointing to her four children who were manfully helping the smallest ones over the rough ground, whispered:

' How can you bring yourself to kill such beautiful, darling children? Have you no heart at all? '

One old man, as he passed by me, hissed:

'Germany will pay a heavy penance for this mass murder of the Jews.'

His eyes glowed with hatred as he said this. Nevertheless he walked calmly into the gas-chamber, without worrying about the others.

One young woman caught my attention particularly as she ran busily hither and thither, helping the smallest children and the old women to undress. During the selection she had had two small children with her, and her agitated behaviour and appearance had brought her to my notice at once. She did not look in the least like a Jewess. Now her children were no longer with her. She waited until the end, helping the women who were not undressed and who had several children with them, encouraging them and calming the children. She went with the very last ones into the gas-chamber. Standing in the doorway, she said:

'I knew all the time that we were being brought to Auschwitz to be gassed. When the selection took place I avoided being put with the able-bodied ones, as I wished to look after the children. I wanted to go through it all, fully conscious of what was happening. I hope that it will be quick. Goodbye!'

From time to time women would suddenly give the most terrible shrieks while undressing, or tear their hair, or scream like maniacs. These were immediately led away behind the building and shot in the back of the neck with a small-calibre weapon.

It sometimes happened that, as the men of the Special Detachment left the gas-chamber, the women would suddenly realise what was happening, and would call down every imaginable curse upon our heads.

I remember, too, a woman who tried to throw her children out of the gas-chamber, just as the door was closing. Weeping she called out:

'At least let my precious children live.'

There were many such shattering scenes, which affected all who witnessed them.

During the spring of 1942 hundreds of vigorous men and women walked all unsuspecting to their death in the gas-chambers, under the blossom-laden fruit trees of the 'Cottage' orchard. This picture of death in the midst of life remains with me to this day.

The process of selection, which took place on the unloading platforms, was in itself rich in incident.

The breaking up of families, and the separation of the men from the women and children, caused much agitation and spread anxiety throughout the whole transport. This was increased by the further separation from the others of those capable of work. Families wished at all costs to remain together. Those who had been selected ran back to rejoin their relations. Mothers with children tried to join their husbands, or old people attempted to find those of their children who had been selected for work, and who had been led away.

Often the confusion was so great that the selections had to be begun all over again. The limited area of standing-room did not permit better sorting arrangements. All attempts to pacify these agitated mobs were useless. It was often necessary to use force to restore order.

As I have already frequently said, the Jews have strongly developed family feelings. They stick together like limpets. Nevertheless, according to my observations, they lack solidarity. One would have thought that in a situation such as this they would inevitably help and protect one another. But no, quite the contrary. I have often known and heard of Jews, particularly those from Western Europe, who revealed the addresses of those members of their race still in hiding.

One woman, already in the gas-chamber, shouted out to a non-commissioned officer the address of a Jewish family. A man who, to judge by his clothes and deportment appeared to be of very good standing, gave me, while actually undressing, a piece of paper on which was a list of the addresses of Dutch families who were hiding Jews.

I do not know what induced the Jews to give such information. Was it for reasons of personal revenge, or were they jealous that those others should survive?

The attitude of the men of the Special Detachment was also strange. They were all well aware that once the actions were completed they, too, would meet exactly the same fate as that suffered by these thousands of their own race, to whose destruction they had contributed so greatly. Yet the eagerness with which they carried out their duties never ceased to amaze me. Not only did they never divulge to the victims their impending fate, and were considerately helpful to them while they undressed, but they were also quite prepared to use violence on those who resisted. Then again, when it was a question of removing the trouble-makers and holding them while they were shot, they would lead them out in such a way that the victims never saw the non-commissioned officer standing there with his gun ready, and he was able to place its muzzle against the back of their necks without their noticing it. It was the same story when they dealt with the sick and the invalids, who could not be taken into the gas-chambers. And it was all done in such a matter-of-course manner that they might themselves have been the exterminators.

Then the bodies had to be taken from the gas-chambers, and after the gold teeth had been extracted, and the hair cut off, they had to be dragged to the pits or to the crematoria. Then the fires in the pits had to be stoked, the surplus fat drained off, and the mountain of burning corpses constantly turned over so that the draught might fan the flames.

They carried out all these tasks with a callous indifference as though it were all part of an ordinary day's work. While they dragged the corpses about, they ate or they smoked. They did not stop eating even when engaged on the grisly job of burning corpses which had been lying for some time in mass graves.

It happened repeatedly that Jews of the Special Detachment would come upon the bodies of close relatives among the corpses, and even among the living as they entered the gas-chambers. They were obviously affected by this, but it never led to any incident.

I myself saw a case of this sort. Once when bodies were being carried from a gas-chamber to the fire-pit, a man of the Special Detachment suddenly stopped and stood for a moment as though rooted to the spot. Then he continued to drag out a body with his comrades. I asked the Capo what was up. He explained that the corpse was that of the Jew's wife. I watched him for a while, but noticed nothing peculiar in his behaviour. He continued to drag corpses along, just as he had done before. When I visited the Detachment a little later, he was sitting with the others and eating, as though nothing had happened. Was he really able to hide his emotions so completely, or had he become too brutalised to care even about this?

Where did the Jews of the Special Detachment derive the strength to carry on night and day with their grisly work? Did they hope that some whim of fortune might at the last moment snatch them from the jaws of death? Or had they become so dulled by the accumulation of horror that they were no longer capable even of ending their own lives and thus escaping from this ' existence '?

I have certainly watched them closely enough, but I have never really been able to get to the bottom of their behaviour.[1]

The Jew's way of living and of dying was a true riddle that I never managed to solve.

All these experiences and incidents which I have described could be multiplied many times over. They are excerpts only, taken from the whole vast business of the extermination, sidelights as it were.

This mass extermination, with all its attendant circumstances, did not, as I know, fail to affect those who took a part in it. With very few exceptions, nearly all of those detailed to do this monstrous ' work ', this ' service ', and who, like myself, have given sufficient thought to the matter, have been deeply marked by these events.

Many of the men involved approached me as I went my rounds through the extermination buildings, and poured out their anxieties and impressions to me, in the hope that I could allay them.

Again and again during these confidential conversations I was asked: is it necessary that we do all this? Is it necessary that hundreds of thousands of women and children be destroyed? And I, who in my innermost being had on countless occasions asked myself exactly this question, could only fob them off and attempt to console them by repeating that it was done on Hitler's order. I had to tell them that this extermination of Jewry had to be, so that Germany and our posterity might be freed for ever from their relentless adversaries.

There was no doubt in the mind of any of us that Hitler's order had to be obeyed regardless, and that it was the duty of the SS to carry it out. Nevertheless we were all tormented by secret doubts.

I myself dared not admit to such doubts. In order to make my subordinates carry on with their task, it was psychologically essential that I myself appear convinced of the necessity for this gruesomely harsh order.

Everyone watched me. They observed the impression produced upon me by the kind of scenes that I have described above, and my reactions. Every word I said on the subject was discussed. I had to

[1] It may be mentioned in this connection that in the summer of 1944 a determined, armed attempt to break out of Birkenau was made by the Jewish Special Detachment with the help of other prisoners from the women's camp, the stores camp called ' Canada ', etc. It proved abortive, however. Four hundred and fifty-five prisoners and four SS non-commissioned officers were killed during this armed uprising.

exercise intense self-control in order to prevent my innermost doubts and feelings of oppression from becoming apparent.

I had to appear cold and indifferent to events that must have wrung the heart of anyone possessed of human feelings. I might not even look away when afraid lest my natural emotions got the upper hand. I had to watch coldly, while the mothers with laughing or crying children went into the gas-chambers.

On one occasion two small children were so absorbed in some game that they quite refused to let their mother tear them away from it. Even the Jews of the Special Detachment were reluctant to pick the children up. The imploring look in the eyes of the mother, who certainly knew what was happening, is something I shall never forget. The people were already in the gas-chamber and becoming restive, and I had to act. Everyone was looking at me. I nodded to the junior non-commissioned officer on duty and he picked up the screaming, struggling children in his arms and carried them into the gas-chamber, accompanied by their mother who was weeping in the most heart-rendering fashion. My pity was so great that I longed to vanish from the scene: yet I might not show the slightest trace of emotion.

I had to see everything. I had to watch hour after hour, by day and by night, the removal and burning of the bodies, the extraction of the teeth, the cutting of the hair, the whole grisly, interminable business. I had to stand for hours on end in the ghastly stench, while the mass graves were being opened and the bodies dragged out and burned.

I had to look through the peep-hole of the gas-chambers and watch the process of death itself, because the doctors wanted me to see it.

I had to do all this because I was the one to whom everyone looked, because I had to show them all that I did not merely issue the orders and make the regulations but was also prepared myself to be present at whatever task I had assigned to my subordinates.

The Reichsführer SS sent various high-ranking Party leaders and SS officers to Auschwitz so that they might see for themselves the process of extermination of the Jews. They were all deeply impressed by what they saw. Some who had previously spoken most loudly about the necessity for this extermination fell silent once they had actually seen the ' final solution of the Jewish problem '. I was repeatedly asked how I and my men could go on watching these operations, and how we were able to stand it.

My invariable answer was that the iron determination with which we must carry out Hitler's orders could only be obtained by a stifling of all human emotions. Each of these gentlemen declared that he was glad the job had not been given to him.

Even Mildner[1] and Eichmann, who were certainly tough enough, had no wish to change places with me. This was one job which nobody envied me.

I had many detailed discussions with Eichmann concerning all matters connected with the 'final solution of the Jewish problem', but without ever disclosing my inner anxieties. I tried in every way to discover Eichmann's innermost and real convictions about this 'solution'.

Yes, every way. Yet even when we were quite alone together and the drink had been flowing freely so that he was in his most expansive mood, he showed that he was completely obsessed with the idea of destroying every single Jew that he could lay his hands on. Without pity and in cold blood we must complete this extermination as rapidly as possible. Any compromise, even the slightest, would have to be paid for bitterly at a later date.

In the face of such grim determination I was forced to bury all my human considerations as deeply as possible.

Indeed, I must freely confess that after these conversations with Eichmann I almost came to regard such emotions as a betrayal of the Führer.

There was no escape for me from this dilemma.

I had to go on with this process of extermination. I had to continue this mass murder and coldly to watch it, without regard for the doubts that were seething deep inside me.

I had to observe every happening with a cold indifference. Even those petty incidents that others might not notice I found hard to forget. In Auschwitz I truly had no reason to complain that I was bored.

If I was deeply affected by some incident, I found it impossible to go back to my home and my family. I would mount my horse and ride, until I had chased the terrible picture away. Often, at night, I would walk through the stables and seek relief among my beloved animals.

It would often happen, when at home, that my thoughts suddenly

---

[1] Head of the Gestapo office for the Kattowitz district, in which Auschwitz was located.

turned to incidents that had occurred during the extermination. I then had to go out. I could no longer bear to be in my homely family circle. When I saw my children happily playing, or observed my wife's delight over our youngest, the thought would often come to me: how long will our happiness last? My wife could never understand these gloomy moods of mine, and ascribed them to some annoyance connected with my work.

When at night I stood out there beside the transports, or by the gas-chambers or the fires, I was often compelled to think of my wife and children, without, however, allowing myself to connect them closely with all that was happening.

It was the same with the married men who worked in the crematoria or at the fire-pits.

When they saw the women and children going into the gas-chambers, their thoughts instinctively turned to their own families.

I was no longer happy in Auschwitz once the mass exterminations had begun.

I had become dissatisfied with myself. To this must be added that I was worried because of anxiety about my principal task, the never-ending work, and the untrustworthiness of my colleagues.

Then the refusal to understand, or even to listen to me, on the part of my superiors. It was in truth not a happy or desirable state of affairs. Yet everyone in Auschwitz believed that the commandant lived a wonderful life.

My family, to be sure, were well provided for in Auschwitz. Every wish that my wife or children expressed was granted them. The children could live a free and untrammelled life. My wife's garden was a paradise of flowers. The prisoners never missed an opportunity for doing some little act of kindness to my wife or children, and thus attracting their attention.

No former prisoner can ever say that he was in any way or at any time badly treated in our house. My wife's greatest pleasure would have been to give a present to every prisoner who was in any way connected with our household.

The children were perpetually begging me for cigarettes for the prisoners. They were particularly fond of the ones who worked in the garden.

My whole family displayed an intense love of agriculture and particularly for animals of all sorts. Every Sunday I had to walk them all across the fields, and visit the stables, and we might never miss out the kennels where the dogs were kept. Our two horses and the foal were especially beloved.

The children always kept animals in the garden, creatures the prisoners were forever bringing them. Tortoises, martens, cats, lizards: there was always something new and interesting to be seen there. In summer they splashed in the paddling pool in the garden, or in the Sola.[1] But their greatest joy was when Daddy bathed with them. He had, however, so little time for all these childish pleasures. Today I deeply regret that I did not devote more time to my family. I always felt that I had to be on duty the whole time. This exaggerated sense of duty has always made life more difficult for me than it actually need have been. Again and again my wife reproached me and said: ' You must think not only of the service always, but of your family too.'

Yet what did my wife know about all that lay so heavily on my mind? She has never been told.

When, on Pohl's suggestion, Auschwitz was divided up, he gave me the choice of being commandant of Sachsenhausen or head of DI.[2]

It was something quite exceptional for Pohl to allow any officer a choice of jobs. He gave me twenty-four hours in which to decide. It was really a kindly gesture in good will, a recompense, as he saw it, for the task I had been given at Auschwitz.

At first I felt unhappy at the prospect of up-rooting myself, for I had become deeply involved with Auschwitz as a result of all the difficulties and troubles and the many heavy tasks that had been assigned to me there.

But then I was glad to be free from it all.

On no account did I wish to have another camp. I had truly had enough of the life, after a total of nine years in camp service, of which three and a half years had been spent at Auschwitz.

So I chose the position of chief of DI. There was nothing else for me to do. I was not allowed to go to the front. The Reichsführer SS had twice and firmly forbidden this.

[1] The river Sola, which flows into the Vistula a few miles north of Auschwitz, formed the eastern boundary of the Auschwitz camp area.

[2] Hoess's predecessor as head of Department DI in the Economic-Administration Head Office was Arthur Liebehenschel. He became commandant of Auschwitz I. He proved, incidentally, a considerably less cruel and brutal commandant than Hoess had been.

I did not at all care for an office job, but Pohl had told me that I could organise the department as I saw best.

When I took up my post, on 1 December, 1943, Glücks also gave me a completely free hand. Glücks was not pleased with my appointment, which brought me, of all people, so closely in contact with himself. Nevertheless, he bowed to the inevitable, since this was Pohl's wish.

I had to regard my job, if I were not to look upon it as a nice, easy billet, as one in which I was primarily concerned to assist the commandants, and I saw all my functions from the point of view of the camps themselves. In fact I intended that the activities of the DI should be precisely the reverse of what they had hitherto been.

Above all I wanted my office to be in close and permanent contact with the camps and by personal visits I intended to form a first-hand judgment of their difficulties and grievances, so that I would be in a position to exert pressure on the higher authorities concerning what could and should be done for them.

In my new office I could now, thanks to the documents, orders and entire correspondence filed there, follow the development of all the camps since Eicke's inspectorate, and obtain a complete picture.

There were many camps of which I had no personal knowledge at all. The entire correspondence between the Inspector of Concentration Camps and the camps themselves, unless solely concerned with the distribution of labour or with matters of health or administration, was filed in the DI offices. It was thus possible to gain a bird's eye view of all the camps. But no more than that. What actually happened in the camps, what they looked like, was not to be found in the documents and archives. That could only be discovered by walking through the camps oneself and keeping one's eyes open. And this was what I proposed to do.

I spent a lot of time travelling on duty. This was usually at Pohl's request, for he regarded me as an expert on what went on inside the camps.

I was thus able to see the reality in the camps, the hidden defects and shortcomings. Maurer of DII[1] was Glücks's deputy and virtually the Inspector, and he and I were able to put right much that was wrong. But by 1944 it was too late for drastic change. The camps became increasingly overcrowded, with all the usual by-products that followed this state of affairs.

[1] See Appendix 6.

It is true that tens of thousands of Jews were moved from Auschwitz for the new armaments project, but this was only a question of
out of the frying-pan and into the fire. Knocked together with great
speed and under unbelievably difficult conditions, the buildings,
constructed by officials exactly in accordance with the principles
laid down in the manuals, presented a picture of unrelieved squalor.
In addition there was the heavy work to which the prisoners were
unaccustomed and the ever diminishing scale of rations. The prisoners
would have been spared a great deal of misery if they had been taken
straight into the gas-chambers at Auschwitz. They soon died,
without making any substantial contribution to the war effort and
often without having done any work at all.

I drafted numerous reports on the subject, but pressure on the
part of the Reichsführer SS ('more prisoners for armaments') was
too strong. He was intoxicated by the weekly rise in the figures of
prisoners employed. And he no longer looked at the mortality rate.
In past years a rise in the death rate had always infuriated him. Now
he said nothing.

If Auschwitz had followed my constantly repeated advice, and
had only selected the most healthy and vigorous Jews, then the
camp would have produced a really useful labour force and one that
would have lasted, although it is true that it would have been
numerically smaller. As it was, the numbers on paper were high, but
a majority percentage had to be subtracted to obtain a true picture.
The sick cluttered up the camps, depriving the able-bodied of food
and living space and doing no work, and in fact their presence made
many of those who could work incapable of it.

No slide-rule was necessary to calculate what the final result would
be. But I have already said enough about this, and have written a
detailed account in my descriptions of the various persons concerned.[1]

By reason of my appointment I was now in more immediate and
direct contact with the Reich Security Head Office. I got to know all
the influential officials in the various departments responsible for the
concentration camps.

Their views, however, varied from office to office. I have already
given a detailed account of the chief of Amt IV,[2] but I was never able
to discover his own real opinions, since he hid behind the Reichsführer SS.

[1] See Appendices 2 to 9.
[2] Heinrich Müller, the head of the Gestapo. See Appendix 4.

Sub-section IVb (Protective Custody)[1] was still bogged down in its old, pre-war routine. A great deal of energy was devoted to fighting the paper war and far too little to the actual requirements of the real war. Many officials in this sub-section should have been dismissed from their posts.

In my opinion, the arrest, on the outbreak of the war, of those public officials who had hitherto been antagonistic to the régime was a mistake. It only served to create more enemies for the State. Those who were considered untrustworthy could have been arrested much earlier, for there was plenty of time during the years of peace. But the protective custody sub-section was bound by the reports of the controlling offices.

I had many struggles with this sub-section, despite the fact that I was personally on good terms with its chief.

The sub-section that was concerned with the Western and Northern territories, including special prisoners from these areas, was very difficult to deal with, because these territories were of direct interest to the Reichsführer SS. The greatest caution was needed here. The prisoners were to be given special consideration and employed so far as possible on lighter work, etc.

The sub-section concerned with the Eastern territories was less troublesome. Eastern prisoners, apart from the Jews, formed the majority in all the camps. It was therefore they who provided the main labour force for use in the armaments programme.

Execution orders came in an unending stream. Today I can see more clearly. My requests for help in remedying the deficiencies of Auschwitz by putting a stop to new deliveries were shelved by the Reich Security Head Office, since they would not, or perhaps did not wish to, show any consideration for the Poles. All that mattered was that the actions of the Security Police should be completed. What happened to the prisoners afterwards was a matter of indifference to the Reich Security Head Office, since the Reichsführer SS attached no particular importance to it.

[1] Hoess is, inexplicably enough, confused about the organisation in which he worked. According to an organisation-plan of the Reich Security Head Office dated 1 October, 1943, there was no Sub-section (Referat) IVb. There was a Department (*Amtsgruppe*) VIb of the Reich Security Head Office, which had four sub-sections, the first three of which dealt with Catholicism, Protestantism, the sects and freemasonry, while the fourth (Eichmann) was responsible for Jewish matters. A special administrative sub-section for protective custody matters formed part of Department IVc, under Dr Berndorff, and was referred to as Sub-section IV C2.

The sub-section concerned with the Jews, controlled by Eichmann and Gunther, had no doubts about its objective. In accordance with the orders given by the Reichsführer SS in the summer of 1941, all Jews were to be exterminated. The Reich Security Head Office raised the strongest objections when the Reichsführer SS, on Pohl's suggestion, directed that able-bodied Jews were to be sorted out from the rest.

The Reich Security Head Office was always in favour of the complete extermination of all Jews, and saw in the creation of each new work camp, and in every further thousand Jews selected for work, the danger that circumstances might arise that would set them free and keep them alive.

No department had a greater interest in raising the Jewish death-rate than the Jewish sub-section of the Reich Security Head Office.

As against that, Pohl had been authorised by the Reichsführer SS to provide as many prisoners as possible for the armaments industry. Accordingly he laid the greatest emphasis on the delivery of the maximum number of prisoners, and this also meant that as many Jews capable of work as possible were to be removed from the transports earmarked for extermination.

He also attached the greatest importance to the preservation of this labour force alive, although without much success.

The Reich Security Head Office and the Economic-Administration Head Office were thus at loggerheads.

Nevertheless, Pohl appeared to be the stronger, for he was backed by the Reichsführer SS who, bound in his turn by his promises to the Führer, was constantly and ever more urgently demanding prisoners to work in the armaments factories.

On the other hand the Reichsführer SS also wished to see as many Jews as possible destroyed.

From 1941 onwards, when Pohl took over the concentration camps, the camps were incorporated into the Reichsführer SS's armaments programme.

As the war situation grew ever more total, the Reichsführer SS's demands for prisoner labour became more ruthless.

The bulk of the prisoners were those from the East and, later, the Jews. They were mainly sacrificed to the armaments programme.

The concentration camps were a bone of contention between the Reich Security Head Office and the Economic-Administration Head Office.

The Reich Security Head Office delivered prisoners with the object of destroying them. It was a matter of indifference to them whether this objective was realised straight away by execution or by way of the gas-chambers, or rather more slowly through diseases brought about by the unwarrantable conditions in the concentration camps, which were deliberately not put right.

The Economic-Administration Head Office wanted the prisoners preserved for the armaments industry. Since, however, Pohl allowed himself to be led astray by the Reichsführer SS's continual demands for ever more labour, he unintentionally played into the hands of the Reich Security Head Office. For because of his insistence on the fulfilment of these demands, thousands of prisoners died at their work, since virtually all the basic necessities of life for such masses of prisoners were lacking.

I guessed at the time that this was happening, but was reluctant to believe it.

But today I can see the picture more clearly.

I have now described what was the true and only background to it all, the dark shadows that lay behind the concentration camps.

Thus the concentration camps were intentionally, though sometimes unintentionally, transformed into huge-scale extermination centres.

The Reich Security Head Office issued to the commandants a full collection of reports concerning the Russian concentration camps. These described in great detail the conditions in, and the organisation of, the Russian camps, as supplied by former prisoners who had managed to escape. Great emphasis was placed on the fact that the Russians, by their massive employment of forced labour, had destroyed whole peoples. For example, if, during the construction of a canal, the inmates of one camp were expended, thousands of fresh kulaks or other unreliable elements would be produced, who after a time would be expended in their turn.

Was the purpose of these reports to accustom the commandants gradually to their new task? Or was it to render them insensitive to the conditions gradually developing in their own camps?

As DI one of my regular jobs was to undertake distasteful enquiries in the various concentration camps, and even more often in the work camps. These were not always pleasant for the commandants. I was also responsible for the necessary changes in personnel, as for example at Bergen-Belsen. Up till then the Inspectorate of Concentration Camps had paid no attention to this camp. It was used by the Reich Security Head Office mainly for the so-called 'delicate' Jews, and it was only regarded as a temporary transit camp. The commandant, Sturmbannführer Haas, a grim, taciturn man, directed and governed the place as he saw fit. He had actually been for a time at Sachsenhausen, in 1939, as commander of the protective custody camp, but he came from the General-SS and had not much knowledge of concentration camps.

He made no attempt to improve the state of the buildings or the grim hygienic conditions prevailing at Bergen-Belsen, which was an old prisoner-of-war camp taken over from the Army. He had to be relieved of his post in the autumn of 1944 because of the way he neglected the camp and carried on with women, and I had to go there and install Kramer,[1] previously commandant of Auschwitz II, in his place. The camp was a picture of wretchedness. The barracks and the store-rooms and even the guards' quarters were completely neglected. Sanitary conditions were far worse than at Auschwitz.

By the end of 1944 it was no longer possible to do much in the way of building, although I managed to extract a most capable architect from Kammler. We could only patch up and improvise. Despite all his efforts, Kramer was not able to rectify the results of Haas's negligence. Thus when Auschwitz was evacuated, and a large proportion of the prisoners came to Bergen-Belsen, the camp was at once filled to overflowing and a situation arose which even I, accustomed as I was to Auschwitz, could only describe as dreadful. Kramer was powerless to cope with it. Even Pohl was shocked when he saw the conditions, during our lightning tour of all the concentration camps which the Reichsführer SS had ordered us to undertake. He at once commandeered a neighbouring camp from the Army so that there would at least be room to breathe, but conditions there were no better. There was hardly any water, and the drains simply emptied into the adjoining fields. Typhus and spotted

[1] Joseph Kramer, a member of the SS-Totenkopf organisation, had been employed on concentration camp duties since 1934. In 1940 he was, for five months, Hoess's adjutant at Auschwitz. Transferred to Natzweiler, he returned in May 1944 to Auschwitz, where he succeeded Hartjenstein, who then became commandant of Natzweiler, as commandant of Auschwitz II or Auschwitz-Birkenau. In December 1944 he was made commandant of Bergen-Belsen, where he remained until the end.

typhus were rampant. A start was immediately made on the building of mud huts, to provide additional accommodation.[1]

But it was all too little and too late. A few weeks after our visit the prisoners from Mittelbau[2] began to arrive, so it was little wonder that the British found only dead or dying or persons stricken with disease, and scarcely a handful of healthy prisoners in a camp that was in an unimaginably disgusting condition.

The war, and above all the war in the air, produced a cumulative effect on all the camps. Each new shortage as it appeared caused a further deterioration in their general condition. The building of work camps in connection with important armaments projects— always rush jobs—suffered particularly on account of such shortages and dislocations.

The air war and the bombing attacks on the armaments factories caused countless deaths among the prisoners. Although the Allies did not attack any concentration camp, as such, that is to say the

[1] Bergen-Belsen was created in the spring of 1943 as a concentration camp for privileged Jews, by which was meant the so-called 'exchange' Jews, persons with British or American nationality or with papers of a neutral power, as well as Jews who were believed to have some sort of bargaining value. Until late in 1944 the number of Jews in Bergen-Belsen did not exceed 15,000 and at that time conditions in the camp were relatively good, certainly far better than in the other camps. But in the winter of 1944–1945 Bergen-Belsen was made into a reception camp for sick prisoners. During the evacuation of the camps located in the East and West, Auschwitz, Sachsenhausen, Natzweiler, etc., a steady stream of prisoners, most of whom were sick, began to pour into Bergen-Belsen, until its population reached some 50,000, living in the most appalling conditions and with a daily death roll of 250 or 300. The camp was liberated by the British on 15 April, 1945.

[2] The visit in question took place in March 1945. 'Mittelbau' was the name given, in the summer of 1943, to the complex of work camps, underground factories, etc., controlled by the Mittelwerke Company and located in the Harz Mountains, principally near Salza. The major part of the work was the production of V-weapons, and very large numbers of prisoners were employed on this, being drawn in the main from Buchenwald concentration camp. This complex of camps was also known as Dora, and the living and working conditions that prevailed there, even as early as 1943, were catastrophic. On 28 October, 1944, the majority of the prisoners engaged on work in this area were concentrated into one camp, which was called Dora, and which then contained some 24,000 persons, while a further 8,000 prisoners who continued to live in work camps were now controlled from Dora. By the spring of 1945 Dora, or Mittelbau, contained some 50,000 prisoners, despite an exceptionally high mortality rate. When in April of 1945 American troops approached the southern Harz mountains, Himmler ordered that all the inmates of Dora be gassed in the subterranean installations. A series of accidents prevented the implementation of this order, and finally in mid-April the inmates were evacuated to Bergen-Belsen.

actual protective custody camp, yet prisoners were employed in all the more important war factories. They thus shared the fate of the civilian population.

From the beginning of the intensified air offensive in 1944, not a day passed without casualty reports being received from the camps as a result of air raids. I cannot give a rough estimate of the total number, but it must have run into many thousands. I myself lived through plenty of air attacks, usually not in the safety of a ' hero's cellar '. Attacks of unprecedented fury were made on factories where prisoners were employed. I saw how the prisoners behaved, how guards and prisoners cowered together and died together in the same improvised shelters, and how the prisoners helped the wounded guards.

During such heavy raids, all else was forgotten. They were no longer guards or prisoners, but only human beings trying to escape from the hail of bombs.

I myself have passed unscathed, though often badly shaken, through countless raids. I have seen the bombs rain down on Hamburg and Dresden and often on Berlin. I once escaped certain death during an accident in Vienna. On the journeys which formed part of my duties, my train was often subjected to low-level air attack. The Economic-Administration Head Office and the Reich Security Head Office were repeatedly hit with bombs, but were always patched up again. Neither Müller nor Pohl would let themselves be driven out of their offices. The homeland too, or at any rate the larger towns, had become the front line. The total number of lives lost as a result of the air war can certainly never be calculated. In my estimate it must be several millions.[1] The casualty figures were never made known, and were always kept strictly secret.

I am constantly reproached for not having refused to carry out the Extermination Order, this gruesome murder of women and children. I have given my answer at Nuremburg: what would have happened to a group-captain who refused to lead an air attack on a town which he knew for certain contained no arms factory, no industrial plant of value to the war effort and no military installations? An attack in which he knew for sure that his bombs must kill principally women and children? He would surely have been court-martialled. People

---

[1] The Federal German Statistical Office has estimated (1956) the total number of civilian dead in all Germany throughout the war, killed by air action, at 410,000.

say that this is no comparison. But in my opinion the two situations are comparable. I was a soldier and an officer, just as was that group-captain. Some say that the Waffen-SS was not a military organisation, but a kind of party militia. However, we were just as much soldiers as were the members of the other three armed services.

These perpetual air-attacks were a heavy burden on the civilian population and especially on the women. The children were evacuated to remote districts, free from the threat of air raids. The effect was not only physical—the whole life in the big towns was thrown into confusion, but also and to a very great extent psychological.

Careful observation of the faces and the demeanour of the people in the public shelters or in the cellars of their homes revealed their mounting nervousness and fear of death, as the onslaught approached and the bomb-carpet came closer. How they clung to each other, wives seeking the protection of husbands, as whole buildings shook or began to collapse.

Even Berliners, who are not so easily got down, were in the end worn out. Day after day and night after night their nerves were strained in the cellars and shelters.

This war of nerves, this psychological battering, could not have been borne by the German people for very much longer.

I have sufficiently described the activities of Department DI, the Inspectorate of Concentration Camps, in my description of the departmental heads and of the various officials.[1] I have nothing to add to these portraits.

Would the concentration camps have been organised differently under another Inspector? I think probably not. For nobody, however energetic and strong-willed, could have dealt with the conditions created by the war, and none could have successfully opposed the inflexible will of the Reichsführer SS. No SS officer would have dared to act against, or to circumvent, the intentions of the Reichsführer SS. Even when the concentration camps were being created and set up by a man as strong-willed as Eicke, the voice of the Reichsführer SS was always the real and decisive power behind him.

The concentration camps became what they were during the war entirely and solely because such was the intention of the Reichsführer SS. It was he who issued the directives to the Reich Security Head Office, and he alone could do so. The Reich Security Head Office was a purely executive body. I firmly believe that not a

[1] See Appendices 8 and 9.

single important large-scale action by the Security Police was inaugurated without the prior approval of the Reichsführer SS. In most cases he was both the proposer and the instigator of such actions. The entire SS was the tool which Heinrich Himmler, the Reichsführer SS, used in order to realise his will.

The fact that from 1944 on he had to compete with a force stronger than himself, namely the war, in no way affects the truth of this statement.

During my official tours of the arms factories where prisoners were employed, I obtained an insight into our armaments production. I saw, and also heard from the works managers, a great deal that truly astounded me. Especially in the aeroplane industry. From Maurer, who often had to deal with the Armaments Ministry, I heard of delays that could never be made good, of large-scale failures, of mistakes in planning which took months to put right. I knew of cases where well-known and important figures in the armaments industry were imprisoned and even executed, because of failure. This gave me a lot to think about.

Although our leaders were continually talking about new inventions and new weapons, these produced no visible results in the actual conduct of the war. In spite of our new jet fighters, the weight of the enemy air offensive continued to increase. A few dozen fighter squadrons were all we had to send up against streams of bombers consisting of anything up to two and a half thousand heavy machines.

Our new weapons were in production and had even been tested in action. But to win the war, a new system of armaments production must be created. Whenever a factory was mass-producing a finished article at full speed, it was likely to be levelled to the ground in the space of a few minutes. The transfer underground of the factories manufacturing the ' decisive ' weapons was not envisaged before 1946 at the earliest. Even then nothing would be accomplished, because the supply of raw materials and the removal of the finished product would, as before, be at the mercy of the enemy air force.

The best example of this was the manufacture of V-weapons at Mittelbau. The bombers destroyed the whole of the permanent way within miles of the workshops hidden in the mountains. Months of painstaking work were thus rendered vain. The heavy V1s and V2s were immobilised in the hillsides. No sooner were temporary tracks laid than they, too, were destroyed.

By the end of 1944 it was the same story everywhere.

The Eastern Front was continuously being 'withdrawn' and the German soldier in the East no longer stood firm. The Western Front, too, was being forced back.

Yet the Führer spoke of holding firm at all costs. Goebbels spoke and wrote about believing in miracles. Germany will conquer!

For my part I had grave doubts whether we could win the war. I had seen and heard too much. Certainly we could not win this way. But I dared not doubt our final victory, I must believe in it. Even though sturdy commonsense told me plainly and unambiguously that we must lose. My heart clung to the Führer and his ideals, for those must not perish.

My wife often asked me during the spring of 1945, when everyone saw that the end was coming: 'How on earth can we win the war? Have we really got some decisive weapon in reserve?' With a heavy heart I could only say that she must have faith, for I did not dare tell what I knew. I could not discuss with anyone what I knew, and what I had seen and heard. I am convinced that Pohl and Maurer, who both saw more than I did, had the same thoughts as myself. But no one dared talk about this to anyone else. This was not so much because they feared being charged with spreading despondency, as because nobody wished to believe what he knew was in fact the truth. It was impossible that our world should perish. We *had* to win.

Each of us worked on with bitter determination, as though victory depended on our labours. And when, in April, the Oder Front collapsed, we devoted the greatest effort to keeping the prisoners at full pitch in the war factories that still remained to us. We used every means in our power. We even considered turning out emergency war materials in our extremely primitive substitute camps. Any man in our sphere who neglected his work on the grounds that it did not matter any more was roughly dealt with. Maurer wished a member of his staff brought before an SS court-martial on this account, even though Berlin was already encircled and we were preparing to pull out.

I have referred on many occasions to the mad evacuation of the concentration camps.

The scenes I saw, and which resulted from the evacuation order, made such an impression on me that I shall never forget them.

When Pohl received no further reports from Baer during the

evacuation of Auschwitz, he sent me post-haste to Silesia to put matters in order. I first found Baer at Gross-Rosen,[1] where he was making preparations for the reception of the prisoners. He had no idea where his camp might be wandering. The original plan had had to be scrapped because of the Russian push to the south. I immediately drove on, in the hope of reaching Auschwitz in time to make sure that the order for the destruction of everything important had been properly carried out. But I was only able to get as far as the Oder, near Ratibor, for the Russian armoured spearheads were already fanning out on the far side of that river.

On all the roads and tracks in Upper Silesia west of the Oder I now met columns of prisoners, struggling through the deep snow. They had no food. Most of the non-commissioned officers in charge of these stumbling columns of corpses had no idea where they were supposed to be going. They only knew that their final destination was Gross-Rosen. But how to get there was a mystery. On their own authority they requisitioned food from the villages through which they passed, rested for a few hours, then trudged on again. There was no question of spending the night in barns or schools, since these were all crammed with refugees. The route taken by these miserable columns was easy to follow, since every few hundred yards lay the bodies of prisoners who had collapsed or been shot. I directed all the columns I could reach to go westwards, into the Sudetenland, so as to avoid the incredibly chaotic bottle-neck near Neisse. I gave strict orders to the men in charge of all these columns that they were not to shoot prisoners incapable of further marching. They were to hand them over in the villages to the *Volkssturm*.[2] During the first night, on the road near Leobschütz, I constantly came upon the bodies of prisoners who had just been shot, and which were therefore still bleeding. On one occasion, as I stopped my car by a dead body, I heard revolver shots quite near. I ran towards the sound, and saw a soldier in the act of stopping his motor cycle and

[1] Gross-Rosen, near Schweidnitz in Lower Silesia, had been a concentration camp since May 1941. In 1944 it contained some 12,000 inmates. Gross-Rosen with its numerous subsidiary camps scattered throughout Lower Silesia, East Saxony and the Sudetenland, was to receive the inmates from Auschwitz according to the evacuation plan. However, as early as 21 March, 1945, Gross-Rosen had itself to be evacuated, and was moved to Reichenau in Bohemia, where the camp was finally liberated on 5 April, 1945.

[2] The 'People's Levy' called out at the very end of the war, roughly equivalent to the British Home Guard of 1940.

shooting a prisoner leaning against a tree. I shouted at him, asking him what he thought he was doing, and what harm the prisoner had done him. He laughed impertinently in my face, and asked me what I proposed to do about it. I drew my pistol and shot him forthwith. He was a sergeant-major in the Air Force.

Every now and then I also met officers from Auschwitz, who had managed somehow or other to get hold of a vehicle, I posted them at cross-roads, to collect these wandering columns of prisoners, and move them westwards, eventually perhaps by train. I saw open coal trucks, loaded with frozen corpses, whole trainloads of prisoners who had been shunted on to open sidings and left there without food or shelter. Then again there were groups of prisoners, often without guards, who had escaped or whose guards had simply vanished. They too were making their way peacefully westwards. I also met unaccompanied British prisoners-of-war doing the same: they were determined on no account to fall into the hands of the Russians. I saw SS-men and prisoners huddled together on the refugees' vehicles. I came upon columns of building workers and agricultural labourers. No one knew where he was trying to go. Gross-Rosen was the final destination of them all. There was deep snow at the time and it was very cold. The roads were blocked by Army and Air Force columns, and by the crowds of refugees. The slippery surface caused innumerable car accidents.

Beside the roads were not only dead prisoners, but also refugees, women and children. Outside one village I saw a woman sitting on a tree stump, and singing to her child as she rocked it in her arms. The child had been dead for a long time and the woman was mad. Many women struggled through the snow pushing perambulators stacked high with their belongings. They had only one aim, to get away and not to fall into the hands of the Russians.

Gross-Rosen was crammed to overflowing. Schmauser[1] had already arranged for it to be evacuated. I travelled to Breslau to tell him what was happening and to urge him to stop the evacuation. He showed me the wireless message from the Reichsführer SS which made him responsible for seeing that not a single healthy prisoner remained in any camp under his authority.

[1] Heinrich Schmauser, an SS general, was Leader of the Southeast District (Silesia) and simultaneously senior SS and Police Leader in this province. As such he was responsible for the carrying out of Himmler's orders for the evacuation of Auschwitz and of the Silesian Camps.

At the railway station in Gross-Rosen the transports coming in were immediately sent on. Only the smallest ones could be fed. Gross-Rosen itself had no more food.

Dead SS-men lay peacefully in the open cars between dead prisoners. Those still alive sat on top of them, chewing their piece of bread. Terrible scenes, best not described.

I lived through the evacuation of Sachsenhausen and of Ravensbrück. The scenes were the same here. By good fortune it was warmer and dry, so the columns could sleep in the open. But after two or three days there was no food left. The Red Cross helped by distributing food parcels. There was no more food to be found in the villages, through which columns of refugees had been passing for weeks on end. In addition there was the constant menace of low-flying planes, which systematically shot up every road.

Until the very end I tried my utmost to bring some order into this chaos. But it was all in vain. We ourselves had to flee. Since the end of 1944 my family had been living in the immediate neighbourhood of Ravensbrück. I was therefore able to take them with me when the Inspectorate of Concentration Camps moved himself. We went first of all towards the Darss,[1] then after two days we headed for Schleswig-Holstein. All this was in accordance with the orders of the Reichsführer SS. What we were supposed to do for him, or what duties we were still intended to perform, we could not imagine. I had to look after Frau Eicke and her daughter and children, and several other families too, and see that they did not fall into the hands of the enemy. Our flight was a gruesome journey. We travelled by night, without lights, along roads crowded with vehicles moving bumper to bumper. I had to be constantly on the look-out to see that all our lorries remained together, for I was responsible for the whole column. Glücks and Maurer took another route, via Warnemunde. In Rostock two of my large lorries containing all the wireless equipment broke down, and by the time they were repaired the enemy tanks had nabbed them. For days on end we scurried from one clump of trees to the next, for the enemy's low-flying planes were continually machine-gunning this principal escape route.

In Wismar Keitel himself stood in the street, arresting deserters from the front. On the way we heard, in a farmhouse that the Führer was dead.

When we heard this, my wife and I were simultaneously struck by

[1] A peninsula in the Baltic, west of Rügen.

the same thought: now we, too, must go! With the Führer gone, our world had gone. Was there any point in going on living? We would be pursued and persecuted wherever we went. We wanted to take poison. I had obtained some for my wife, lest she and the children fall alive into the hands of the Russians in the event of their making an unexpected advance.

Nevertheless, because of the children, we did not do this. For their sake we wanted to take on our own shoulders all that was coming. But we should have done it. I have always regretted it since. We would all have been spared a great deal, especially my wife and the children. How much more suffering will they have to endure? We were bound and fettered to that other world, and we should have disappeared with it.

After her flight, Frau Thomsen, who had been our children's governess at Auschwitz, had gone to live with her mother at St Michaelisdonn in Holstein. I now brought my family there. I had no idea at that time where we, the Concentration Camp Inspectorate, were to go. I took my eldest child along, as he wanted to stay with me, and we still hoped we might have some active role to play, even in the last unoccupied patch of Germany and in the final hours.

We reported for the last time at Flensburg, where the Reichsführer SS had withdrawn with other members of the government. There was no more talk of fighting. Every man for himself was now the order of the day. I shall never forget my last meeting with the Reichsführer SS. He was beaming and in the best of spirits; yet the world, our world, had crumbled beneath our feet. He said: ' Well, gentlemen, this is the end. You know what you now have to do.' So far I understood him, since these words were in accordance with what he had been preaching to the SS for years. Self-sacrifice for the ideal. But then he gave us his last order: hide in the Army!

Such was our farewell message from the man to whom I had looked up so respectfully, in whom I had had such implicit trust, whose orders and utterances had been gospel to me.

Maurer and I looked at each other in dumb astonishment. Our thoughts were identical. We were both veteran Nazis and SS officers, and had grown up in our ideals. Had we been alone, we would have committed some act of despair. But we had to look after our department chiefs, the officers and men of our staff, and our poor families.

Glücks was already half dead. We carried him to the naval hospital under another name. Gebhardt[1] took charge of the women and children with the intention of getting them to Denmark. The rest of the departmental staff were issued with false papers that would enable them to vanish into the navy. I myself, under the name of boatswain's mate Franz Lang, went to the island of Sylt, with orders to report to the Naval Intelligence School there. I sent my son back to my wife, along with my driver and car.

Since I knew a certain amount about naval life, I was able to make myself inconspicuous. There was not much work to be done, so I had time to ponder deeply on what had happened.

By chance I heard one day, on the wireless, the news of Himmler's arrest and his death by poison. I, too, had my phial of poison always with me. But I decided to wait on events.

The Naval Intelligence School was removed to the internment district between the Kiel Canal and the Schlei. The British moved the SS-men from their zone to the School, and concentrated them on the Friesian Islands. So I was quite close to my family, whom I was able to see quite often. My eldest boy visited me every few days. Since my profession was given as farmer, I was soon released. I passed through all the British control points without difficulty, and was sent by the labour office to work on a farm near Flensburg. I liked the work and I was completely independent, for the farmer was still being held by the Americans. I worked there for eight months. With the help of my wife's brother, who worked in Flensburg, I was able to keep in touch with my wife.

I learnt through my brother-in-law that I was being hunted for by the British Field Security Police. I also heard that they were keeping a close watch on my family, and repeatedly searched the house.

I was arrested on 11 March, 1946.

My phial of poison had been broken two days before.

When I was aroused from sleep, I thought at first I was being attacked by robbers, for many robberies were taking place at that

---

[1] Professor Dr Karl Gebhardt was a childhood friend of Himmler's. He was in the Oberland Bund and took part in the abortive Munich putsch of 1923. In 1933 Himmler took him into the SS. As head of the Hohenlychen Medical Institute in Brandenburg, which later became an SS hospital, he was one of the senior SS medical men in Germany. He was also Himmler's principal adviser in medical matters. Shortly before the end of the war he was appointed President of the German Red Cross. During the so-called 'Doctors' Trial' at Nuremberg he was condemned to death for the part he had played in medical experiments carried out on concentration camp inmates.

M

time. That was how they managed to arrest me. I was maltreated by the Field Security Police.

I was taken to Heide where I was put in those very barracks from which I had been released by the British eight months earlier.

At my first interrogation, evidence was obtained by beating me. I do not know what is in the record, although I signed it.[1] Alcohol and the whip were too much for me. The whip was my own, which by chance had got into my wife's luggage. It had hardly ever touched my horse, far less the prisoners. Nevertheless, one of my interrogators was convinced that I had perpetually used it for flogging the prisoners.

After some days I was taken to Minden-on-the-Weser, the main interrogation centre in the British Zone. There I received further rough treatment at the hands of the English public prosecutor, a major.[2]

The conditions in the prison accorded with this behaviour.

After three weeks, to my surprise, I was shaved and had my hair cut and I was allowed to wash. My handcuffs had not previously been removed since my arrest.

On the next day I was taken by lorry to Nuremburg, together with a prisoner of war who had been brought over from London as a witness in Fritsche's[3] defence. My imprisonment by the International Military Tribunal was a rest-cure compared to what I had been through before. I was accommodated in the same building as the principal accused, and was able to see them daily as they were taken to the court. Almost every day we were visited by representatives of all the Allied nations. I was always pointed out as an especially interesting animal.

I was in Nuremberg because Kaltenbrunner's counsel had demanded me as a witness for his defence. I have never been able to grasp, and it is still not clear to me, how I of all people could have helped to exonerate Kaltenbrunner. Although the conditions in prison were, in every respect, good—I read whenever I had the time, and there was a well stocked library available, the interrogations were extremely unpleasant, not so much physically, but far

---

[1] A typewritten document of eight pages, which Hoess signed at 2.30 am on 14 March, 1946. It does not differ substantially from what he later said or wrote in Nuremberg or Cracow.

[2] See page 18 of Lord Russell's Introduction for details of this interview.

[3] Hans Fritsche, a Radio commentator and a close colleague of Goebbels, was one of the principal accused before the Nuremberg Tribunal.

more because of their strong psychological effect. I cannot really blame the interrogators—they were all Jews.

Psychologically I was almost cut in pieces. They wanted to know all about everything, and this was also done by Jews. They left me in no doubt whatever as to the fate that was in store for me.

On 25 May, my wedding anniversary as it happened, I was driven with von Burgsdorff[1] and Bühler[2] to the aerodrome and there handed over to Polish officers. We flew in an American plane via Berlin to Warsaw. Although we were treated very politely during our journey, I feared the worst when I remembered my experiences in the British Zone and the tales I had heard about the way people were being treated in the East. Also the expressions and gestures of the spectators at the airfield on our arrival were not exactly reassuring. In prison several of the officials immediately came at me, and showed me their Auschwitz tattoo numbers. I could not understand them, but it was obvious that they were not extending friendly greetings towards me. Nevertheless I was not beaten. My imprisonment was very strict and completely isolated. I was frequently interrogated. I was kept there for nine weeks. The time weighed heavily on me, for I had absolutely no distractions, not being allowed either to read or to write.

On 30 July I was taken to Cracow with seven other Germans. We had to wait for some time in the station there until the car had arrived. Quite a large crowd collected, and the people hurled insults at us. Göth[3] was recognised at once. If the car had not come soon, they would have stoned us seriously. During the first few weeks we were treated quite well, but then suddenly the attitude of the prisoner-officials changed completely and overnight. From their behaviour

[1] Dr Curt von Burgsdorff had served as Under-Secretary of State for Administration in the Protectorate Bohemia-Moravia from 1939 to 1942. From December 1943 until January 1945 he was Governor of the Cracow District in the General Gouvernement. Found guilty merely of participation in the 'criminal fascist government', he was given the minimum sentence by the Polish People's Court, and, since he had already been in prison for three years awaiting trial, was immediately discharged and sent back to Germany.

[2] The reference is apparently to Secretary of State, Dr Josef Bühler, formerly deputy for the General-Governement in Cracow. He was condemned to death in Warsaw on 20 July, 1948.

[3] Göth, an SS officer, had been directly responsible for the liquidation of the Cracow ghetto in March, 1943. Later he was in command of the Jewish camp at Plaszow, near Cracow. In the autumn of 1944 proceedings for embezzlement were instigated against him in an SS court. On 5 September, 1946, he was condemned to death by the Polish People's Court in Cracow.

and their conversation, the meaning of which was clear to me though I could not understand what they said, I gathered that they wanted to ' finish me off '. I was given only the smallest piece of bread, and less than a spoonful of thin soup. I was no longer given a second helping, although almost every day there was food left over which was divided among the inmates of the adjoining cells. If an official wanted to unlock my door, he was immediately whistled back. It was here that I became acquainted with the power of prisoners in position of authority over their fellows. They ran everything. They provided irrefutable proof of my contentions concerning the immense and often evil power which those prisoners with official positions exercise over different categories of warders.

If the public prosecutor's office had not intervened, it would have been the end of me, not only physically but first of all from a psychological point of view. They had nearly got me at the end of my tether.

It was not a question of feeble hysteria. I can stand up to a lot, and had taken plenty of hard knocks during my life. The mental torture inflicted by the three devils was too much for me. And I was not the only one to be persecuted in this way. Some of the Polish prisoners were severely maltreated by them as well. They have long since departed, and a welcome quiet now reigns.

I must admit that I had never expected such decent and considerate treatment as I received in Polish custody, once the public prosecutor had intervened.

What are my opinions today concerning the Third Reich?

What do I think of Himmler and his SS, the concentration camps and the Security Police? How do I feel about all that was done in this sphere, and through which I passed ?

I remain, as I have always been, a convinced National-Socialist in my attitude to life. When a man has adhered to a belief and an attitude for nigh on twenty-five years, has grown up with it and become bound to it body and soul, he cannot simply throw it aside because the embodiments of this ideal, the National-Socialist State and its leaders have used their powers wrongly and even criminally, and because as a result of this failure and mis-direction his world has collapsed and the entire German people been plunged for decades into untold misery. I, at least, cannot.

From the documents published and from the Nuremberg trials I can see that the leaders of the Third Reich, because of their policy of force, were guilty of causing this vast war and all its consequences. I see that these leaders, by means of exceptionally effective propaganda and of limitless terrorism, were able to make the whole German people so docile and submissive that they were ready, with very few exceptions, to go wherever they were led, without voicing a word of criticism.

In my opinion the necessary extension of living space for the German people could have been obtained by peaceful means. However, I am convinced that wars can never be prevented, and that others will occur in the future.

In order to disguise a policy of force it is necessary to use propaganda so that a clever distortion of all the facts, the policies and measures of the rulers of the State can be made palatable. Terrorism must be used from the outset, to stifle all doubt and opposition.

In my view, real opponents can be overcome by presenting the better alternative.

Himmler was the crudest representative of the leadership principle. Every German had to subordinate himself unquestioningly and uncritically to the leaders of the State, who alone were in a position to understand the real needs of the people and to direct them along the right path.

Anyone who did not submit to this principle must be eliminated from public life. With this purpose in mind Himmler trained and formed his SS, and created the concentration camps, the German police, and the Reich Security Head Office.

In Himmler's view, Germany was the one State in Europe that had the right to exercise supremacy. All the other countries were second-rate. The predominantly Nordic races were to be favourably treated, with the aim of incorporating them into Germany. The Eastern races were to be split up, to be made insignificant, and to become slaves.

The concentration camps before the war had to be depositories in which to segregate opponents of the State. The fact that they incidentally became re-education centres for a-socials of every kind, and in this performed valuable service to the country as a whole, was a consequence of the cleaning-up process.

Similarly, they were necessary for the preventive war on crime.

When war came, they were turned into centres for the extermination, by direct or indirect means, of those elements in the conquered countries which continued to oppose their conquerors and oppressors.

I have already repeatedly expressed my attitude regarding the 'enemies of the State'.

But the extermination of those population elements which remained hostile was in any case a mistake. If the peoples of the occupied territories had been treated with decency and common-sense, their resistance movements could have been reduced to insignificance. There would then have been few serious opponents left.

I also see now that the extermination of the Jews was funda-mentally wrong. Precisely because of these mass exterminations, Germany has drawn upon herself the hatred of the entire world. It in no way served the cause of anti-Semitism, but on the contrary brought the Jews far closer to their ultimate objective.

The Reich Security Head Office was only the executive, the long arm, of Himmler the police chief. The Reich Security Head Office and the concentration camps were only the tools that were used to carry out the wishes of Himmler, or the intentions of Adolf Hitler, as the case might be.

In these pages, and also in my sketches of the leading personalities concerned,[1] I have sufficiently explained how the horrors of the concentration camps could come about.

I for my part never sanctioned them. I myself never maltreated a prisoner, far less killed one. Nor have I ever tolerated maltreatment by my subordinates.

When during the course of this investigation I have had to listen to descriptions of the fearful tortures that were enacted in Auschwitz and also in other camps, my blood runs cold. I knew very well that prisoners in Auschwitz were ill-treated by the SS, by their civilian employers, and not least of all by their fellow-prisoners. I used every means at my disposal to stop this. But I could not. The commandants of other camps, who had a similar outlook to myself, but whose camps were far smaller and far easier to supervise, found themselves equally impotent in this respect.

Nothing can prevail against the malignancy, wickedness and brutality of the individual guard, except keeping him constantly under one's personal supervision. And the worse the guards and supervisory personnel, the more they oppress the prisoners. The truth of this has been abundantly confirmed to me during my present imprisonment.

[1] See Appendices 3 to 9.

In the British Zone I had plenty of opportunity to study the three categories of guards at very close quarters. At Nuremberg maltreatment by individual guards was impossible, since there all the prisoners were under the permanent supervision of the prison duty officers. Even while changing planes in Berlin I only met with ill-treatment from strangers encountered by chance in the lavatory.

In the Warsaw prison, which, so far as I was able to observe and judge from the confines of my cell, was conducted on strict and exact lines, there was one supervisor, and only one who, as soon as he came on duty, ran from cell to cell, wherever there were Germans, and proceeded to beat them up indiscriminately. Apart from von Burgsdorff, who had his face slapped on several occasions, every German got a taste of his fists. He was a young man of eighteen or twenty, whose eyes gleamed with a fanatical hatred. He said he was a Polish Jew, though he did not look like one. He certainly never grew tired of beating us. His activities were only interrupted by signals from his colleagues warning him of the approach of a stranger. I am certain that none of the higher officials nor the governor of the prison approved of his behaviour. I was occasionally asked by visiting officials how I was treated, but I always kept quiet about this, because he was the only man who acted in this way. The other supervisors were more or less strict and unfriendly, but none of them laid a hand on me.

So it can be seen that even in a small prison the governor is unable to prevent such behaviour; how much more difficult was it in a concentration camp the size of Auschwitz!

I was certainly severe and strict. Often perhaps, when I look at it now, too severe and too strict.

In my digust at the errors and abuses that I discovered, I may have spoken many hard words that I should have kept to myself. But I was never cruel, and I have never maltreated anyone, even in a fit of temper. A great deal happened in Auschwitz which was done ostensibly in my name, under my authority and on my orders, which I neither knew about nor sanctioned. But all these things happened in Auschwitz and so I am responsible. For the camp regulations say: the camp commandant is *fully* responsible for *everything* that happens in his sphere.

My life is now nearly at its end. I have given an account here of everything that was important in that life, of all those things that impressed me most strongly and which affected me most deeply.

It is the absolute truth, as I saw it and experienced it. I have omitted much that is irrelevant, and much I have forgotten, and much I can no longer remember very clearly.

I am no writer and I have never been particularly skilled with the pen. I am sure that I must have frequently repeated myself, and perhaps I have not always made myself sufficiently clear.

I have also lacked the calm and mental balance required for a task of this nature.

I have written down what came to my mind, often not in sequence, but nothing is invented.

I have described myself as I was and as I am.

I have led a full and varied life. I have followed my star wherever it led me. Life has given me some hard and rough knocks, but I have always managed to get along. I have never given in.

Since returning from the war to which I went as a youngster and from which I came back a man, I have had two lights to guide me: my fatherland and, later, my family. My unalterable love for my country brought me into the NSDAP and the SS.

I regarded the National-Socialist attitude to the world as the only one suited to the German people. I believed that the SS was the most energetic champion of this attitude and that the SS alone was capable of gradually bringing the German people back to its proper way of life.

My second worship was my family. To them I was securely anchored. My thoughts were always with their future, and our farm was to become their permanent home. In our children both my wife and I saw our aim in life. To bring them up so that they could play their part in the world, and to give them all a steady home, was our one task in life.

So now my thoughts turn chiefly to my family. What will become of them?

It is this uncertainty concerning my family's future that makes my imprisonment so hard to bear.

I gave myself up for lost from the beginning and I am concerned no longer about my personal fate, but only about that of my wife and children, for what will happen to them?

Fate has played strange tricks on me. How often have I escaped death by a hair's breadth? During the First World War, or in the Freikorps, accidents at work, the car smash on the autobahn in 1941, when I ran into an unlighted lorry and yet was able, in the fraction of a second left to me, to wrench my wheel around so that the impact came on the side and we all three escaped with cuts and bruises, although the front of the car looked like a concertina. Then there was the riding accident in 1942, when I was thrown on to a rock with the heavy stallion on top of me, and my ribs were broken. And there were the air raids too, when time and again my life did not seem worth a farthing. Yet I always managed to survive. There was that other car accident too, shortly before the evacuation of Ravensbrück. Everyone thought I was dead, and it seemed impossible that I should recover, yet I did.

Then the phial of poison that broke just before my arrest.

On every occasion fate has intervened to save my life, so that at last I might be put to death in this shameful manner.

How greatly I envy those of my comrades who died a soldier's death.

Unknowingly I was a cog in the wheel of the great extermination machine created by the Third Reich. The machine has been smashed to pieces, the engine is broken and I, too, must now be destroyed.

The world demands it.

I could never have brought myself to make this confession of my most secret thoughts and feelings, had I not been approached with a disarming humanity and understanding that I had never dared to expect.

It is because of this humane understanding that I have tried to assist as best I can in throwing some light on matters that seemed obscure.

But whenever use is made of what I have written, I beg that all those passages relating to my wife and my family, and all my tender emotions and secret doubts, shall not be made public.

Let the public continue to regard me as the blood-thirsty beast, the cruel sadist and the mass murderer; for the masses could never imagine the commandant of Auschwitz in any other light.

They could never understand that he, too, had a heart and that he was not evil.

These writings consist of 114 pages. I have written them voluntarily and without compulsion.

Cracow. February 1947   *Rudolf Hoess*

Appendices

APPENDIX ONE

The final solution of the Jewish question in Auschwitz concentration camp

IN the summer of 1941, I cannot remember the exact date, I was suddenly summoned to the Reichsführer SS, directly by his adjutant's office. Contrary to his usual custom, Himmler received me without his adjutant being present and said in effect:

'The Führer has ordered that the Jewish question be solved once and for all and that we, the SS, are to implement that order.

'The existing extermination centres in the east are not in a position to carry out the large actions which are anticipated. I have therefore earmarked Auschwitz for this purpose, both because of its good position as regards communications and because the area can easily be isolated and camouflaged. At first I thought of calling in a senior SS officer for this job, but I changed my mind in order to avoid difficulties concerning the terms of reference. I have now decided to entrust this task to you. It is difficult and onerous and calls for complete devotion notwithstanding the difficulties that may arise. You will learn further details from Sturmbannführer Eichmann of the Reich Security Head Office who will call on you in the immediate future.

'The departments concerned will be notified by me in due course. You will treat this order as absolutely secret, even from your superiors. After your talk with Eichmann you will immediately forward to me the plans of the projected installations.

'The Jews are the sworn enemies of the German people and must be eradicated. Every Jew that we can lay our hands on is to be destroyed now during the war, without exception. If we cannot now obliterate the biological basis of Jewry, the Jews will one day destroy the German people.'

On receiving these grave instructions, I returned forthwith to Auschwitz, without reporting to my superior at Oranienburg.

Shortly afterwards Eichmann came to Auschwitz and disclosed to me the plans for the operations as they affected the various countries concerned. I cannot remember the exact order in which they were to take place. First was to come the eastern part of Upper Silesia and the neighbouring parts of Polish territory under German rule, then, depending on the situation, simultaneously Jews from Germany and Czechoslovakia, and finally the Jews from the West: France, Belgium and Holland. He also told me the approximate numbers of transports that might be expected, but I can no longer remember these.

We discussed the ways and means of effecting the extermination. This could only be done by gassing, since it would have been absolutely impossible to dispose by shooting of the large numbers of people that were expected, and it would have placed too heavy a burden on the SS men who had to carry it out, especially because of the women and children among the victims.

Eichmann told me about the method of killing people with exhaust gases in lorries, which had previously been used in the east. But there was no question of being able to use this for these mass transports that were due to arrive in Auschwitz. Killing with showers of carbon monoxide while bathing, as was done with mental patients in some places in the Reich, would necessitate too many buildings and it was also very doubtful whether the supply of gas for such a vast number of people would be available. We left the matter unresolved. Eichmann decided to try and find a gas which was in ready supply and which would not entail special installations for its use, and to inform me when he had done so. We inspected the area in order to choose a likely spot. We decided that a peasant farmstead situated in the north-west corner of what later became the third building sector at Birkenau would be the most suitable. It was isolated and screened by woods and hedges, and it was also not far from the railway. The bodies could be placed in long, deep pits dug in the nearby meadows. We had not at that time thought of burning the corpses. We calculated that after gas-proofing the premises then available, it would be possible to kill about 800 people simultaneously with a suitable gas. These figures were borne out later in practice.

Eichmann could not then give me the starting date for the operation because everything was still in the preliminary stages and the Reichsführer SS had not yet issued the necessary orders.

Eichmann returned to Berlin to report our conversation to the Reichsführer SS.

A few days later I sent to the Reichsführer SS by courier a detailed location plan and description of the installation. I have never received an acknowledgment or a decision on my report. Eichmann told me later that the Reichsführer SS was in agreement with my proposals.

At the end of November a conference was held in Eichmann's Berlin office, attended by the entire Jewish Section, to which I, too, was summoned. Eichmann's representatives in the various countries reported on the current stage of the operation and the difficulties encountered in executing it, such as the housing of the prisoners, the provision of trains for the transports and the planning of time-tables, etc. I could not find out when a start was to be made, and Eichmann had not yet discovered a suitable kind of gas.

In the autumn of 1941 a secret order was issued instructing the Gestapo to weed out the Russian *Politruks,* commissars and certain political officials from the prisoner-of-war camps, and to transfer them to the nearest concentration camp for liquidation. Small drafts of these prisoners were continually arriving in Auschwitz and they were shot in the gravel pit near the Monopoly buildings[1] or in the courtyard of Block II. When I was absent on duty my representative, Hauptsturmführer Fritsch, on his own initiative, used gas for killing these Russian prisoners of war. He crammed the underground detention cells with Russians and, protected by a gas mask, discharged Cyclon B gas into the cells, killing the victims instantly.

Cyclon B gas was supplied by the firm of Tesch & Stabenow and was constantly used in Auschwitz for the destruction of vermin, and there was consequently always a supply of these tins of gas on hand. In the beginning, this poisonous gas, which was a preparation of prussic acid, was only handled by employees of Tesch & Stabenow under rigid safety precautions, but later some members of the Medical Service were trained by the firm in its use and thereafter the destruction of vermin and disinfection were carried out by them.

During Eichmann's next visit I told him about this use of Cyclon B and we decided to employ it for the mass extermination operation.

[1] Buildings in the base camp, where articles of clothing and equipment for the SS rank and file were stored.

The killing by Cyclon B gas of the Russian prisoners-of-war transported to Auschwitz was continued, but no longer in Block II, since after the gassing the whole building had to be ventilated for at least two days.

The mortuary of the crematorium next to the hospital block was therefore used as a gassing room, after the door had been made gas-proof and some holes had been pierced in the ceiling through which the gas could be discharged.

I can however only recall one transport consisting of nine hundred Russian prisoners being gassed there and I remember that it took several days to cremate their corpses. Russians were not gassed in the peasant farmstead which had now been converted for the extermination of the Jews.

I cannot say on what date the extermination of the Jews began. Probably it was in September 1941, but it may not have been until January 1942. The Jews from Upper Silesia were the first to be dealt with. These Jews were arrested by the Kattowitz Police Unit and taken in drafts by train to a siding on the west side of the Auschwitz-Dziedzice railway line where they were unloaded. So far as I can remember, these drafts never consisted of more than 1,000 prisoners.

On the platform the Jews were taken over from the police by a detachment from the camp and were brought by the commander of the protective custody camp in two sections to the bunker, as the extermination building was called.

Their luggage was left on the platform, whence it was taken to the sorting office called Canada situated between the DAW[1] and the timber-yard.

The Jews were made to undress near the bunker, after they had been told that they had to go into the rooms (as they were also called) in order to be de-loused.

All the rooms, there were five of them, were filled at the same time, the gas-proof doors were then screwed up and the contents of the gas containers discharged into the rooms through special vents.

After half an hour the doors were re-opened (there were two doors in each room), the dead bodies were taken out, and brought to the pits in small trolleys which ran on rails.

[1] After Auschwitz had been built, the German Armaments Works (DAW) built a branch factory inside the camp, where a labour force of up to 2,500 prisoners was employed.

The victims' clothing was taken in lorries to the sorting office. The whole operation, including assistance given during undressing, the filling of the bunker, the emptying of the bunker, the removal of the corpses, as well as the preparation and filling up of the mass graves, was carried out by a special detachment of Jews, who were separately accommodated and who, in accordance with Eichmann's orders, were themselves liquidated after every big action.

While the first transports were being disposed of, Eichmann arrived with an order from the Reichsführer SS stating that the gold teeth were to be removed from the corpses and the hair cut from the women. This job was also undertaken by the special detachment.

The extermination process was at that time carried out under the supervision of the commander of the protective custody camp or the *Rapportführer*. Those who were too ill to be brought into the gas-chambers were shot in the back of the neck by a small calibre weapon.

An SS doctor also had to be present. The trained disinfectors (SDG'S) were responsible for discharging the gas into the gas chamber.

During the spring of 1942 the actions were comparatively small, but the transports increased in the summer, and we were compelled to construct a further extermination building. The peasant farmstead west of the future site of crematoria III and IV was selected and made ready. Two huts near Bunker I and three near Bunker II were erected, in which the victims undressed. Bunker II was the larger and could hold about 1,200 people.

During the summer of 1942 the bodies were still being placed in the mass graves. Towards the end of the summer, however, we started to burn them; at first on wood pyres bearing some 2,000 corpses, and later in pits together with bodies previously buried. In the early days oil refuse was poured on the bodies, but later methanol was used. Bodies were burnt in pits, day and night, continuously.

By the end of November all the mass graves had been emptied. The number of corpses in the mass graves amounted to 107,000, This figure not only included the transports of Jews gassed up to the time when cremation was first employed, but also the bodies of those prisoners in Auschwitz who died during the winter of 1941–2, when the crematorium near the hospital building was out of action for a considerable time. It also included all the prisoners who died in the Birkenau camp.

During his visit to the camp in the summer of 1942, the Reichsführer SS watched every detail of the whole process of destruction from the time when the prisoners were unloaded to the emptying of Bunker II. At that time the bodies were not being burnt.

He had no criticisms to make, nor did he discuss the matter. Gauleiter Bracht and the Obergruppenführer Schmauser were present with him.

Shortly after the visit of the Reichsführer SS, Standartenführer Blobel arrived from Eichmann's office with an order from the Reichsführer SS stating that all the mass graves were to be opened and the corpses burnt. In addition the ashes were to be disposed of in such a way that it would be impossible at some future time to calculate the number of corpses burnt.

Blobel had already experimented with different methods of cremation in Culenhof and Eichmann had authorised him to show me the apparatus he used.

Hössler and I went to Culenhof on a tour of inspection. Blobel had had various makeshift ovens constructed, which were fired with wood and petrol refuse. He had also attempted to dispose of the bodies with explosives, but their destruction had been very incomplete. The ashes were distributed over the neighbouring countryside after first being ground to a powder in a bone mill.

Standartenführer Blobel had been authorised to seek out and obliterate all the mass graves in the whole of the eastern districts. His department was given the code number ' 1005 '. The work itself was carried out by a special detachment of Jews who were shot after each section of the work had been completed. Auschwitz concentration camp was continuously called upon to provide Jews for department ' 1005 '.

On my visit to Culenhof I was also shown the extermination apparatus constructed out of lorries, which was designed to kill by using the exhaust gases from the engines. The officer in charge there, however, described this method as being extremely unreliable, for the density of the gas varied considerably and was often insufficient to be lethal.

How many bodies lay in the mass graves at Culenhof or how many had already been cremated, I was unable to ascertain. Standartenführer Blobel had a fairly exact knowledge of the number of mass graves in the eastern districts, but he was sworn to the greatest secrecy in the matter.

Originally all the Jews transported to Auschwitz on the authority of Eichmann's office were, in accordance with orders of the Reichsführer SS, to be destroyed without exception. This also applied to the Jews from Upper Silesia, but on the arrival of the first transports of German Jews, the order was given that all those who were able-bodied, whether men or women, were to be segregated and employed on war work. This happened before the construction of the women's camp, since the need for a women's camp in Auschwitz only arose as a result of this order.

Owing to the extensive armaments industry which had developed in the concentration camps and which was being progressively increased, and owing to the recent employment of prisoners in armaments factories outside the camps, a serious lack of prisoners suddenly made itself felt, whereas previously the commandants in the old camps in the Reich had often had to seek out possibilities for employment in order to keep all their prisoners occupied.

The Jews, however, were only to be employed in Auschwitz camp. Auschwitz-Birkenau was to become an entirely Jewish camp and prisoners of all other nationalities were to be transferred to other camps. This order was never completely carried out, and later Jews were even employed in armaments industries outside the camp, because of the lack of any other labour.

The selection of able-bodied Jews was supposed to be made by SS doctors. But it repeatedly happened that officers of the protective custody camp and of the labour department themselves selected the prisoners without my knowledge or even my approval. This was the cause of constant friction between the SS doctors and the officers of the labour department. The divergence of opinion among the officers in Auschwitz was developed and fostered by the contradictory interpretation of the Reichsführer SS's order by authoritative quarters in Berlin. The Reich Security Head Office (Müller and Eichmann) had, for security reasons, the greatest interest in the destruction of as many Jews as possible. The Reichsartz SS, who laid down the policy of selection, held the view that only those Jews who were completely fit and able to work should be selected for employment. The weak and the old and those who were only relatively robust would very soon become incapable of work, which

N

would cause a further deterioration in the general standard of health, and an unnecessary increase in the hospital accommodation, requiring further medical personnel and medicines, and all for no purpose since they would in the end have to be killed.

The Economic Administration Head Office (Pohl and Maurer) was only interested in mustering the largest possible labour force for employment in the armaments industry, regardless of the fact that these people would later on become incapable of working. This conflict of interests was further sharpened by the immensely increased demands for prisoner labour made by the Ministry of Supply and the Todt Organisation. The Reichsführer SS was continuously promising both these departments numbers which could never be supplied. Standartenführer Maurer (the head of department DII), was in the difficult position of being able only partially to fulfil the insistent demands of the departments referred to, and consequently he was perpetually harassing the labour office to provide him with the greatest possible number of workers.

It was impossible to get the Reichsführer SS to make a definite decision in this matter.

I myself held the view that only really strong and healthy Jews ought to be selected for employment.

The sorting out process proceeded as follows. The railway carriages were unloaded one after the other. After depositing their baggage, the Jews had to pass individually in front of an SS doctor, who decided on their physical fitness as they marched past him. Those considered capable of employment were immediately taken off into the camp in small groups.

Taking an average of all the transports, between twenty-five and thirty per cent were found fit for work, but this figure fluctuated considerably. The figure for Greek Jews, for example, was only fifteen per cent, whereas there were transports from Slovakia with a fitness rate of a hundred per cent. Jewish doctors and administrative personnel were without exception taken into the camp.

It became apparent during the first cremations in the open air that in the long run it would not be possible to continue in that manner. During bad weather or when a strong wind was blowing, the stench of burning flesh was carried for many miles and caused the whole neighbourhood to talk about the burning of Jews, despite official counter-propaganda. It is true that all members of the SS detailed for the extermination were bound to the strictest secrecy over the whole operation, but, as later SS legal proceedings showed, this was not always observed. Even the most severe punishment was not able to stop their love of gossip.

Moreover the air defence services protested against the fires which could be seen from great distances at night. Nevertheless, burnings had to go on, even at night, unless further transports were to be refused. The schedule of individual operations, fixed at a conference by the Ministry of Communications, had to be rigidly adhered to in order to avoid, for military reasons, obstruction and confusion on the railways concerned. These reasons led to the energetic planning and eventual construction of the two large crematoria, and in 1943 to the building of two further smaller installations. Yet another one was planned, which would far exceed the others in size, but it was never completed, for in the autumn of 1944, the Reichsführer SS called an immediate halt to the extermination of the Jews.

The two large crematoria I and II were built in the winter of 1942–3 and brought into use in the spring of 1943. They had five three-retort ovens and could cremate about 2,000 bodies in less than twenty-four hours. Technical difficulties made it impossible to increase their capacity. Attempts to do this caused severe damage to the installations, and on several occasions put them out of action altogether. Crematoria I and II both had underground undressing rooms and gas-chambers in which the air could be completely changed. The bodies were taken to the ovens on the floor above by means of a lift. The gas-chambers could hold about 3,000 people, but this number was never reached, since the individual transports were never as large as that.

The two smaller crematoria III and IV were capable, according to calculations made by the constructional firm of Topf of Erfurt, of burning about 1,500 bodies within twenty-four hours. Owing to the war-time shortage of materials the builders were compelled to economise during the construction of crematoria III and IV and they were therefore built above ground and the ovens were of a less solid construction. It soon became apparent, however, that the flimsy build of these two four-retort ovens did not come up to the requirements. Number III failed completely after a short time and later ceased to be used altogether. Number IV had to be repeatedly shut down, since after its fires had been burning for from four to six weeks, the ovens or the chimneys burnt out. The gassed bodies were mostly burnt in pits behind crematorium IV.

The provisional structure number I was demolished when work was started on building section III of Birkenau.

Crematorium II, later designated bunker V, was used up to the last and was also kept as a stand-by when breakdowns occurred in crematoria I to IV. When larger numbers of transports were being received, gassing was carried out by day in number V and numbers I to IV were used for those transports which arrived during the night. The capacity of number V was practically unlimited, so long as cremations could be carried out both by day and night. Because of enemy air attacks, no further cremations were permitted during the night after 1944. The highest total of people gassed and cremated within twenty-four hours was rather more than 9,000. This figure was attained in the summer of 1944, during the action in Hungary, using all the installations except number III. On that day, owing to delays on the line, five trains arrived, instead of three, as expected, and in addition the carriages were more crowded than usual.

The crematoria were erected at the end of the two main thorough-fares in Birkenau camp, firstly in order not to increase the area of the camp and consequently the safety precautions required, and secondly so that they would not be too far from the camp, since it was planned to use the gas-chambers and undressing rooms as bath houses when the extermination actions came to an end.

The buildings were to be screened from view by a wall or hedges. Lack of material prevented this from being done. As a temporary measure, all extermination buildings were hidden under camouflage nets.

The three railway tracks between building sectors I and II in Birkenau camp were to be reconstructed as a station and roofed in and the lines were to be extended to crematoria III and IV, so that the unloading would also be hidden from the eyes of unauthorised people. Once again shortage of materials prevented this plan from being carried out.

Because of the increasing insistence of the Reichsführer SS on the employment of prisoners in the armaments industry, Obergruppen-führer Pohl found himself compelled to resort to Jews who had become unfit for work. The order was given that if the latter could be made fit and employable within six weeks, they were to be given special care and feeding. Up to then all Jews who had become incapable of working were gassed with the next transports, or killed by injection if they happened to be lying ill in the sick block. As far as Auschwitz-Birkenau was concerned, this order was sheer mockery. Everything was lacking. There were practically no medical supplies. The accommodation was such that there was scarcely even room for those who were most seriously ill. The food was completely insufficient, and every month the Food Ministry cut down the supplies still further. But all protests were unavailing and an attempt to carry out the order had to be made. The resultant overcrowding of the healthy prisoners could no longer be avoided. The general standard of health was thereby lowered, and diseases spread like wildfire. As a result of this order the death-rate was sent up with a jerk and a tremendous deterioration in the general conditions developed. I do not believe that a *single* sick Jew was ever made fit again for work in the armaments industry.

During previous interrogations I have put the number of Jews who arrived in Auschwitz for extermination at two and a half millions. This figure was supplied by Eichmann who gave it to my superior officer, Gruppenführer Glücks, when he was ordered to make a report to the Reichsführer SS shortly before Berlin was surrounded. Eichmann, and his permanent deputy Günther, were the only ones who possessed the necessary information on which to calculate the total number destroyed. In accordance with orders given by the Reichsführer SS, after every large action all evidence in Auschwitz on which a calculation of the number of victims might be based had to be burnt.

As head of Department DI I personally destroyed every bit of evidence which could be found in my office. The heads of other offices did the same.

According to Eichmann, the Reichsführer SS and the Reich Security Head Office also had all their data destroyed.

Only his personal notes could give the required information. It is possible that, owing to the negligence of some department or other, a few isolated documents, teleprinter messages, or wireless messages have been left undestroyed, but they could not give sufficient information on which to make a calculation.

I myself never knew the total number and I have nothing to help me make an estimate of it.

I can only remember the figure involved in the larger actions, which were repeated to me by Eichmann or his deputies.

From Upper Silesia and Polish territory under

German rule ...	...	...	...	...	250,000
Germany and Theresienstadt ...		...	...	...	100,000
Holland ...	...	...	...	...	...	95,000
Belgium ...	...	...	...	...	...	20,000
France ...	...	...	...	...	...	110,000
Greece ...	...	...	...	...	...	65,000
Hungary ...	...	...	...	...	...	400,000
Slovakia ...	...	...	...	...	...	90,000

I can no longer remember the figures for the smaller actions, but they were insignificant in comparison with the numbers given above.

I regard a total of two and a half millions as far too high. Even Auschwitz had limits to its destructive possibilities.

Figures given by former prisoners are figments of the imagination and lack any foundation.

'Action Reinhardt' was the code name given to the collection, sorting and utilisation of all articles which were acquired as the result of the transports of Jews and their extermination.

Any member of the SS who laid hands on this Jewish property was by order of the Reichsführer SS, punished with death.

Valuables worth many millions of pounds were seized.

An immense amount of property was stolen by members of the SS and by the police, and also by prisoners, civilian employees and railway personnel. A great deal of this still lies hidden and buried in the Auschwitz-Birkenau camp area.

When the Jewish transports unloaded on arrival, their luggage was left on the platform until all the Jews had been taken to the extermination buildings or into the camp. During the early days all the luggage would then be brought by a transport detachment to the sorting office, Canada I, where it would be sorted and disinfected. The clothing of those who had been gassed in bunkers I and II or in crematoria I to IV was also brought to the sorting office.

By 1942, Canada I could no longer keep up with the sorting. Although new huts and sheds were constantly being added and prisoners were sorting day and night, and although the number of persons employed was constantly stepped up and several trucks (often as many as twenty) were loaded daily with the items sorted out, the piles of unsorted luggage went on mounting up. So in 1942, the construction of Canada II warehouse was begun at the west end of building sector II at Birkenau. A start was also made on the erection of extermination buildings and a bath house for the new arrivals. Thirty newly-built huts were crammed to capacity immediately after completion, while mountains of unsorted effects piled up between them. In spite of the augmented labour gangs, it was out of the question to complete the job during the course of the individual actions, which always took from four to six weeks. Only during the longer intervals was it possible to achieve some semblance of order.

Clothing and footwear were examined for hidden valuables (although only cursorily in view of the quantities involved) and then stored or handed over to the camp to complete the inmates' clothing. Later on, it was also sent to other camps. A considerable part of the clothing was passed to welfare organisations for resettlers and later for victims of air raids. Large and important munition plants received considerable quantities for their foreign workers.

Blankets and mattresses, etc., were also sent to the welfare organisations. In so far as the camp required articles of this nature they were retained to complete their inventory, but other camps also received large consignments.

Valuables were taken over by a special section of the camp command and sorted out by experts, and a similar procedure was followed with the money that was found.

The jewellery was usually of great value, particularly if its Jewish owners came from the west: precious stones worth thousands of pounds, priceless gold and platinum watches set with diamonds, rings, earrings and necklaces of great rarity. Currency from all countries amounted to many thousands of pounds. Often tens of thousands of pounds in value, mostly in thousand dollar notes, were found on single individuals. Every possible hiding place in their clothes and luggage and on their bodies was made use of.

When the sorting out process that followed each major operation had been completed, the valuables and money were packed into trunks and taken by lorry to the Economic Administration Head Office in Berlin and thence to the Reichsbank, where a special department dealt exclusively with items taken during actions against the Jews. Eichmann told me on one occasion that the jewellery and currency were sold in Switzerland, and that the entire Swiss jewellery market was dominated by these sales.

Ordinary watches were likewise sent in their thousands to Sachsenhausen. A large watchmaker's shop had been set up there, which employed hundreds of prisoners and was directly administered by

Department DII (Maurer). The watches were sorted out and repaired in the workshop, the majority being later despatched for service use by front-line SS and army troops.

Gold from the teeth was melted into bars by the dentists in the SS hospital and forwarded monthly to the Sanitary Head Office.

Precious stones of great value were also to be found hidden in teeth that had been stopped.

Hair cut from the women was sent to a firm in Bavaria to be used in the war effort.

Unserviceable clothing was sent for salvage, and useless footwear was taken to pieces and remade as far as possible, what was left over being converted into leather dust.

The treasures brought in by the Jews gave rise to unavoidable difficulties for the camp itself. It was demoralising for the members of the SS, who were not always strong enough to resist the temptation provided by these valuables which lay within such easy reach. Not even the death penalty or a heavy prison sentence was enough to deter them.

The arrival of these Jews with their riches offered undreamed of opportunities to the other prisoners. Most of the escapes that were made were probably connected with these circumstances. With the assistance of this easily acquired money or watches and rings, etc., anything could be arranged with the SS men or the civilian workers. Alcohol, tobacco, food, false papers, guns and ammunition were all in the day's work. In Birkenau the male prisoners obtained access to the women's camp at night by bribing some of the female supervisors. This kind of thing naturally affected the whole camp discipline. Those who possessed valuables could obtain better jobs for themselves, and were able to buy the goodwill of the Capos and block seniors, and even arrange for a lengthy stay in the hospital where they would be given the best food. Not even the strictest supervision could alter this state of affairs. Jewish gold was a catastrophe for the camp.

In addition to Auschwitz there existed, so far as I am aware, the following extermination centres for Jews:

Culendorf near Litzmannstadt ...	Engine exhaust gases	
Treblinka on the Bug	,, ,, ,,
Sobibor near Lublin	,, ,, ,,
Belzec near Lemberg	,, ,, ,,
Lublin (Maidenek)	Cyclon B

I myself have only seen Culenhof and Treblinka. Culenhof had ceased to be used, but in Treblinka I saw the whole operation.

The latter had several chambers, capable of holding some hundreds of people, built directly by the railway track. The Jews went straight into the gas-chambers without undressing, by way of a platform which was level with the trucks. A motor room had been built next to the gas-chambers, equipped with various engines taken from large lorries and tanks. These were started up and the exhaust gases were led by pipes into the gas-chambers, thereby killing the people inside. The process was continued for half an hour until all was silent inside the rooms. In an hour's time the gas-chambers were opened up and the bodies taken out, undressed and burnt on a framework made of railway lines.

The fires were stoked with wood, the bodies being sprayed every now and then with petrol refuse. During my visit all those who had been gassed were dead. But I was told that the performance of the engines was not always uniform, so that the exhaust gases were often insufficiently strong to kill everyone in the chambers. Many of them were only rendered unconscious and had to be finished off by shooting. I heard the same story in Culenhof and I was also told by Eichmann that these defects had occurred in other places.

In Culenhof, too, the Jews sometimes broke the sides of the trucks in an attempt to escape.

Experience had shown that the preparation of prussic acid called Cyclon B caused death with far greater speed and certainty, especially if the rooms were kept dry and gas-tight and closely packed with people, and provided they were fitted with as large a number of intake vents as possible. So far as Auschwitz is concerned, I have never known or heard of a single person being found alive when the gas-chambers were opened half an hour after the gas had been inducted.

The *extermination process in Auschwitz* took place as follows:

Jews selected for gassing were taken as quietly as possible to the crematoria, the men being separated from the women. In the undressing room, prisoners of the special detachment, detailed for this purpose, would tell them in their own language that they were going to be bathed and deloused, that they must leave their clothes neatly together and above all remember where they had put them, so that they would be able to find then again quickly after delousing. The prisoners of the special detachment had the greatest interest in seeing that the operation proceeded smoothly and quickly. After undressing, the Jews went into the gas-chambers, which were furnished with showers and water pipes and gave a realistic impression of a bath house.

The women went in first with their children, followed by the men who were always the fewer in number. This part of the operation nearly always went smoothly, for the prisoners of the special detachment would calm those who betrayed any anxiety or who perhaps had some inkling of their fate. As an additional precaution these prisoners of the special detachment and an SS man always remained in the chamber until the last moment.

The door would now be quickly screwed up and the gas immediately discharged by the waiting disinfectors through vents in the ceilings of the gas-chambers, down a shaft that led to the floor. This ensured the rapid distribution of the gas. It could be observed through the peep-hole in the door that those who were standing nearest to the induction vents were killed at once. It can be said that about one-third died straight away. The remainder staggered about and began to scream and struggle for air. The screaming, however, soon changed to the death rattle and in a few minutes all lay still. After twenty minutes at the latest no movement could be discerned. The time required for the gas to have effect varied according to the weather, and depended on whether it was damp or dry, cold or warm. It also depended on the quality of the gas, which was never exactly the same, and on the composition of the transports which might contain a high proportion of healthy Jews, or old and sick, or children. The victims became unconscious after a few minutes, according to their distance from the intake shaft. Those who screamed and those who were old or sick or weak, or the small children, died quicker than those who were healthy or young.

The door was opened half an hour after the induction of the gas, and the ventilation switched on. Work was immediately begun on removing the corpses. There was no noticeable change in the bodies and no sign of convulsions or discoloration. Only after the bodies had been left lying for some time, that is to say after several hours, did the usual death stains appear in the places where they had lain. Soiling through opening of the bowels was also rare. There were no signs of wounding of any kind. The faces showed no distortion.

The special detachment now set about removing the gold teeth and cutting the hair from the women. After this, the bodies were taken up by lift and laid in front of the ovens, which had meanwhile been stoked up. Depending on the size of the bodies, up to three corpses could be put into one oven retort at the same time. The time required for cremation also depended on this, but on an average it took twenty minutes. As previously stated, crematoria I and II could cremate about 2,000 bodies in twenty-four hours, but a higher number was not possible without causing damage to the installations. Numbers III and IV should have been able to cremate 1,500 bodies in twenty-four hours, but, as far as I know, these figures were never attained.

During the period when the fires were kept burning continuously, without a break, the ashes fell through the grates and were constantly removed and crushed to powder. The ashes were taken in lorries to the Vistula, where they immediately *drifted away* and dissolved. The ashes taken from the burning pits near bunker II and crematorium IV were dealt with in the same way.

The process of destruction in bunkers I and II was exactly the same as in the crematoria, except that the effects of the weather on the operation were more noticeable.

The whole of the work in connection with the extermination process was performed by special detachments of Jews.

They carried out their grisly task with dumb indifference. Their one object was to finish the work as quickly as possible so that they could have a longer interval in which to search the clothing of the gassed victims for something to smoke or eat. Although they were well fed and given many additional allowances, they could often be seen shifting corpses with one hand while they gnawed at something they held in the other. Even when they were engaged in the most gruesome work of digging out and burning the corpses buried in the mass graves, they never stopped eating.

Even the cremation of their near relations failed to shake them.

When I went to Budapest in the summer of 1943 and called on Eichmann, he told me about the further actions which had been planned in connection with the Jews.

At that period there were rather more than 200,000 Jews from the Carpathian-Ukraine, who were detained there and housed in some brickworks, while awaiting transport to Auschwitz.

Eichmann expected to receive from Hungary, according to the estimate of the Hungarian police, who had carried out the arrests, about 3,000,000 Jews.

The arrests and transportation should have been completed by 1943, but because of the Hungarian government's political difficulties, the date was always being postponed.

In particular the Hungarian army, or rather the senior officers, were opposed to the extradition of these people and gave most of the male Jews a refuge in the labour companies of the front line divisions, thus keeping them out of the clutches of the police. When in the autumn of 1944, an action was started in Budapest itself, the only male Jews left were the old and the sick.

Altogether there were probably not more than half a million Jews transported out of Hungary.

The next country on the list was Rumania. According to the reports from his representative in Bucharest, Eichmann expected to get about 4,000,000 Jews from there.

Negotiations with the Rumanian authorities, however, were likely to be difficult. The anti-Semitic elements wanted the extermination of the Jews to be carried out in their own country. There had already been serious anti-Jewish rioting, and abducted Jews had been thrown into the deep and isolated ravines of the Carpathians and killed. A section of the government, however, was in favour of transporting unwanted Jews to Germany.

In the meantime Bulgaria was to follow with an estimated two and a half million Jews. The authorities there were agreeable to the transport, but wanted to wait on the result of the negotiations with Rumania.

In addition, Mussolini was supposed to have promised the extradition of the Italian Jews and those from the Italian occupied part of Greece, although not even an estimate had been made of their numbers. But the Vatican and the Royal Family, and consequently all those opposed to Mussolini, wanted at all costs to prevent these Jews from being surrendered.

Eichmann did not count on getting these Jews.

Finally there was Spain. Influential circles were approached by German representatives over the question of getting rid of the Jews. But Franco and his followers were against it. Eichmann had little faith in being able to arrange for an extradition.

The course taken by the war destroyed these plans and saved the lives of millions of Jews.

Cracow, November 1946   *Rudolf Hoess*

APPENDIX TWO

My meetings with Himmler

I ALREADY knew the Reichsführer SS, Heinrich Himmler, slightly during the years 1921 and 1922, when, as courier of my Freikorps I had a great deal to do with Ludendorff. General Ludendorff was the protector and secret head of all the nationalist movements with their disguised military or semi-military organisations, which were forbidden by the peace treaty. Himmler was also a member of a Freikorps in Bavaria and it was in Ludendorff's house that I got to know him.

Later on, in 1930, at an assembly of the Atamanen in Saxony (Himmler belonged to the association as Gauführer of Bavaria), I became more closely acquainted with him. . . .

In 1940 Himmler suddenly arrived in Sachsenhausen concentration camp. Shortly before he reached the guard, he met a detachment of prisoners who passed him leisurely pulling a trolley. Neither the sentry nor the prisoners recognised the Reichsführer SS sitting in his car, and therefore did not take off their caps. Himmler drove past the guard and went straight to the protective custody camp. As I was just on the point of going into the camp (I was commander of the protective custody camp at the time), I was able to report to him at once on behalf of the camp. He was very irritated and his first question, after giving a curt greeting, was, ' Where is the commandant? ' After some time, the commandant, Sturmbannführer Eisfeld, appeared on the scene, but meanwhile Himmler had already entered the protective custody camp, snapping angrily that he, Himmler, had up to then been accustomed to another kind of discipline in the concentration camps, and that apparently prisoners were no longer required to salute.

He refused to listen to the commandant's explanation and exchanged no further words with him. He made a brief inspection of the detention block, where some special prisoners had been placed, and then immediately drove off again. Two days later Eisfeld was dismissed from his position as commandant of Sachsenhausen and Oberführer Loritz (formerly commandant of Dachau and then section leader of the General SS in Klagenfurt) was recalled to concentration camp service to replace him. Himmler had previously removed Loritz from Dachau because he was too severe with the prisoners, and also because he had not concerned himself sufficiently with the affairs of the camp.

In 1942 Loritz was once again, on the same grounds, removed from Sachsenhausen on Pohl's suggestion. . . .

My personal meetings with Himmler during my membership of the SS were as follows:

In June 1934, during an inspection of the Pomeranian SS, Himmler asked me whether I would like to join the active SS in a concentration camp. It was only after much deliberation with my wife (for we wanted to settle on the land) that I agreed to do this, because I wanted to be on active service once more. On the 1 December, 1934, I was summoned to Dachau by the Inspector of Concentration Camps, Eicke.

In 1936 Himmler held a grand inspection of the whole SS organisation, including that of the concentration camp in Dachau, at which all Gauleiters, Reichsleiters and all SS and SA Gruppenführer were present. I was *Rapportführer* at that time and deputised for the commander of the protective custody camp, who was absent. Himmler is in the best of spirits because the whole inspection has gone off without a hitch. The Dachau concentration camp is also going well at that moment. The prisoners are well fed, clean and well clothed and housed. Most of them are busy in the workshops and the number of sick is hardly worth mentioning. The total strength of about 2,500 is accommodated in ten brick-built huts. The sanitary arrangements are ample. There is a plentiful supply of water. Underwear is changed once a week and bed linen once a month. One-third of the complement consists of political prisoners and two-thirds of professional criminals, a-socials and forced labour prisoners, homosexuals and about 200 Jews.

During the inspection, Himmler and Bormann address me and both ask me if I am satisfied with my job and enquire after my family. In a short time I am promoted to Untersturmführer.

During this inspection, Himmler, following his usual practice, chose a few prisoners and in front of the assembled guests asked them the reasons for their arrest. There were some communist leaders who admitted quite honestly that they were, and would continue to remain, communists. Some professional criminals, however, considerably minimised their catalogue of punishments, and their memory had to be jogged by a rapid inspection of the prison record cards. These proceedings were typical of Himmler's visits and I had repeated experience of them. Himmler punished those who had lied by giving them extra work for a few Sundays. . . .

My next meeting with Himmler was in the summer of 1938 in Sachsenhausen concentration camp.

The Minister of the Interior, Dr Frick, was inspecting a concentration camp for the first time. He was accompanied by various senior administrative officials and the chief constables of the larger cities. Himmler attended and gave a commentary on the organisation.

At that time I was adjutant to the commandant, and during the whole inspection stood near to Himmler and was able to observe him closely. He was in the best of humour and obviously pleased that he was at last able to show the Minister of the Interior and his officials one of the secret and notorious concentration camps. He was overwhelmed with questions, all of which he answered calmly and amiably although often sarcastically. He gave evasive, but even more genial, answers to inconvenient questions such as those relating to the numbers of prisoners and so on (the total number of those held in concentration camps was kept secret in accordance with orders of the Reichsführer SS).

Sachsenhausen concentration camp then held, I believe, 4,000 prisoners, most of them professional criminals, who were accommodated in well constructed wooden huts, divided into dormitories and living rooms. The food was acknowledged to be good and plentiful. The clothing was sufficient and always clean, for an up-to-date laundry had been installed in the camp.

The hospital building with its surgeries was exemplary. The number of sick was small.

Apart from the cell building, which in all camps was forbidden to be shown to unauthorised visitors, since it was mostly occupied by special prisoners of the Reich Security Head Office, all the buildings and the whole camp organisation were thrown open to inspection. It is certain that nothing remained hidden from the critical eyes of those experienced officials of the government and the police. Frick showed great interest, and declared at dinner that it made him ashamed to think that he was then, in 1938, seeing a concentration camp for the first time. The Inspector of Concentration Camps, Eicke, gave a description of the other camps and their special characteristics.

Although there was little time to spare, and he was perpetually surrounded by questioners, Himmler still found an opportunity to speak to me personally and to enquire especially after my family. He never omitted to do this, and one was given the feeling that it was not done merely out of politeness.

I have already described the next meeting, in January 1940. This was when the incident took place concerning the prisoners who failed to salute.

In November 1940 I made my first verbal report to Himmler over Auschwitz in the presence of Sturmbannführer Vogel from Dept. WV of the Economic Administration Head Office. I gave a detailed account and bluntly referred to all those grievances which were causing irritation at that time, but which were insignificant compared with the catastrophic conditions of the years to come. He scarcely referred to this, but only said that it was primarily up to me as commandant to arrange for assistance, but how I was to set about it was my own affair. Besides, there was a war on and a lot of things had to be improvised; and even in the concentration camp one must not expect to live under peacetime conditions. The front line soldier also had to give up a great deal, so why not the prisoners as well?

My constantly expressed fears over the danger of disease arising from the inadequate sanitary arrangements, were curtly dismissed with the remark: ' You look too much on the dark side of things.'

His interest was only aroused when I discussed the camp area as a whole and produced maps to illustrate what I was saying. His attitude changed at once. He talked with animation about future plans, and gave one directive after another or made notes about everything that was to be done with the land in question.

Auschwitz was to become *the* agricultural research station for the eastern territories. Opportunities were opened up to us, which we had never before had in Germany. Sufficient labour was available. All essential agricultural research must be carried out there. Huge laboratories and plant nurseries were to be set out. All kinds of stock-breeding was to be pursued there. Vogel was to take immediate steps to gather a force of specialists; to build fisheries and to drain the lands, and to construct a dam on the Vistula would present difficulties compared to which the grievances in the camp previously described would become insignificant. On his next visit to Auschwitz he wanted to see everything for himself. He remained absorbed in his agricultural planning, down to the smallest details, until the adjutant on duty drew his attention to the fact that an important official had been waiting for a long time to see him.

Himmler's interest in Auschwitz was indeed stimulated, but it was not directed towards remedying the evil conditions or preventing them from occurring in the future, but rather towards increasing them because of his refusal to acknowledge their existence.

My friend Vogel was thrilled by the bold design for constructing the agricultural research stations. I was too—as a farmer. But as camp commandant I saw all my plans for making Auschwitz a clean and healthy place begin to dwindle. Only his announced intention of making a further visit left me with a vague hope. I felt that a personal inspection would induce him to remedy the obvious deficiencies and grievances.

In the meantime I continued to construct and ' improvise ' in an attempt to avert the worst of the evils.

My efforts met with little success, for I could not keep step with the rapid expansion of the camp or the constant increase in the numbers of the prisoners. No sooner was a building erected that could normally accommodate over 200 people than a further transport consisting of a thousand or more prisoners would be drawn up at the platform. Protests to the Inspector of Concentration Camps or the Reich Security Head Office or to the Chief of Police in Cracow were of no avail. ' The actions ordered by the Reichsführer SS must be carried out', was the reply that was always given.

At last, on the 1 March, 1941, Himmler arrived in Auschwitz. He was accompanied by the Gauleiter Bracht, the administrative Presidents, the SS and police officers of Silesia, high executives of IG Farben Industrie and the Inspector of Concentration Camps, Glücks. The latter had arrived beforehand and constantly warned me against reporting anything disagreeable to the Reichsführer SS! And I had nothing to say that was not disagreeable. With the help of plans and maps I explained to Himmler the layout of the land that was being taken over and the extensions that had been made, and gave him an account of the present position. I could not, of course, describe to him, in the presence of all those strangers, the

o

shortcomings which weighed so heavily on my mind. Nevertheless, during the tour which we afterwards made of the district, when I was alone in the car with Himmler and Schmauser, I made up for this by telling him about them candidly and in detail. But it did not have the effect for which I had hoped. Even when we went through the camp and I drew his attention, in an indirect manner, to the worst of the grievances, such as the overcrowding and lack of water and so on, he hardly listened to me. When I repeatedly begged him to stop sending any more drafts, he snubbed me abruptly. I could not expect any kind of help from him. On the contrary, when we were in the canteen in the SS hospital block, he started to discuss in earnest the new tasks that he had for Auschwitz.

This was the construction of the prisoner-of-war camp for 100,000 prisoners. Himmler had already talked about this during our tour and had given a rough indication of the site. The Gauleiter raised objections and the administrative president tried to put a stop to it on account of the lack of water and drainage difficulties. Himmler dismissed these objections with a smile: ' Gentlemen, it will be built. My reasons for constructing it are far more important than your objections. Ten thousand prisoners are to be provided for the IG Farben Industrie according to their requirements and to the progress made in the constructional work. Auschwitz concentration camp is to be expanded to hold a peacetime establishment of 30,000 prisoners. I intend to transfer here afterwards important branches of the armaments industry. The space for this is to be kept clear. In addition there will be the agricultural research stations and farms!' And all this was to be accomplished, when there was already an acute shortage of building materials in Upper Silesia. The Gauleiter drew Himmler's attention to this and received the reply: 'What have the SS requisitioned the brickworks for, and the cement factory, too? They will have to be made more productive, or the concentration camp will be forced to start some undertakings on its own account!

'Problems of water supply and drainage are purely technical matters, which the specialists have to work out, but they cannot be raised as objections. Every means will have to be taken to accelerate the constructional work. You must improvise as much as possible, and any outbreak of disease will have to be checked and ruthlessly stamped out!

'The delivery of drafts to the camp, however, cannot, on principle, be halted. The actions, which I have ordered my security police to undertake, must go on. I do not appreciate the difficulties in Auschwitz.' Then turning to me, he said: 'It is up to you to manage somehow.'

Shortly before his departure. Himmler found time to pay a visit to my family and gave me instructions to enlarge the house in view of its use as an official residence. He was once more genial and talkative, in spite of his abruptness and irritation during our conversations a little earlier on.

Glücks had been shocked by the way I had repeatedly raised objections to the pronouncements of the Reichsführer SS. He, too, could not help me. Nor was he able to arrange for any assistance by transferring personnel and so on. He had no better officers or junior officers available and he could not expect other camp commandants to exchange good material for bad.

' You won't find it so hard and you'll manage all right,' were the words with which my interview with my superior officer ended. . . .

In the summer of 1941, Himmler summoned me to Berlin to inform me of the fateful order that envisaged the mass extermination of Jews from almost every part of Europe, and which resulted in Auschwitz becoming the largest human slaughter house that history had ever known. . . .

My next meeting with Himmler was in the summer of 1942 when he visited Auschwitz for the second and last time. The inspection lasted for two days and Himmler examined everything in great detail. There were present, among others, Gauleiter Bracht, Obergruppenführer Schmauser and Dr Kammler.

After his arrival in the camp we went to the SS officers' mess where I had to explain the layout of the camp with the aid of maps. Then we went to the architects' office where Kammler produced designs and models with which to explain the constructional work which had been proposed or which was already under way, but he did *not* pass in silence over the difficulties which stood in the way of these plans or which might even prevent their realisation. Himmler listened with interest, enquired about some technical details and expressed agreement with the scheme as a whole, but he showed no concern over the difficulties which Kammler had repeatedly brought to his notice. Afterwards a tour was made of the whole of the camp's sphere of interest. First an inspection was made of the agricultural areas and the work of reclamation, the building of the dam, the laboratories and plant breeding establishments in Raisko, the stock breeding centres and the tree nurseries. Then Birkenau was visited, including the Russian camp, the gypsy sector and also a Jewish sector. He then climbed the gate tower and had the different parts of the camp pointed out to him and also the water drainage systems which were being built, and he was shown the extent of the proposed expansion. He saw the prisoners at work and inspected their living quarters and the kitchens and the hospital accommodation. I constantly drew his attention to the defects in the camp, and he saw them as well. He saw the emaciated victims of disease (the causes of which were bluntly explained by the doctors), he saw the crowded hospital block, he learnt of the mortality among the children in the gypsy camp, and he saw children there suffering from the terrible disease called Noma. He also saw the overcrowded huts and the primitive and insufficient latrines and wash houses. The doctors told him about the high rate of sickness and death and, above all, the reasons for it. He had everything explained to him in the most exact manner and saw it all precisely as it really was, and he remained silent. He took me back to Birkenau furious at my perpetual complaints of the miserable conditions in the camp and said: ' I want to hear no more about difficulties! An SS officer does not recognise difficulties; when they arise, his task is to remove them at once by his own efforts! *How* this is to be done is *your* worry and not mine! ' Kammler and Bischoff were told much the same sort of thing.

After the inspection in Birkenau, he watched the whole process of destruction of a transport of Jews, which had just arrived. He also spent a short time watching the selection of the able-bodied Jews, without making any objection. He made no remark regarding the process of extermination, but remained quite silent. While it was going on he unobtrusively observed the officers and junior officers engaged in the proceedings, including myself.

He then went on to look at the synthetic rubber factory. He inspected the buildings just as carefully as he did the prisoners and the work they were doing. He made enquiries concerning the health of these prisoners. Kammler then heard him say: ' You complain about difficulties, but look at what IG Farben Industrie have done in one year, and under similar difficulties! ' He never mentioned the quotas, or the more favourable opportunities, or the thousands of skilled workers (about 30,000 at that time) which IG Farben Industrie had at their disposal. Himmler made enquiries concerning the working capabilities of the prisoners, and received evasive replies on the part of the IG Farben Industrie. Whereupon he told me that I must by all means increase their efficiency! How this was to be done was, once more, to be my affair, in spite of the fact that earlier on he had heard from the Gauleiter and the IG Farben Industrie that in a short time they would have to reckon with a serious cut in rations issued for prisoners, and that he had also seen for himself the general condition of the prisoners.

From the synthetic rubber factory we went to the sewer gas installation, where progress had stopped owing to the impossibility of overcoming the shortage of materials.

It was one of the worst spots in Auschwitz, and it affected everyone. The drainage water from the base camp was discharged, without any purification worth mentioning, directly into the Sola. The population was constantly exposed to the danger of infection, because of the diseases which were always rampant in the camp. The Gauleiter described the position with great clarity, and asked in unmistakable terms for assistance. 'Kammler will apply all his energies to the problem,' was Himmler's reply.

The Kok-saghyz (natural rubber) plantation, which he visited next, was of far greater interest to him.

Himmler always found it more interesting and more pleasant to hear positives rather than negatives. The SS officer counted himself lucky and enviable, who had only positives to report, or who was skilful enough to represent negatives as positives!

In the evening on the first day of the inspection a dinner was given which was attended by the visitors and by all the officers of the Auschwitz command.

Before dinner, Himmler had everyone introduced to him. If a man interested him, he would talk with him about his family and work. During dinner he questioned me about different officers whom he had noticed.

I seized the opportunity to tell him about the troubles I had with my staff and how many of the officers were completely unfit to serve in a concentration camp or to command troops. I begged him to give me some replacements and to increase the strength of the guards.

'You will be amazed,' he replied, 'at the impossible officer-material with which you will have to be satisfied in the end! I need every officer, junior officer and man, who is capable of serving in the front line. For the same reasons it is impossible to increase the strength of the guard. You will have to think up some technical ways of economising in guards. You must use some more dogs for this purpose. I will get my expert in dog-handling to call on you in a few days and explain the new method of using dogs as a substitute for guards. The numbers of escapes from Auschwitz is unusually high, and is unprecedented in a concentration camp. I approve of every means, I repeat *every* means, being used to prevent these escapes. This escape disease, which has become rampant in Auschwitz, must be eradicated!'

After this dinner party the Gauleiter invited the Reichsführer SS, Schmauser, Kammler, Caesar and myself to his house near Kattowitz. Himmler was to stay there overnight, since he had some important matters concerning population registers and resettlement to discuss with the Gauleiter on the following morning.

Himmler expressed a wish that my wife, too, should come to the Gauleiter's house.

Although during the day Himmler was occasionally very ill-humoured and angry and even downright unfriendly, yet this evening, and among this small company, he was a changed person.

He was in the best of spirits, took a leading part in the conversation and was extremely amiable, especially towards the ladies, the Gauleiter's wife and my own wife. He talked on every possible subject which came up in the conversation. He discussed the education of children and new buildings and books and pictures. He spoke about his experiences with the front-line divisions of the SS, and about his visits to the front with the Führer.

He deliberately avoided saying one word about day-to-day events or about service matters, and ignored the attempts of the Gauleiter to get him to do so.

It was fairly late before the guests departed. Very little was drunk during the evening. Himmler, who scarcely ever touched alcohol, drank a few glasses of red wine and smoked, which was also something he did not usually do. Everyone was under the spell of his good humour and lively conversation. I had never known him like that before.

On the second day I called for him and Schmauser at the Gauleiter's house, and the inspection was continued. He inspected the base camp, the kitchens, the women's camp (which then included the first row of the block from the headquarters building up to block 11), the workshops, the stables, Canada and DAW, the butcher's shop and the bakery, the timberyard and the troops' supply depot. He inspected everything with care, observed the prisoners closely and made precise enquiries concerning the different types of confinement and the numbers involved.

He refused to be guided, but on that morning requested to be shown first one thing and then another. In the women's camp he saw the cramped quarters, the insufficient latrine accommodation, and the deficient water supply, and he got the administrative officer to show him the stocks of clothing. Everywhere he saw the deficiencies. He had every detail of the rationing system and the extra allowances for the heavy workers explained to him.

In the women's camp he attended the whipping of a female criminal (a prostitute, who was continually breaking in and stealing whatever she could lay her hands on) in order to observe its effect. Before any woman was whipped, permission had to be obtained from Himmler personally. Some women were produced to him, who had been imprisoned for insignificant offences, and he set them free. He talked with some female Jehovah's Witnesses and discussed with them their fanatical beliefs.

After the inspection, he held a final conference in my office and, in Schmauser's presence, addresses me, more or less, in the following words:

' I have now made a thorough inspection of Auschwitz. I have seen everything and I have seen enough of the deficiencies and difficulties and I have heard enough of them from you. I can, however, do nothing to alter them. You will have to manage as best you can. We are now in the middle of a war and we must learn to think in terms of war. The actions, which I have ordered the security police to carry out, will not be stopped under any circumstances, least of all because of the lack of accommodation and so on, which I have been shown. Eichmann's programme will continue to be carried out and will be intensified month by month. You must see to it that swift progress is made with the building of Birkenau. The gypsies are to be destroyed. The Jews who are unfit for work are to be destroyed with the same ruthlessness. Soon the labour camps at the armaments factories will absorb the first large contingents of able-bodied Jews, and that will give you some breathing space again. Armaments factories will also be built in Auschwitz camp, so prepare yourselves for that. Kammler will give you far-reaching support in matters connected with their construction.

'The agricultural experiments will be intensively pursued, for the results are urgently required.

'I have seen your work and the results you have achieved, and I am satisfied and thank you for your services. I promote you to Obersturmbannführer!'

So ended Himmler's great inspection of Auschwitz. He saw everything and knew what the ultimate results would be. Was his remark, 'Even I cannot help,' intentional?

After the conference in my office, I took him round my house and showed him my furniture, in which he took a great interest, and he spent some time in animated conversation with my wife and children.

I drove him to the aerodrome where he bade me a brief farewell and flew back to Berlin. . . .

On the 3 May, 1945, I met Himmler for the last time. What remained of the Inspectorate of Concentration Camps had been ordered to follow Himmler to Flensburg. Glücks, Maurer and myself duly reported to him there. He had just come from a conference with the surviving members of the government. He was hale and hearty, and in the best of humour. He greeted me and at once gave the following orders: 'Glücks and Hoess are to disguise themselves as non-commissioned officers of the army and make their way across the green frontier to Denmark as stragglers, and hide themselves in the army. Maurer and what is left of the Inspectorate of Concentration Camps are to disappear into the army in the same way. All further matters will be dealt with by Standartenführer Hintz, the police president of Flensburg.' He shook each of us by the hand. We were dismissed!

He had with him at the time Professor Gebhardt and Schellenberg of the Reich Security Head Office. Like Gebhardt, Glücks said that Himmler intended to go into hiding in Sweden.

APPENDIX THREE

Eichmann

SS Obersturmbannführer Adolf Eichmann was head of the Jewish section IV B 4 in the Reich Security Head Office

EICHMANN originally came from Linz and was therefore on friendly terms with Kaltenbrunner during the time of the illegal SS activities in Austria. After the occupation he went to the SD and later to the Gestapo. Finally he joined Müller in Section IV of the Reich Security Head Office.

Eichmann had concerned himself with the Jewish question since his youth and had an extensive knowledge of the literature on the subject. He lived for a long time in Palestine in order to learn more about the Zionists and the growing Jewish state. Eichmann knew all the places where Jews had settled and also their approximate numbers, which latter were kept a secret even from the Jews themselves. He also knew the habits and customs of the orthodox Jews, as well as the views of the assimilated Jews of the West.

It was because of his special knowledge that he was made head of the Jewish section.

I myself first got to know him after I had received from the Reichsführer SS the orders for the destruction of the Jews, when he visited me in Auschwitz to discuss the exact details of the extermination process.

Eichmann was a vivacious, active man in his thirties, and always full of energy. He was constantly hatching new plans and perpetually on the look out for innovations and improvements. He could never rest. He was obesssed with the Jewish question and the order which had been given for its final solution.

Eichmann had to make continual reports to the Reichsführer SS, directly and by word of mouth, concerning the preparation and completion of the individual actions. He was the only person in a position to give the exact figures involved.

He kept almost everything in his memory. His memoranda

consisted of a few pieces of paper which he always carried with him, inscribed with signs that were unintelligible to anyone else. Even his permanent representative in Berlin, Günther, could not always furnish detailed information. Eichmann was constantly away on service matters and it was only rarely that he could be found in his Berlin office.

The arrangements for an action against the Jews were made by members of Eichmann's staff stationed in the countries concerned, who were thus fairly well acquainted with the country and able to prepare the necessary groundwork for him. Wisliceni, for example, operated in Slovakia, Greece, Rumania, Bulgaria and Hungary. The negotiations with the governments of the countries concerned were conducted by the German diplomatic representatives, in most cases by specially commissioned delegates from the Foreign Office.

Those governments which agreed to the extradition of the Jews appointed a department to organise their arrest and delivery. Eichmann then discussed the details of transportation direct with this department and gave them the benefit of his experience on matters connected with their arrest. In Hungary, for example, the action was carried out by the Ministry for Internal Affairs and the police. Eichmann and his colleagues supervised the operation, and intervened if it was being done too slowly or too carelessly. Eichmann's staff also had to make transport available and arrange time tables with the Ministry of Transport.

On Pohl's orders I made three visits to Budapest in order to obtain an estimate of the number of able-bodied Jews that might be expected. This gave me the opportunity of observing Eichmann's methods of negotiating with the Hungarian government departments and the army. His manner of approach was extremely firm and matter-of-fact, but nevertheless amiable and courteous and he was liked and made welcome wherever he went. This was confirmed by the innumerable private invitations he received from the chiefs of these departments. Only the Hungarian army showed no pleasure in Eichmann's visits. The army sabotaged the surrender of the Jews whenever they could, but they did it in such a manner that the Hungarian government was unable to intervene. The majority of the Hungarian population, particularly in eastern Hungary, were unfavourably disposed towards the Jews and there cannot have been many Jews in that part, in 1943, who escaped being rounded up.

If they did, it was only because they were lucky enough to make their way across the Carpathians to Rumania.

Eichmann was absolutely convinced that if he could succeed in destroying the biological basis of Jewry in the east by complete extermination, then Jewry as a whole would never recover from the blow. The assimilated Jews of the West, including America, would, in his opinion, be in no position (and would have no desire), to make up this enormous loss of blood and there would therefore be no future generation worth mentioning. He was strengthened in these views by the continual efforts of the leader of the Hungarian Jews, a fanatical Zionist, to persuade Eichmann to exclude from the transports Jews with large families. Eichmann repeatedly had long discussions with this Zionist leader on all questions relating to the Jews. Moreover it was interesting to hear that this man had up-to-date knowledge concerning Auschwitz and the number of transports, and of the process of selection and extermination. Eichmann's journeys and his dealings with the authorities of the various countries were also kept under continuous observation. The leader of the Jews in Budapest was able to tell Eichmann exactly where he had been in recent weeks and with whom he had been negotiating.

Eichmann was completely obsessed with his mission and also convinced that this extermination action was necessary in order to preserve the German people in the future from the destructive intentions of the Jews. This was the way in which he regarded his task, and he employed all his energy in fulfilling the plans for extermination which the Reichführer SS had made.

Eichmann was also a determined opponent of the idea of selecting from the transports Jews who were fit for work. He regarded it as a constant danger to his scheme for a 'final solution', because of the possibility of mass escapes or some other event occurring which would enable the Jews to survive. In his view action should be taken against every Jew that could be got hold of, and such actions ought to be pursued to their conclusion as quickly as possible, since it was impossible to anticipate the final result of the war. Already in 1943 he had doubts in a complete German victory and believed that the end would be inconclusive. . . .

APPENDIX FOUR

Müller

SS Gruppenführer and Lieutenant-General of the Police, Müller was head of Department IV in the Reich Security Head Office and Deputy Chief of the Security Police and SD

MÜLLER served as an officer in the First World War and later joined the Bavarian police. After Hitler had assumed power, he was transferred to the Bavarian political police under Best, who installed him in the office of the State Secret Police in Berlin.

He quickly assumed a prominent position in this office under Heydrich, and finally became head of the Gestapo himself.

Müller was a police official by choice. It was only after the assumption of power that he became a member of the party, and it was comparatively late before he was enrolled into the SS.

His specialist knowledge of police methods (he always was an active executive) and his aptitude for the job were particularly useful in the development of the Gestapo. He also played a decisive part in its organisation.

It was Müller's principle to remain in the background, for he did not care to be associated with any kind of operations or actions. Yet it was he who organised all the larger and more important actions taken by the security police, and it was he who planned their execution.

After Heydrich's departure he became the leading personality of the Reich Security Head Office. Kaltenbrunner was *only* the chief and concerned himself principally with the SD.

Müller was always well informed about the major political events in the Reich. He had many trusted friends in every kind of official position, especially in the economic sphere, with whom he kept in contact through third parties. He was adept at working behind the scenes.

Müller had only visited a concentration camp on a few occasions and had never inspected them all. Nevertheless he was always kept up to date on matters concerning them, and it was not for nothing that the head of the political department in each camp was a member of the police.

Eicke and Müller had got on very well with each other ever since the time when Eicke was commandant of Dachau and Müller was working with the Bavarian political police.

It was impossible to find out what Müller's personal opinions were on matters concerning concentration camp prisoners. All his pronouncements on such questions began with: ' the Reichsführer SS wishes that ', or ' the Reichsführer SS orders '. His own point of view could never be discovered.

As adjutant at Sachsenhausen, and camp commandant at Auschwitz, and later more especially as head of department D1, I very often had dealings with him. But I never knew of a single occasion on which he said: ' I decide this—I order that—I want this.' He always hid himself behind the Reichsführer SS or the chief of the security police and the SD, although the initiated knew that his was the deciding voice and that the Reichsführer SS or Kaltenbrunner completely depended on him in all questions concerning the prisoners. It was he who decided what appointments should be made and who should be dismissed, and he also had the final word in the executions, so far as they were determined by the Reich Security Head Office: that is to say that in important cases he submitted the orders for execution to the Reichsführer SS for signature.

He had an accurate knowledge of the far-reaching and delicate question of the special prisoners. He knew the exact details of each of these numerous prisoners and where they were accommodated and their particular weaknesses.

Müller was a tremendously versatile and tenacious worker. He was seldom away on duty and could always be contacted by day or by night, on Sundays and holidays as well, either in his office or at his home.

He had two adjutants and two clerks, whom he kept busy alternately day and night.

He answered every enquiry promptly, mostly through the Reichsführer SS, ' since he must always first obtain the decision of the Reichsführer SS! '

I knew from Eichmann and Günther, who had much more to do with him than I had, that he controlled the actions against the Jews in their more important respects, even though he gave Eichmann a fairly free hand in the matter.

As I have already said, he was well informed about all the concentration camps and always possessed an accurate knowledge about Auschwitz, which he had personally never seen. He knew every detail, whether it concerned Birkenau or the crematoria, or the numbers of prisoners or the mortality figures, with an exactitude that often astonished me.

My personal requests that he should slow down the actions so that the defects in the camps could be remedied were of no avail, for he always sheltered behind the strict order of the Reichsführer SS that ' the actions which I have ordered are to be ruthlessly carried out'. I tried everything I could to move him in this matter, but in vain, although in other respects I managed to achieve a great deal with him, where others never succeeded, especially later on when as D1 he placed much reliance on my judgment. I now believe that they did not want to remedy the conditions in Auschwitz, so that the effects of the actions could be increased by their indifference.

Müller might have had the power to stop the actions, or to slow them down, and he might have been able to convince the Reichsführer SS of the need for this. But he failed to do so, although he knew exactly what the results would be, because it was contrary to their intentions. That is how I see it today, although at the time I could not appreciate the attitude of the Reich Security Head Office.

Müller repeatedly said to me: ' The Reichsführer SS is of the opinion that the release of political prisoners during the war must be refused for security reasons. Requests for release must therefore be reduced to a minimum and only submitted in exceptional cases.' ' The Reichsführer SS has ordered that, on principle, all prisoners of foreign nationality are not to be released for the duration of the war.' ' The Reichsführer SS desires that even in the case of negligible acts of sabotage by prisoners of foreign nationality, the death penalty shall be demanded, as a deterrent to others.'

After what I have said above, it is not difficult to guess who was behind these orders and wishes.

Altogether one can say that the Reich Security Head Office, or at least the executive, and all that it achieved, was Müller.

As a person, Müller was very correct in his attitude, obliging and friendly. He never stood on his seniority or rank, but it was impossible to have any close, personal contact with him. This was confirmed to me time and again by those of his colleagues who had worked with him for several years.

Müller was the ice-cold executive or organiser of all the measures which the Reichsführer SS deemed necessary for the security of the Reich.

APPENDIX FIVE

Pohl

The Chief of the Economic Administration Head Office, SS Obergruppen-füher Oswald Pohl has been known to me since my appointment to Dachau on the 1 December, 1934

POHL was a native of Kiel and a paymaster in the navy. He was a veteran member of the party and belonged to the naval SA. The Reichsführer SS removed him from there in 1934 and installed him as administrative chief of the SS.

Although this office played only a small part in affairs under the guidance of his predecessors, Pohl managed in a very short time to make himself indispensable to the Reichsführer SS and to make his office feared and all-powerful. For example his auditors, who were selected by himself and received his support and were responsible only to him, were held in terror by the administrative heads of every department. Pohl's methods did, however, instil order and accuracy into the administration of the SS and resulted in the dismissal of any administrative official whom he found careless or unreliable.

Under Pohl's predecessors, the more senior officers were fairly independent in money matters and did much as they pleased. Pohl got the Reichsführer SS to issue instructions that permission had to be obtained for all payments made by the general SS and that such payments would be audited by him. This caused a lot of ill-feeling and irritation, but with characteristic energy Pohl succeeded in getting his way and, as a result, obtained for himself an enormous influence over the affairs of every SS unit. Even the most obstinate cranks among the senior SS officers, such as Sepp Dietrich and Eicke, had to draw in their horns and ask Pohl when they wanted money for some extra-budgetary expenditure.

Each SS unit had an exactly calculated yearly budget, which had to be observed with the most scrupulous accuracy. Pohl's blood-hounds, the auditors, would unearth every penny that had been over or under spent.

Pohl's main objective from the beginning, however, was gradually to make the SS financially independent of the State and the Party, by means of its own business undertakings and thus to guarantee the Reichsführer SS the necessary freedom of action in his planning. It was a task with a far-reaching objective, which Pohl was convinced could be accomplished and for which he laboured unremittingly. He was the guiding spirit behind almost all of the business undertakings of the SS. To start with there were the German Armaments Works (DAW), the porcelain factory (Allach), the quarries, clinker works, brickyards and cement factories forming the German Mineral and Stone Works (Dest), and the clothing factories. There was the WIII German Provisions Combine, incorporating bakeries, butchers, retail grocers and canteens, the numerous spas, the agricultural and forestry undertakings, the printing works and publishing companies, all of which already represented a considerable economic strength. Yet this was only a beginning.

Pohl had already made plans for industrial undertakings of great magnitude, which would put even the IG Farben Industrie in the shade. Pohl also had the necessary energy to bring these schemes to completion.

The Reichsführer SS needed an enormous amount of money for his research and experimental establishments alone, and Pohl had always produced it. The Reichsführer SS was very liberal in allowing money to be spent for exceptional purposes, and Pohl financed everything. He was easily able to do this, since the business undertakings of the SS, in spite of the large capital investment they required, produced an immense amount of money.

The Waffen SS, the concentration camps, the Reich Security Head Office, the police and later some other service departments, were financed by the State. Budgetary discussions were conducted on Pohl's behalf by Gruppenführer Frank, his adlatus and general factotum.

The negotiations with the Exchequer over the budget were veritable trials of strength, for without money provided by the State, not one new company of the Waffen SS could be formed. Frank was clever and tenacious and managed to get all that he wanted, often after negotiations lasting for weeks on end. He had been trained by Pohl, and Pohl stood behind his shoulder. Later on Frank reorganised the administration of the entire police force, which had become completely fossilised. After the attempt on the

P

Führer's life, Frank became administrative chief of the army. Pohl stood in the background and directed.

The headquarters and administration of the SS were situated in Munich during the first few years after the assumption of power. During the same period, Pohl lived in Dachau in the immediate neighbourhood of the camp. He therefore came into contact with the concentration camp and the prisoners from the start, and was able to acquire a thorough knowledge of their needs. Because of his intense interest in the construction of industrial indertakings in Dachau concentration camp, he spent much time in the camp and on Sundays enjoyed making a tour of inspection of the entire camp area. He deliberately avoided entering the actual protective custody camp, so as not to give the Inspector of Concentration Camps, Eicke, any possible ground for complaining to the Reichsführer SS. Pohl and Eicke were both powerful personalities, and there was constant friction between them which often deveploped into violent quarrels. They held contrary opinions on almost every question that came within their competence. This was the case in questions concerning the treatment of prisoners, so far as they affected Pohl, on matters such as their accommodation, provisioning and clothing and their employment in the industrial undertakings. During the whole time that I knew Pohl, up to the final collapse, he always showed the same approach to all questions concerning the prisoners. It was his opinion that a prisoner who was given good and warm living quarters, and was sufficiently well fed and clothed, would work industriously on his own account, and that punishment was only necessary as a last resort.

On Pohl's initiative a garden of medicinal herbs was started in Dachau. Pohl was an enthusiastic believer in diet reform. Spices and medicinal herbs of all kinds were bred and cultivated in this garden, with the object of weaning the German people from the foreign spices that were a danger to health, and from the synthetic medicines, and of accustoming them instead to the use of unharmful, pleasant-tasting German spices and natural, medicinal herbs for all kinds of bodily infirmities. The use of these spices was made obligatory for all SS and police formations. Later on, during the war, almost the entire army received these spices from Dachau. Pohl found many opportunities in this herb garden of discussing with the prisoners the reasons for their arrest, and of hearing about their life in the camp. In this way he was always in the know about what was going on in Dachau concentration camp. Even in later years he visited the herb garden almost every month, and always lived there when he was in Munich or when he had some business to transact in the neighbourhood.

Pohl persistently supported requests for the release of prisoners who were known to him, when he believed that they had been wrongly imprisoned, or when he considered that the length of their sentences was unjustifiable. This brought him into irreconcilable hostility with Eicke and the Reich Security Head Office, and later on with Kaltenbrunner. Pohl was never afraid to make a complaint, and in especially bad cases he would go to the Reichsführer SS himself, which he otherwise avoided doing. But he met with little success, for in matters relating to releases the Reichsführer SS deferred on principle to the opinions of the Reich Security Head Office.

In 1941 the concentration camps were incorporated in Department D of the Economic Administration Head Office, and placed under Pohl's authority.

Through his contacts with the industrial undertakings which were concerned with all the camps, and through the heads of those undertakings and their temporary inspector Maurer, and also through the chiefs of the department groups and of departments A, B, C and W, Pohl was kept well informed about all the camps.

After he had taken over the concentration camps, Pohl immediately started to reform them in accordance with his ideas. First of all, some of the camp commandants had to go, either because they failed to comply with Pohl's new instructions, or because, like Loritz, they were (in Pohl's opinion) no longer tolerable for service in a concentration camp.

Pohl's main demands were: decent treatment of the prisoners, elimination of all arbitrary handling of the prisoners by subordinate members of the SS, improvements in the system of provisioning, the supply of warmer clothing for the winter, sufficient accommodation, and improvement of the sanitary arrangements. All of these improvements were proposed with the object of keeping the prisoners sufficiently fit to do the work demanded of them!

Pohl constantly inspected all the concentration camps and also a large proportion of the labour camps. He saw the deficiencies and tried whenever he could to remedy them. If he discovered somewhere that an officer or a junior officer was at fault he would deal ruthlessly with him, without regard to his person or position. His inspections were mostly unheralded and very thorough. He would not let himself be taken around, but insisted on seeing everything for himself. Regardless of time, or people, or meals, he rushed from one place to another. He had a prodigious memory. Figures, which he had been told only once, he never forgot. He was always on the look out for things which he had seen and to which he had objected on previous inspections.

Next to Dachau, Auschwitz received his special attention. He spent a great deal of energy in connection with the construction and development of the camp. Kammler often said to me that Pohl began every building conference in Berlin by first asking how matters were going at Auschwitz. The SS department concerned with raw materials had a voluminous file of demands, memoranda and angry letters from Pohl regarding Auschwitz. I must have been the only SS officer in the whole SS who possessed such a comprehensive blanket authority for procuring everything that was needed in Auschwitz.

Later on as D1 he was perpetually harrying me about defects that he had found in the concentration camps and labour camps, which he had not been able to clear up, and demanding that the culprits be discovered and the worst of the abuses be rectified.

But so long as Himmler's basic attitude remained unchanged, any attempts to improve the conditions were hopeless from the start.

Anyone who had distinguished himself by his proficiency could come to Pohl at any time with requests or wishes, and he would give him all the help that he could.

Pohl was very capricious and often went from one extreme to the other. It was inadvisable to contradict him when he was in a bad humour, for this would result in a snub. But when he was in a good humour, even the most disagreeable and unpleasant things could be told him and he would not take them amiss. It was not easy to work with him in his immediate presence for any length of time, and his adjutants were changed frequently and often with startling suddenness.

Pohl liked to show his position and his power. His uniform was deliberately simple and he wore no decorations, although Himmler forced him to wear the German Cross and the Knight's Cross to the War Service Cross, with which he was later decorated.

In spite of his age (he was over fifty) he was exceptionally brisk and active, and tremendously tough. To accompany him on a duty journey was not an unmixed blessing.

Pohl's behaviour towards the Reichsführer SS was peculiar. He did everything through Himmler. Every letter and every teleprinter message was despatched under Himmler's name, and yet Pohl only went to him in person when he was summoned.

For Pohl, every wish expressed by the Reichsführer SS, and they were not few in number, was a command. I have never known of an occasion when Pohl criticised or even expressed disapproval of an order from Himmler. An order from the Reichsführer SS was something that was settled and fixed, and had to be carried out exactly as it stood. Nor did he like there to be any discussion as to the interpretation or impracticability of these orders, which were often very obscure. This was especially so with regard to Kammler and Glücks, both of whom were very talkative; they were often bluntly reproved in this connection, although in other respects Pohl allowed them to take many liberties. *In spite of his commanding personality Pohl was the most willing and obedient executive of all the wishes and plans of the Reichsführer SS, Heinrich Himmler.*

APPENDIX SIX

Maurer

SS Standartenführer Gerhard Maurer was the chief of department DII in the Economic Administration Head Office

HE was a business man and a veteran member of the Party and the SS. He originally came from Saxony. Before 1933 he held a senior position as accountant in his local SS unit.

In 1934 he took an administrative post in the SS in Munich, and Pohl brought him into the auditing department. His skill as an auditor had already been noticed by Pohl, and he was employed in the newly established Central Administrative Office concerned with the commercial undertakings of the SS, of which Pohl later made him inspector.

Maurer thus gained a knowledge of the concentration camps and took a particular interest in matters connected with the industrial employment of the prisoners. He obtained an insight into the peculiarities of the commandants and commanders of the protective custody camps and their negative attitude towards these industrial schemes. Most of the older commandants and commanders felt that the prisoners employed in the commercial undertakings were too well treated and also that the heads of these undertakings were learning too much from the prisoners about what went on in the camps. They played many tricks on the executives of these industries. They would, for example, suddenly remove skilled men and employ them on outside work, or retain them in the camp, or they would send them prisoners who were quite unfit for work.

Maurer dealt ruthlessly with these schemes by giving Pohl many reports which he found useful. On Maurer's instigation and in order to avoid these unedifying intrigues, Pohl later made the camp commandants directors of all the commercial undertakings set up in the camp. They received a considerable monthly allowance for this according to the size of the industries, and later they received a share of the profits. As a result, the commandants paid more attention to these industries, and their subordinates were forced to recognise their needs.

It was Maurer, however, who persuaded Pohl to introduce a system of bonus payments. Later, in 1944, Maurer drew up, at Pohl's request, the regulations for the payment of prisoners, which laid down that every prisoner was to be paid according to the work he had done. These regulations however, were never carried into effect.

Soon after the incorporation of the Concentration Camp Inspectorate into the Economic Administration Head Office, Maurer became chief of department DII, concerned with the employment of prisoners. Maurer proceeded to organise this office with great thoroughness. He installed an employment officer in each camp, who was responsible to him and was thoroughly instructed in his task of procuring prison labour for the war industries. This officer also had to make a record of every prisoner's trade or profession and to take strict care that each prisoner was employed according to his abilities. Most of the commanders of the protective custody camps, as well as the *Rapportführer* and labour officers, tried to sabotage the work of the employment officer, because they wanted to continue to have independent control over the prisoners' employment. At first this caused a lot of friction, but Maurer took severe action whenever any incidents of this kind were brought to his notice.

Maurer was an energetic man and had sharp eyes and ears. If anything was wrong in the camp he would notice it at once and either make the commandant aware of it, or report the matter to Pohl.

Pohl had complete confidence in Maurer. When Glücks wanted to keep something unpleasant from Pohl, Maurer would always tell him about it.

After Liebehenschel's departure, Maurer became Glücks's deputy. By this appointment, Pohl to all intents and purposes handed the inspectorate over to Maurer. Glücks gradually entrusted all the most important matters to Maurer. He was Inspector in name only.

I had already known Maurer when I was at Dachau and Sachsenhausen, but we got to know each other better during my time as commandant of Auschwitz. We always got on with each other and worked together very well. I was able to bring many things to

Pohl's attention through Maurer, which it was impossible to do through Glücks. We shared the same views on almost all problems concerning the prisoners and the conduct of the camp. Only on the question of selecting the able-bodied Jews from the rest did we hold contrary opinions. Maurer wanted to employ as many Jews as possible, even those who would probably only be able to work for a short time, whereas I wanted only the fittest and strongest to be selected, for reasons which I have often explained. We never agreed on this matter, and although the results of Maurer's attitude became plain enough later on, he refused to grasp their significance.

Maurer had watched the development of Auschwitz from the start and I had drawn his attention to the deficiencies on every visit he made. He observed them for himself as well. He reported them all to Pohl, who was then inspector of the industrial undertakings, but it had no effect.

Maurer was always in favour of treating the prisoners well. During his factory inspections he often talked with the prisoners about their accommodation and feeding and about the way they were treated. By doing so, however, he often harmed the prisoners more than he helped them, since the Capos were always lurking in the background.

Maurer displayed enormous energy in pursuing his main task of obtaining labour for the armaments industry. He travelled a great deal, inspecting the start of an undertaking in one place, or the progress of one somewhere else, or solving difficulties which arose between the industrial chiefs and the labour company officers and hearing complaints about the prisoners' work or from the industrial employers about their ill treatment. There were hundreds of matters with which he had to deal. There was the eternal pressure from the Armaments Ministry and the Todt Organisation for more prisoners, and the everlasting cry from Auschwitz about the many, too many transports. Maurer had his full measure of work. But it was never too much for him and in spite of his lively manner he maintained an unruffled composure.

As a result of his continual requests to be employed at the front, and on Kammler's instigation, he was given the post of commissary to Kammler's Special Services Division from January to the middle of April 1945; it afterwards became an artillery corps.

Maurer had an understanding for all matters concerning the prisoners, even though he always regarded them from the point of

view of their employment as a labour force. He would never appreciate that the selection or retention of too many Jews for employment
resulted *directly* in a deterioration in the general conditions in Auschwitz, followed by a similar deterioration in all the other camps.
Yet the truth of this could not be doubted.

APPENDIX SEVEN

Globocnik

SS Gruppenführer Globocnik was head of the SS and Police in Lublin

SHORTLY after the beginning of the Russian campaign, the Reichs-führer SS ordered a concentration camp to be set up in Lublin. The Inspector of Concentration Camps, Glücks, took over from Globocnik the land which had been selected for this purpose, together with the beginnings of the camp, and installed Koch (hitherto commandant of Buchenwald) as its commandant. Globoc-nik then promised to supply Glücks with enormous quantities of blankets and sheets and footwear and also cooking utensils and surgical instruments and medicines, for use in the concentration camp. Eventually Glücks came to Auschwitz and authorised me to go to Lublin and select the supplies that I needed. I visited Globocnik straight away, accompanied by my administrative officer, Wagner. After much dashing about, we were able to collect a certain amount of supplies that could be of use in Auschwitz. I cannot now remem-ber of what they consisted but they included some surgical apparatus and instruments and also some medicines. At any rate the spoils were miserably small compared with the amount that Globocnik had promised. They were articles which had been requisitioned in the Lublin area and indiscriminately heaped together in a factory building.

It was during this transaction that I got to know Globocnik. He assumed a great air of importance, with his instructions from the Reichsführer SS to set up police strong-points in the territories which had been taken over. He worked out fantastic plans for a series of strong-points stretching to the Urals. He could see no difficulties in this, and he waved aside all objections. He wanted to destroy every Jew in this area on the spot, except those whom he needed for work on ' his ' police positions. He proposed to put all their property into a collecting centre and utilise it for the SS. He talked about all this in his Viennese dialect in an easy-going way sitting in front of his fire in the evening, as though it were a most innocent adventure. I was rather shocked by Globocnik, who according to Glücks's account was supposed to be extremely competent and to be held in high regard by the Reichsführer SS.

My first impressions were correct. Globocnik was a pompous busybody, whose object was to put himself in the foreground and to describe his fanciful plans as though they had to a large extent already been put into practice. It was he and only he who could get things done properly, whether it was a question of exterminating the Jews or resettling the Poles or the utilisation of sequestered property. He was able to spin the most extraordinary yarns to Himmler. The latter believed him and continued to keep him, although he became unbearable and was attacked from all sides by the SD and the General Governor and the District Governor.

I do not know what led to his final dismissal. He left Lublin and went to Trieste as a senior SS and police officer. I know nothing about his activities there.

The second occasion on which I had anything to do with him was in Lublin in the spring of 1943. There had been a dispute between us over some machines and tools which he had got the local DAW (at that time subordinate to him) to deliver to the DAW at Auschwitz. He had described some ancient junk as being the most up-to-date machinery and had used the same description in his report to Pohl.

Since he had personally given orders for these swindles he did not feel very happy about it, but he dismissed the affair, without comment and gave me five really modern and most urgently needed machines for the Auschwitz DAW.

My administrative officer, Möckel, had to settle accounts with his department, which had also advised Pohl that the promised equipment had either not been delivered or had been delivered only in negligible quantities. Promises were made of deliveries on a grand scale, but they came to nothing.

At that time, the chief of the SS Personnel Head Office, SS Obergruppenführer von Herff arrived in Lublin to make the acquaintance of the officers of Globocnik's department. Globocnik took the opportunity of showing him all his model establishments. He began by getting him to inspect the large quantities of Jewish property collected in the former aircraft factory and ' his ' Jewish workshops where the most hopeless commodities were turned out, ranging from brushes to foot-mats. Everything he did was done in a way that can only be described as flashy. The Jews there, who had really organised it all, had effectively deceived Globocnik and his officers. They created as many supervisory positions as possible for themselves and then proceeded to conduct their own businesses. This was confirmed to me, later on, by Globocnik's staff officer Höfle. . . .

As might be expected, he regarded the Lublin concentration camp as 'his' camp. He issued orders and instructions to the commandants which completely contradicted those given by the concentration camp inspectorate or by Pohl. This was the cause of perpetual dissension. Globocnik, however, always managed to get his way with the Reichsführer SS by pointing out to him the special position that Lublin occupied. He hardly bothered about instructions that came from the Reich Security Head Office. He organised 'his own' police actions, when it suited him. He carried out executions at his own discretion. He built labour camps for the prisoners, just where he liked, without bothering in the least about Pohl or DII, for to him they were always 'his' camps and 'his' prisoners. In the same way he regarded Sobibor, Belczek and Treblinka as 'his' extermination centres.

Eichmann, who had known Globocnik during the time of the SS's illegal activities prior to the invasion of Austria, was greatly bothered by him. While I spent my time arguing with Eichmann about slowing down the transports of Jews to Auschwitz, Globocnik was saying that he could not get hold of enough. He wanted to be in the forefront with 'his' exterminations and 'his' collections of valuables.

As his adviser on exterminations, he had SA Oberführer Oldenburg, from the Führer's Chancellery, who before the war had devised methods of liquidating mental patients.

Among Globocnik's extermination centres, I saw Treblinka on the same tour of inspection.

The training camp in Trawniki was also a creation of Globocnik's. He wanted to form a separate unit of Russian guards, and had obtained the consent of the Reichsführer SS.

As might have been expected, these guards, who were called police were unreliable. A company of them was given to me for Auschwitz. After a short time fifteen fled, taking with them all the weapons and ammunition they could lay their hands on, and during the chase that followed they engaged their pursuers with fire, which resulted in the deaths of three junior officers. All of them were recaptured, except three who managed to make their escape. The company was immediately disbanded and distributed among all the concentration camps.

His staff officer, Höfle, came to Oranienburg in 1944 and should have taken over the position of commander of a protective custody camp. In spite of the lack of suitable officers, even Glücks refused him the post. He had been too long under Globocnik's tuition. I learnt from Höfle something about Globocnik and his machinations.

Globocnik wanted to create a large German settlement in 'his territory'. With this in mind, he chose the district around Zamosch. He promised the Reichsführer SS that he would move 50,000 new German settlers there within a year, as a model for the large settlements which it was intended to build later on in the far eastern districts. He wanted to collect the necessary cattle and machines required for this purpose in the shortest possible space of time. But the district he had chosen was then occupied by Polish peasants. He therefore began straight away to evacuate them. He was quite indifferent as to where they were to go, but left that for the UWZ or the Reich Security Head Office or the BDS in Cracow to work out. His main concern was to get the area ready to receive the 50,000 new settlers. According to Höfle's descriptions this re-settlement organised by Globocnik must have been catastrophic. Moreover, the German settlers themselves were by no means satisfied. Their hopes were unfulfilled and they worked themselves to death under the unusual conditions, waiting endlessly for Globocnik to give them assistance.

In the summer of 1943 Globocnik visited Auschwitz on Himmler's orders to inspect the crematoria and examine the method of extermination. He was not, however, particularly struck by what he saw. His own installations were far quicker in operation and he began to quote figures to emphasise the daily rate of extermination (for example, I remember he talked of *five* trains arriving daily at Sobibor) and the enormous amount of property which he had collected. He recklessly exaggerated at every opportunity.

I always had the impression that he believed what he was saying. I knew from Eichmann that, for technical reasons connected with the railway, only two trains at the most could arrive at Sobibor each day.

After the incorporation of Austria, Globocnik became Gauleiter in Vienna. He caused so much mischief, however, that he soon had to be removed.

He was in reality a good natured person, and in my opinion his deceptions were due to his pomposity and self-importance. Whether or not he made anything for himself out of the confused muddle of the Reinhardt action in Lublin, I do not know, but I would not put it past him. The officers and men of ' his territory ' certainly did well out of it. The special SS tribunals were given plenty of work and not a few death sentences were pronounced.

It had become almost a mania with Globocnik to requisition and utilise everything that was within his reach. He wanted to be able to supply the Reichsführer SS with an immense amount of money, and to excel even Pohl by means of ' his business undertakings '. He was completely unscrupulous and he never even considered whether ' his requisitioning ' was right or not. This attitude naturally affected his subordinates, and since hardly any control was exercised over them, many organised their own requisitioning and made a flourishing business out of it, or else they stole whatever they could lay their hands on.

Globocnik's staff was nothing less than a collection of misfits. But they nevertheless managed to make themselves indispensable and liked by him, which was not very difficult considering his poor knowledge of human nature. When their misdeeds had to be covered up, Globocnik gave them his help, both out of good nature and so that his own intrigues would not come to light.

The Reichsführer SS believed his assurances that everything in his domain was in exemplary order and exceedingly prosperous.

APPENDIX EIGHT

Eicke

The first Inspector of Concentration Camps was SS Obergruppenführer Theodor Eicke

HE can be regarded as the actual founder of all the concentration camps, with the exception of Dachau. It was he, too, who gave them their form and shape.

Eicke came from the Rhineland and during the First World War fought on every front and was many times wounded and decorated. When the Rhineland was occupied he took a leading part in the resistance movement against the French. He was sentenced to death in his absence by a French military tribunal and remained in Italy until 1928. When he returned home he went to the NSDAP and became an SS man.

In 1933 the Reichsführer SS took him out of the general SS and made him Colonel and commandant of Dachau, from which post two of his predecessors had already been sacked for incompetence. He at once set about reorganising the camp in accordance with his own ideas.

Eicke was an inflexible Nazi of the old type. All his actions sprang from the knowledge that National Socialism had made many sacrifices and had fought a long battle before coming to power, and that this power had now to be used against every enemy of the new State. He regarded the concentration camps in this light.

In his view, the prisoners were sworn enemies of the state, who were to be treated with great severity and destroyed if they showed resistance. He instilled the same attitude of mind into his officers and men. At the beginning of Eicke's period of service as commandant, the majority of the guards came from the Bavarian country constabulary and they also occupied most of the important posts. To Eicke, the police were like a red rag to a bull especially the country constabulary, who had made life so difficult for the Nazis during their early struggles. In a very short time he replaced all the police (except two, whom he brought into the SS) with SS-men and chased the 'laponesten', as they were called in camp slang, out of the camp.

The prisoners were treated harshly and were flogged for the slightest misdemeanour. Floggings were carried out in the presence of the assembled guards (at least two companies of them had to be present) with the intention, as he saw it, of toughening up the men. In particular, the recruits were regularly forced to witness these proceedings.

At that time, the inmates consisted almost exclusively of political prisoners from the Bavarian communist and social-democratic parties, and from the Bavarian people's party.

Eicke's instructions from first to last were: behind the wire lurks the enemy, watching everything you do, so that he can use your weaknesses for his own advantage. Do not let yourselves be taken in, but show the enemy your teeth. Anyone who displays the slightest sympathy with these enemies of the State must vanish from our ranks. My SS men must be tough and ready for all eventualities and there is no room among us for weaklings.

Eicke did not, however, tolerate independent action by his men against the prisoners. They were to be treated harshly but fairly and they were to be punished only on his orders. He organised the supervision of the protective custody camp and so had it under his control.

Little by little he built up the whole camp and gave it the form, which was later used as a model for all the other concentration camps.

He made the guards into a tough body of men, who were correct in the performance of their duties, but who were also quick with their weapons, if an ' enemy of the State ' should escape.

He punished any lapse on the part of the guard, with great severity. Yet his men loved 'papa Eicke', as they called him. In the evenings he sat with them in the canteen or in their barracks. He spoke with them in their own language, and went into all their troubles and worries, and taught them how to become what *he* wanted, hard, tough fellows, who would shrink at nothing that he ordered them to do.

' Every order is to be carried out, however harsh it may be! ' That is what he required and what he preached in all his instructions to his men. And these instructions stayed fast and became part of their flesh and blood. The men who were guards at the time when Eicke was commandant of Dachau were the future commanders of protective custody camps, *Rapportführers* and other senior camp officials. They never forgot the instructions that Eicke had given them. The prisoners were enemies of the State, so far as they were concerned, and would always remain so.

Eicke knew his men and he knew how to go to work on them, and the training he gave them was far-sighted.

In 1934 he became the first Inspector of Concentration Camps. To begin with he directed affairs from Dachau, but later he went to Berlin in order to be near the Reichsführer SS.

He now started with great enthusiasm to remould the existing camps Esterwegen, Sachsenburg, Lichtenburg and Columbia on the Dachau model. Officers and men from Dachau were constantly transferred to the other camps in order to inject them with the ' Dachau spirit ' and with a dose of Prussian militarism.

The Reichsführer SS gave him a completely free hand, knowing that there was no more suitable person to whom he could entrust the camps. Himmler had often emphasised his complete agreement with Eicke's views concerning the concentration camps and the ' enemies of the State '.

In Berlin, Eicke became convinced that the jolly, comradely, Bavarian type of military 'instruction', with plenty of sociable evenings and a lot of Bavarian beer, was quite insufficient for the training of a really efficient soldier, capable of being employed in any capacity.

He therefore looked for a Prussian ' instructor ' and found one in Schulze, a police captain, whom he then charged with the task of instilling some Prussian spirit into the easy-going Bavarian methods, and of giving the officers and men some of the old Prussian type of military training. It caused a lot of ill-feeling in Dachau, when the ' Prussian pig ' initiated his more rigorous system of training. The older members of the Dachau guard were never able to get over it and they obstructed Schulze to such a degree that after a year they succeeded in getting rid of him.

He was told that the reason for his sudden dismissal was that although he was an excellent officer and had achieved exceptional results by his methods of training, yet he was not a National-Socialist or SS-man and therefore did not understand how to handle the men properly!

Eicke retained his habit, both when he was Inspector and

Q

afterwards, of talking with the guards and the lower ranks, without their superior officers being present. In this way, he enjoyed a popularity and devotion in the eyes of his men which was exceptional even in the SS (where a special value was placed on comradeship), and which was keenly observed by the Reichsführer SS. The superior officers greatly disapproved of this habit of Eicke's. For one thing, Eicke got to know all that went on in the camp and nothing of any importance was hidden from him. For another, he was kept constantly informed about the behaviour of the SS officers, both on and off duty, and the SS-men naturally made use of this opportunity to tell some malicious tales. Many SS officers had to answer to Eicke for matters which existed only in the imagination of the SS-men who had recounted them.

Eicke, however, attained his object and got all the camps completely under his control.

Later on he had letter boxes put up in every camp, which could only be opened by him and which gave every SS-man a means of communicating reports, complaints and denunciations direct to him. He also had his confidants amongst the prisoners in every camp, who, unknown to the others, informed him of anything that was worth knowing.

From the start of his activities as Inspector of Concentration Camps Eicke placed a special importance on increasing the strength of the guards in the camps.

Up to the end of 1935, the financing of the concentration camps was a matter for the districts concerned, but this did not apply to the financing of the guards. Up till then Eicke had paid his men out of contributions from the exchequer, subsidies from the Party and SS bank credits and canteen profits.

Finally he got the Reichsführer SS to agree that he should ask the Führer to make a decision in the matter. The Führer authorised an establishment of twenty-five companies of 100 men each who were to be financed out of State funds. The financing of the concentration camps remained the responsibility of the various districts, until further notice.

Eicke had now taken the first decisive step towards building up the strength of the guards, which were later called the Death's Head formations.

In the meantime plans and preparations were made for the construction of further concentration camps. The acquisition of suitable sites and the arrangements for the necessary finance gave rise to great difficulties which were nevertheless overcome by Eicke's perseverance.

Sachsenhausen and Buchenwald were created. They were erected from the start by prisoners under Eicke's administration, who were alone responsible for deciding on the way they were to be built. As a result he came into sharp conflict with Pohl, who had meanwhile been put in charge of all SS constructional operations and was responsible for financing them.

The Esterwegen camp was closed down and transferred to Sachsenhausen, similarly Berlin-Columbia. Sachsenburg, Lichtenburg and Bad Sulza were transferred to Buchenwald. Lichtenburg then became a women's camp. In addition, Flossenburg, Mauthausen and Gross-Rosen were also under Eicke's administration before the war. At first these were entirely labour camps, which Eicke had planned for use in the quarries acquired by the SS, but they very soon became independent concentration camps.

Eicke built all these camps autocratically, using the experiences he had gained to assist him in his perpetual battle of opinions with Pohl.

Pohl already wanted more space to accommodate the prisoners and he also foresaw the future development of the camps more clearly than Eicke, who adopted a narrow-minded attitude in this matter. Eicke was in favour of keeping the camps compact, so that they could be more easily guarded, and he was against any substantial enlargement. The following is an example of this, which I experienced for myself when I was adjutant at Sachsenhausen.

It is 1938. Plans have been made for the construction of a new women's camp. Lichtenburg is not suitable for a concentration camp and is far too small. After much search, Pohl and Eicke have picked on an area by the lake near Ravensbrück. The Reichsführer SS has expressed his approval. A conference is arranged to take place between Pohl and Eicke on the site to discuss details of construction. The commandant of Sachsenhausen who is to provide the prisoners for the building work and who has to arrange for their accommodation is summoned to attend, and also myself. The question of the size of the women's concentration camp is still undecided. Eicke estimates that at the very most there will be not more than 2,000 female prisoners. Pohl wants to build for 10,000. Eicke says that he is crazy and that number will never be reached.

Pohl wants the camp to be built in such a way that it can be extended in the future to hold the number of prisoners that he envisaged. Eicke sticks stubbornly to his figure of 2,000 and considers that even this figure is unreasonably high. Eicke wins with his 2,000!

The Ravensbrück women's concentration camp is built and later on has to be perpetually enlarged under the most difficult conditions and in a completely unmethodical manner. Ravensbrück ultimately had to accommodate up to 25,000 women. They were crowded together under the most cramped conditions with the inevitable results. Pohl's judgment was correct and far-seeing. Eicke was always narrow-minded and petty in matters relating to concentration camps.

His inability to see sufficiently far ahead was to blame for the fact that the old camp could not be extended to accommodate the enormous increase in numbers that came to be imprisoned during the war.

The extension of the camp was nevertheless continued, to the detriment of the prisoners, who were packed together even more tightly. I have already sufficiently described the consequences of this overcrowding. Not only was it practically impossible to increase the living accommodation, but the water supply and drainage installations, which were barely adequate under normal conditions, could not be improved in any important respect. Thus the way was laid for future defects, which were to prove impossible to remedy.

In contrast to the narrow-mindedness which Eicke displayed in all matters relating to the concentration camps, he showed an unprecedented liberality in all that concerned the troops. *The strengthening of the Death's Head formations had become his main preoccupation.* The concentration camps with their ' enemies of the State ' were for him only a means to an end.

At later budget conferences he constantly produced overwhelming arguments concerning the danger represented by the ' enemies of the State ' and the consequent necessity for increasing the strength of the guards.

The new barracks, which were under construction, were never big enough or spacious enough for him. The furnishings were never comfortable enough. For every bit of space that was saved in the concentration camp, the troops were given ten times as much in return. He had to square matters with Pohl in order to get the necessary money for furnishing the troops' quarters.

Eicke had no knowledge of human nature and time and again he allowed himself to be deceived by appearances and clever talk by men who knew how to make themselves seem skilful and adept, and he trusted these individuals far too much. His opinions of people were apt to be coloured by chance events or by his moods. If an SS officer had got himself disliked, or if Eicke, for some reason or other, could not tolerate him, then it was best for that officer to arrange to be transferred from Eicke's service as rapidly as possible.

Any officers or junior officers (he hoped to bring the men round to his way of thinking) whom he considered unsuitable for service with the troops would either be removed from his command or (after 1937 when, at his instigation, the troops and the concentration camps were separated from each other), transferred to a post in a concentration camp. As a result, the commandants' staffs were gradually filled with incapable officers and junior officers, whom Eicke did not want to get rid of completely because of the length of time during which they had been a member of the Party or of the SS. The camp commandants would have to worry about them. They were constantly transferred in an effort to find them a suitable post and most of them eventually found their way to Auschwitz, which gradually became used by the Inspector of Concentration Camps as a dumping ground for discarded personnel. If Eicke had only removed these incapable officers entirely out of his command, the concentration camps would later on have been spared a great deal of unpleasantness and brutality. The effects of Eicke's philosophy were to continue to make themselves felt for many years.

It can be ascribed to Eicke's ignorance of human nature that camp commandants such as Koch and Loritz possessed his complete confidence, which could not be displaced even by the most disagreeable incidents. They were allowed to do as they pleased in their camps.

He indulged them in every respect and never interferred with them, even though he was fully informed about all that went on.

After the separation of the troops from the concentration camps, Eicke no longer took such an active interest in the latter as he had previously done. His main preoccupation was with the troops. The work in connection with the expansion of the camps was done on his authority, but he was concerned only with the outside appearances and no longer worried about the internal arrangements. He remained stuck in his ideas about 'enemies of the State', but he was now out of date. Only about ten per cent of the inmates of the concentration camps were political prisoners, the rest being professional criminals, a-socials, and so on. Eicke's later orders and regulations on matters concerning the prisoners were made at his desk and were still based on his Dachau experiences and opinions. He made no more innovations or upheavals. In spite of his inexhaustible capacity for work and his resilience, and in spite of his perpetual urge for improvements and reforms, he had nothing to offer to the concentration camps. His energies were directed towards the troops. His position as Inspector of Concentration Camps *was purely nominal.*

When German troops marched into the Sudetenland, Eicke was with the Upper Bavarian Death's Head formation, as the guard regiment at Dachau was later named. The 4th Regiment assisted in the occupation of Danzig. Isolated units of the Death's Head formation also took part in the Polish campaign. After the campaign Eicke received orders from the Führer to form the Death's Head Division as speedily as possible. He himself was created Lieutenant-General.

At the beginning of the war all the front line Death's Head units in the camps were replaced by reservists from the general SS. This was also tried as a temporary expedient during the occupation of Czechoslovakia. It gave rise to many difficulties, since the veteran reservists had no knowledge whatever about guarding prisoners, and many of them were physically unsuited to the arduous requirements of the service. The professional criminals quickly took advantage of many of them and used them to abet their escape or for similar delinquencies.

Dachau concentration camp was evacuated to enable the Death's Head division to be formed, and the prisoners were transferred to Flossenburg and Mauthausen. After F Division had been formed and marched off to the training ground, the prisoners were brought back.

While the division was being formed, Brigadeführer Glücks, who up till then had been chief of staff to the Inspector of Concentration Camps, was appointed Inspector by order of the Reichsführer SS.

The Death's Head Division first took part in the fighting in France and was then employed in occupation duties on the Spanish frontier, until the campaign against Russia, when it was constantly used where the fighting was fiercest. They were several times encircled, as at Demiansk, and suffered terrible losses.

Eicke's behaviour during the building up of this Division was typical.

The army departments used all their endeavours to impede and delay the build-up. First it was to be a motorised division, then a cavalry division, then it was to be a partially motorised division.

With imperturbable calm Eicke watched all this happening and stole for himself, whenever he could, the weapons and equipment he required. In this way he collected all his heavy artillery from transports destined for Rumania.

The training of active service guards into tough soldiers now began to bear fruit.

The achievements of the Death's Head Division were only made possible because of the iron-clad training which Eicke had given the troops, and because of the affection which they had for Eicke himself.

In the spring of 1942 he was shot down during a reconnaissance flight near Charkov, while he was searching for a tank company, commanded by his son-in-law. All that was found of him was a piece of his uniform, with the Knight's Cross with Oak Leaves and Swords.

In this way he met the soldier's death, which he had sought, ever since the time, a short while before, when his only son had also fallen in battle.

APPENDIX NINE

Glücks

The second Inspector of Concentration Camps was SS Gruppenführer Richard Glücks

GLÜCKS originally came from Dusseldorf and had spent several years before the First World War in the Argentine. When war broke out he got through the British control by smuggling himself on board a Norwegian ship and eventually reported for military service. He served throughout the war as an artillery officer. After the war he was appointed a liaison officer with the armistice commission, and later on joined a Freikorps in the Ruhr district. Up to the time when Hitler assumed power, he was engaged in business activities.

Glücks was one of the early members of the Party and the SS. In the SS he at first spent some years as a staff officer in the Senior Sector West, after which he commanded a regiment of the general SS in Schneidemühl. In 1936 he joined Eicke as a staff officer on the Concentration Camp Inspectorate.

Glücks's attitude of mind was that of the typical office worker who has no knowledge of practical matters. He imagined that he could direct everything from his office desk. Under Eicke, he scarcely made his presence felt in connection with the camps, and the occasional visits which he paid to individual concentration camps, in Eicke's company, had no practical effect on him, for he saw nothing and learnt nothing.

Nor had he any influence with Eicke in this connection in his capacity as staff officer, for Eicke handled these matters himself, mostly through personal contact with the commandants during his inspections of the camps.

But Eicke held him in great esteem and Glücks's opinions on questions dealing with personnel were practically decisive, to the disadvantage of the commandant's staff. Various commandants had repeatedly tried to cold shoulder Glücks, but his status with Eicke remained unassailable.

On the outbreak of war, as I have already stated, the active service guards were transferred for military duties and their places were taken by reservists from the general SS.

In addition, new formations of the Death's Head units were built up from the younger age groups, which were intended at first to be used for strengthening the police and as occupation troops. Eicke became 'General Inspector of the Death's Head Formations and of the Concentration Camps', with Glücks as his chief of staff. When Eicke was given the job of building up the Death's Head Division, the general inspectorate of the Death's Head formations was taken over by the administrative office of the Waffen SS under Jüttner, and Glücks became Inspector of Concentration Camps and also subordinate to the administrative office (later the headquarters office) of the Waffen SS. In 1941 the Inspectorate of Concentration Camps became incorporated in the Economic Administration Head Office as Department D.

The Reichsführer SS never had any particular confidence in Glücks and had often considered employing him in a different capacity. But Eicke and Pohl always warmly supported him, and so he retained his position as Inspector.

The appointment of Glücks as Inspector made no difference to the camps. Glücks always felt that Eicke's arrangements and his orders and instructions should not be disturbed, even when they had obviously become out of date. Moreover he believed that his position as Inspector was only a temporary one. He did not consider himself justified in making the smallest alteration in the existing organisation of the camp without the permission of the Reichsführer SS. Any changes suggested by the commandants were either turned down or shelved. During the whole time he held office he had an almost unbelievable fear of the Reichsführer SS. A telephone call from Himmler would throw him into the utmost confusion. If he had to pay a personal visit to Himmler, he would be useless for anything for several days beforehand. His otherwise imperturbable calm would completely forsake him when Himmler requested him to forward reports or comments.

He therefore avoided everything that might lead to a discussion with Himmler, or even to a refusal, or, worse still, a reprimand.

He was never seriously perturbed over incidents that occurred in the camps, so long as they did not have to be reported to Himmler.

Escapes had to be reported, and when one of these occurred, he was given no rest. The first question he asked when work started in the morning was always: ' How many have got away? ' Auschwitz gave him more trouble than any of the other camps.

His persistent fear of Himmler determined, quite naturally, his whole attitude towards the concentration camps, which, roughly speaking was: do what you like, so long as it doesn't get to the Reichsführer SS.

When he was subordinated to Pohl, he breathed again. Someone stronger than him was now able to deflect the blows. But he never lost his fear of the Reichsführer SS, since the latter would still ask him for reports or summon him to his presence, although Pohl helped him out of many of his difficulties.

He only inspected the camps when there was some very important reason for doing so, or at the request of the Reichsführer SS or of Pohl.

As he often said, he observed nothing during his inspections and he was always glad if the commandant did not spend too long in dragging him round the camp. ' It is the same in every camp. I am never shown what they don't want me to see and the rest I have seen so often that I no longer find it interesting.' He far preferred to sit in the officers' mess and talk about every possible subject except those which were troubling the commandants.

Glücks possessed an unquenchable Rhenish humour and he saw the funny side of everything. He made the most serious matters sound comic, and he laughed over them and forgot them and made no decisions about them. It was impossible to be angry with him, for it was the way he was made.

He never took me seriously. He regarded my perpetual worries and complaints about Auschwitz as grossly exaggerated and he was astonished if he heard from Pohl or Kammler confirmation of my views. He never gave me any kind of help, although he could have done, for example, by transferring the officers and junior officers who had become intolerable in Auschwitz. But he wanted to spare the other commandants. He would do anything to avoid trouble. And Auschwitz brought nothing but trouble to disturb the holy peace of the Inspector of Concentration Camps.

Glücks's inspections of Auschwitz were worthless in practice, and never achieved any results. He had no liking for the place. He found it too straggling and too badly arranged, and it caused him too much unpleasantness. Also the commandant always had so many complaints and requests to make. On two occasions Glücks wanted to get rid of me, or to put a higher ranking officer over me, but he was afraid to do so because of the Reichsführer SS. This was on account of the large number of escapes, which exceeded anything so far experienced in concentration camps, and which were causing him so much trouble with the Reichsführer SS. Auschwitz was a perpetual thorn in Glücks's flesh because it was troublesome and because Himmler took too much interest in it.

He did not want to have anything to do with the extermination actions against the Jews, nor did he like hearing about them. The fact that the catastrophic conditions, which later arose, were directly connected with these actions, was something he could not understand and he adopted the same helpless attitude towards it as he did towards all the difficulties in all the camps and mostly left them to the commandants to settle as best they could. 'Don't ask me so much,' was the reply so often heard at his conferences with the commandants, 'You know much better than I do.' He often asked Liebehenschel just before one of his conferences, 'What on earth shall I say to the commandants? I know nothing.' That was the Inspector of Concentration Camps, the camp commandants' superior officer, who was supposed to give directions and advice on any difficulties which might arise and for which the war alone was responsible! Later on the commandants turned to Pohl for assistance, Glücks very often resented this.

Glücks was too weak, and he did not like to offend his subordinates. In particular he was too indulgent towards the older commandants and officers, who were his favourites. Officers who should have been brought before the SS tribunal, or at least removed from concentration camp service, were retained by him out of sheer good nature.

It was good nature, too, which made him forgive many failures on the part of his staff.

When, after Liebehenschel's departure to Auschwitz, Maurer became Glücks's deputy and at the same time I became head of Department DI, Maurer and I rid headquarters of most of the officers and men of the staff, who up to then had been considered indispensable. There was a certain amount of argument with Glücks over this, but Maurer finally threatened to go to Pohl, and Glücks gave way with a heavy heart.

Gradually he handed over the reins, which he had never held very tightly, to Maurer. Apart from Maurer, whom he had to check when he considered his actions too severe, his only worry then was the Reichsführer SS.

Glücks was the opposite to Eicke in every respect. Both held extreme views and both were responsible for developing the concentration camps in a way that inevitably ended in tragedy.

INDEX